Continuous Delivery and DevOps – A Quickstart Guide
Third Edition

Start your journey to successful adoption of CD and DevOps

Paul Swartout

BIRMINGHAM - MUMBAI

Continuous Delivery and DevOps – A Quickstart Guide
Third Edition

Commissioning Editor: Gebin George
Acquisition Editor: Rahul Nair
Content Development Editor: Deepti Thore
Technical Editor: Varsha Shivhare
Copy Editor: Safis
Project Coordinator: Kinjal Bari
Proofreader: Safis Editing
Indexer: Pratik Shirodkar
Graphics: Tom Scaria
Production Coordinator: Deepika Naik

First published: November 2012
Second edition: December 2014
Third edition: October 2018

Production reference: 2191118

Published by Packt Publishing Ltd.
Livery Place
35 Livery Street
Birmingham
B3 2PB, UK.

ISBN 978-1-78899-547-4

www.packtpub.com

`mapt.io`

Mapt is an online digital library that gives you full access to over 5,000 books and videos, as well as industry leading tools to help you plan your personal development and advance your career. For more information, please visit our website.

Why subscribe?

- Spend less time learning and more time coding with practical eBooks and Videos from over 4,000 industry professionals

- Improve your learning with Skill Plans built especially for you

- Get a free eBook or video every month

- Mapt is fully searchable

- Copy and paste, print, and bookmark content

Packt.com

Did you know that Packt offers eBook versions of every book published, with PDF and ePub files available? You can upgrade to the eBook version at `www.packt.com` and as a print book customer, you are entitled to a discount on the eBook copy. Get in touch with us at `customercare@packtpub.com` for more details.

At `www.packt.com`, you can also read a collection of free technical articles, sign up for a range of free newsletters, and receive exclusive discounts and offers on Packt books and eBooks.

Contributors

About the author

Paul Swartout has spent over 2 decades working in the IT industry. He has worked across several different industries and sectors and within organizations of various sizes, from start-ups to multinational corporates. He is and always has been passionate about quality software and how it is delivered. Since first encountering Agile he has been committed to the adoption and implementation of Agile techniques and approaches to improve the efficiency, output, and lives of everyone involved in software development. He strongly believes that CD and DevOps add massive value to the way software is delivered, and he wants to ensure as many people realize this as possible. Paul lives in a small seaside town in the southwest of the UK.

Firstly, I would like to say a massive thank you to my darling wife Jane who has yet again had to put up with a husband who for the past few months has done little more than spend every spare moment staring at a laptop screen typing things, frowning then typing more things—things which eventually turned into this book.

A big thank you to John Fisher for allowing me to again include his transition curve within the book.

Thank you to everyone who purchased and read the first two editions—without you the opportunity for this third edition would never have come to be.

Lastly I want to thank the global CD and DevOps community for their never ending commitment, passion, enthusiasm and evangelism to bring this amazing way of working to the masses. Keep up the good work.

About the reviewers

Mitesh Soni is an avid learner with 10 years of experience in the IT industry. He is an SCJP, SCWCD, VCP, IBM Urbancode, as well as IBM Bluemix-certified, and a certified Jenkins Engineer. He loves DevOps and cloud computing, and he also has an interest in programming in Java. He finds design patterns fascinating and believes that a picture is worth a thousand words. He occasionally contributes to the clean-clouds and eTutorials World websites.

He believes in the KISS principle. Yes, you read it right. The KISS (Keep It Simple Stupid) principle states that simplicity should be a key goal in design and unnecessary complexity should be avoided. Hence, he follows the KISS principle in life.

Max Manders is a recovering PHP developer and former sysadmin who currently works as Principal Engineer (DevOps) at FanDuel, the leader in online Daily Fantasy Sports. Max enjoys discussing distributed systems, availability and scalability, infrastructure as code, continuous delivery, and automation. With experience of managing large-scale distributed system configuration with Puppet and Chef, Max has started exploring containerization with Docker and Kubernetes.

Max was a co-founder and organizer of Whisky Web, a Scottish conference for the web development and ops community. When he's not writing code or tinkering with the latest monitoring and operations tools, Max enjoys playing jazz and funk trombone. Max lives in Edinburgh with his wife Jo, their cats Ziggy and Maggie, and their hedgehog, Pickle.

Sami Rönkä has a background in software business and has been a keen advocate of DevOps for years. After years of hands-on specialist work, he has moved more into the business and management side and is currently transforming an MSP business into a more agile and development-oriented company using DevOps practices. He has also been reviewing other DevOps-guides for Packt.

Packt is searching for authors like you

If you're interested in becoming an author for Packt, please visit `authors.packtpub.com` and apply today. We have worked with thousands of developers and tech professionals, just like you, to help them share their insight with the global tech community. You can make a general application, apply for a specific hot topic that we are recruiting an author for, or submit your own idea.

Table of Contents

Preface

Continuous Delivery (**CD**) and DevOps have been in the spotlight over the last decade or so. Much has been written about the technical aspects and tooling of CD and DevOps, yet a vast number of so-called IT experts don't really understand what they actually are. More worryingly, they don't seem to know what they are definitely not. Over the pages that make up this book I will be unpicking both CD and DevOps so that you will gain an understanding of what they are, how they came to be, and how they can bring true business value to your business. Strictly speaking, we should consider CD and DevOps as two complementary yet separate approaches:

- Continuous Delivery, as the name suggests, is a way of working whereby quality products, normally software assets, can be built, tested and shipped in quick succession—thus delivering value much sooner than traditional approaches.
- DevOps is a way of working whereby developers and IT system operators work closely, collaboratively, and in harmony towards a common goal with little or no organizational barriers or boundaries between them.

This book will provide you with some insight into how these approaches can help you optimize, streamline, and improve the way you work and, ultimately, how you ship quality software. Included in this book are some tricks and tips based on real-world experiences and observations; they can help you reduce the time and effort needed to implement and adopt CD and DevOps, which, in turn, can help you reduce the time and effort required to consistently ship quality software.

In this revised edition, you'll be introduced to the tools, techniques, and approaches that will assist you in the successful adoption of CD and DevOps. Included within are real-world examples to help you to understand what adoption of CD and DevOps entails from the early stage of preparation, through implementation and scaling, to extending beyond traditional uses, along with some real-world examples and tricks and tips that will help facilitate adoption. You will be provided with clear and concise insights into what CD and DevOps are all about and what quantifiable value they can bring to your business and everyone working within it.

Who this book is for

Everyone involved in traditional software delivery, whether they are IT professionals, C-level executives, product owners, developers, testers, project managers, or the ever inquisitive tech press, perceive a common problem at some point; delivering quality software can be very hard, very painful, and very expensive. It needn't be and it shouldn't be. This book has been written for everyone and anyone who wants to understand how to overcome these hardships and how CD and DevOps adoption can provide much-needed pain relief.

What this book covers

Chapter 1, *The Evolution of Software Delivery*, introduces you to a typical software-based business and details their evolution from a fledgling start-up, through the growing pains following acquisition, to the best of both worlds.

Chapter 2, *Understanding Your Current Pain Points*, introduces you to the tools and techniques that can be used to determine the current pain points within your software delivery process and where they stem from.

Chapter 3, *Culture and Behaviors are the Cornerstones to Success*, highlights the importance of the "human" factors that must be taken into account if you want CD and DevOps to succeed.

Chapter 4, *Planning for Success*, gives you some pointers on how a successful adoption of CD and DevOps can be defined and how this success can be measured.

Chapter 5, *Approaches, Tools, and Techniques*, introduces you to the various tools and techniques (some technical, some not so) that can help with the adoption of CD and DevOps.

Chapter 6, *Avoiding Hurdles*, gives you useful insights, tips, and tricks to help you overcome or avoid the bumps in the road during adoption of CD and DevOps.

Chapter 7, *Vital Measurements*, focuses on the various metrics and measures that can be used to monitor and communicate the relative success of CD and DevOps adoption.

Chapter 8, *You Are Not Finished Just Yet*, covers the less-than-obvious tasks that are important if you want to cement CD and DevOps into your day-to-day work.

Chapter 9, *Expanding Your Opportunity Horizon*, looks into how to evolve CD and DevOps once the adoption has taken hold.

Chapter 10, *CD and DevOps Beyond Traditional Software Delivery*, provides some insight into how you can reuse CD and DevOps tools, techniques, and approaches beyond software delivery.

To get the most out of this book

This book is not focused on a specific demographic or specific type of person. If you've never heard of CD or DevOps, this book will give you an insight into what all the fuss is about. If you have already set out to adopt CD and/or DevOps, then this book can help by providing some useful tips and tricks. If you know everything there is to know about both/either subject, then this book will help reaffirm your choices and might provide some additional things to chew over. All in all, the target audience is quite broad: anyone who wants to understand how to painlessly and regularly ship quality software.

Previous knowledge of DevOps practices, CD, or using DevOps tools is not necessary.

Download the color images

We also provide a PDF file that has color images of the screenshots/diagrams used in this book. You can download it here: http://www.packtpub.com/sites/default/files/downloads/9781788995474_ColorImages.pdf.

Conventions used

There are a number of text conventions used throughout this book.

Warnings or important notes appear like this.

 Tips and tricks appear like this.

Get in touch

Feedback from our readers is always welcome.

General feedback: If you have questions about any aspect of this book, mention the book title in the subject of your message and email us at customercare@packtpub.com.

Errata: Although we have taken every care to ensure the accuracy of our content, mistakes do happen. If you have found a mistake in this book, we would be grateful if you would report this to us. Please visit www.packt.com/submit-errata, selecting your book, clicking on the Errata Submission Form link, and entering the details.

Piracy: If you come across any illegal copies of our works in any form on the Internet, we would be grateful if you would provide us with the location address or website name. Please contact us at copyright@packt.com with a link to the material.

If you are interested in becoming an author: If there is a topic that you have expertise in and you are interested in either writing or contributing to a book, please visit authors.packtpub.com.

Reviews

Please leave a review. Once you have read and used this book, why not leave a review on the site that you purchased it from? Potential readers can then see and use your unbiased opinion to make purchase decisions, we at Packt can understand what you think about our products, and our authors can see your feedback on their book. Thank you!

For more information about Packt, please visit packt.com.

1
The Evolution of Software Delivery

As described in the preface, **Continuous Delivery** (**CD**) and DevOps are complementary ways of working. The former gives anyone who delivers customer value via software the ability to do so rapidly, consistently, and—as the name implies—continuously. The latter helps harmonize the teams that deliver and support said software. Both approaches can help you to optimize, streamline, and improve the way you work, and ultimately how you deliver value by shipping quality software.

It should be pointed out that the true meaning of these approaches have been blurred over the past decade—be that by tech press misunderstanding or recruitment businesses wanting to add 10% on salary rates, or software vendors and consultancies wanting to make their fortune by jumping on the bandwagon.

I have summarized what CD and DevOps **are**, but before we proceed, it may help if I highlight what they **are not**:

- Continuous delivery and continuous deployment are not the same—the former focuses on business value and the latter is the mechanism of shipping software
- A DevOps engineer is not a magical wizard. Software engineers and DevOps engineers are basically the same—the former creates text files that are used to create software assets and the latter creates text files that create environments and configuration to run said software
- DevOps does not replace traditional system operations activities and approaches—it extends, complements, and enhances them
- DevOps does not remove the need for ensuring your software, and the environments in which they run are highly secure—although this can ease the adoption and implementation of SecOps
- CD and DevOps are not the silver bullet to remove all of your process and business issues, although they can help reduce the overall number

One thing you need to take into account is that almost all successful software businesses go through a number of phases of evolution. They normally start life as a small highly-focused team with good ideas, plenty of ambition, and some investment. As they build their market share, reach, and revenue, a period of rapid growth normally follows both in terms of workforce and spend. As the business matures and becomes established, they transition to the next phase of either continued and substantial growth to keep ahead of the competition, or make themselves a target for acquisition—this usually depends on how quickly investors want to see a return.

It's also inevitable that as a business goes through this evolution, the day-to-day business processes will become more complex, which in turn leads to complexity and pain in terms of how software is delivered.

The adoption of CD and DevOps can assist in reducing this complexity and pain; however, the effectiveness and benefits a business can reap are very much dependent on where the business sits on the evolutionary scale. If you are off the mark, then adoption can be more trouble than it is worth, and you may end up making things worse for the overall business. Not only that, but business, are strange and unique creatures—especially those whose raison d'etre is delivering software solutions—and no two are the same; therefore, the adoption needs to be uniquely tailored to fit.

The topics we will cover in this chapter are as follows:

- A more detailed explanation of the various phases of the evolution of software delivery
- The positives and negatives of each phase
- How you can ascertain which phase you are in
- The advantages—some unforeseen—that can come from a CD and DevOps way of working

To make it a little easier to understand what all of this actually means, we'll now dig a little deeper into these phases by following the evolution of a typical software-based business, called ACME systems.

ACME systems – evolution phase 1.0

ACME started out with a couple of things in common with the many thousands of small software businesses scattered around the globe: it had some good ideas and a saw gap in the market that it could exploit to make its fortune. It had a relatively small amount of cash so it needed to move fast to be able to survive and it needed to quickly entice, enlist, and retain customers at all costs. It did this by delivering what the customer wants just before the customer needs it. Deliver too soon, and it may have wasted money on building solutions that the customer decides they no longer want. Deliver too late, and someone else may well have taken the company's market share—and the revenue—away. The keyword here is deliver.

As a small start-up, in the early days, the going is slow and the work is hard: lots of R&D, frantically-built pre-sales prototypes, quick and dirty deliveries, and unrealistic deadlines After many long days, nights, weeks, months, and weekends, things actually start to come together. The customer base starts to grow and the orders—and revenue—start rolling in. After a while, the number of employees are in double figures and the founders have become directors.

So, what has this got to do with CD or DevOps? Well, everything really. The culture, default behaviors, and engineering practices of a small software house are what would be classed as pretty good in terms of CD and DevOps. For example:

- There are next to no barriers between developers and the operations teams—in fact, they are generally one and the same
- Developers have full access to the production environment and can closely monitor their software
- All areas of the business are focused on the same thing, that being to get software into the production environment a quickly as possible, thus delighting customers
- Speed of delivery is crucial
- If things break, everyone swarms around to help fix the problem—even out of hours
- The software evolves quickly and features are added in incremental chunks
- The ways of working are normally very agile
- Communication and collaboration across the business is efficient and, for the most part, effective

There is a reason for stating that the culture, default behaviors, and engineering practices of a small software house would be classed as pretty good rather than ideal. This is because there are many flaws in the way a small software business typically has to operate to stay alive:

- Corners will be cut to hit deadlines, which compromises software design, quality, and elegance
- Application security best practices are given short shrift or even ignored
- Engineering best practices are compromised to hit deadlines
- The concept of technical debt is pretty much ignored
- Testing won't be in the forefront of the developer's mind (even if it were, there may not be enough time to work in a test-first way)
- Source-and version-control systems are not used religiously
- With unrestricted access to the production environment, ad hoc and uncontrolled tweaks and changes can be made to the infrastructure and environmental setup
- Software releasing will be mainly manual and most of the time an afterthought of the overall system design
- At times, a rough and ready prototype may become production code without the opportunity for refactoring
- Documentation is scant or non-existent—any that does exist is probably out of date
- The work-life balance for an engineer working within a small software house is not sustainable and burn out does happen

Let's have a look at the software-delivery process for ACME systems Version 1.0, which, to be honest, shouldn't take too long.

Software-delivery process flow Version 1.0

The following diagram gives an overview of the simple process used by ACME systems to deliver software. It's simple, elegant (in a rough-and-ready kind of way), and easy to communicate and understand:

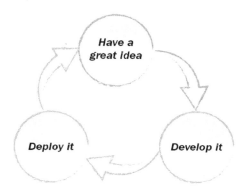

Overview of ACME Version 1.0 software-delivery process

 This very simple process is something that many small software businesses and start-ups will recognize. From a CD and DevOps perspective, there are next to no barriers between those building and delivering the software and those supporting it (we'll cover this later in this chapter).

Let's move forward a few years and see how ACME systems is doing, and gain some insight into the benefits and pitfalls of being the leader of the field.

ACME systems evolution phase 2.0

The business has grown in both size and turnover. The customer base is now global and the ACME software platform is being used by millions of customers on a daily basis. ACME systems as a business is well-established, well-renowned, and recognized as being at the forefront in their area of expertise. However, the level of growth and investment has had an impact on profits—which are still pretty much non-existent.

The board of ACME systems are approached by a larger competitor with an acquisition offer. The board and investors feel this makes good commercial sense and that this will help stabilize the business for the future so the sale is agreed. On the whole, everyone is happy with the deal and most see this as positive recognition that they have at last reached the big time.

At first everything is good—everything is great, in fact. The ACME systems team now has the backing it needs to invest in the business and be able to scale out and obtain a truly global reach. It can also focus on the important things, such as building quality software, scaling out the software platform, investing in new technologies, tools, and R&D. The drier side of business—administration, program and project management, sales, marketing, and so on—can be passed to the new parent company that has all of this in place already.

The ACME engineering team moves forward in excited anticipation. The level of investment is such that the software engineering team doubles in size in a number of months. The R&D team—as it's now called—introduces new development tools and processes to enable the speedy delivery of quality software. Agile is adopted across the R&D team, and the opportunity to fully exploit engineering best practices is realized. The original ACME platform starts to creak and is showing its age, so further investment is provided to re-architect and rewrite the software platform using the latest architectural approaches and technologies. In short, the R&D team feels that it's all starting to come together and it has the opportunity to do things right.

In parallel to this, the ACME engineering team members who looked after the production environments are absorbed into the parent's global operations organization. On the face of it, this seems a very good idea; there are datacenters filled with cutting-edge kit, cloud capabilities, global network capabilities, and scalable infrastructure. Everything that is needed to host and run the ACME platform is there. Like the R&D team, the operations team has more than they could have dreamed of. In addition to the tin and string, the operations team also has resources available to help maintain quality, control change to the platform, and ensure the platform is stable and available 24 x 7.

Sitting above all of this, the parent company also has well-established governance, and program—and project-management functions to control and coordinate the overall end-to-end product delivery schedule and process.

On the face of it, everything seems rosy and the teams are working more effectively than ever. At first, this is true, but very soon things start to take a downward turn. Under the surface, things are not all that rosy:

- It is getting increasingly difficult to deliver software—what took days now takes weeks or even months
- Releases are getting overly complex and larger as the new ACME platform rapidly grows and more features are added and changes are made
- Despite the advances in re-architecting the ACME platform, there still remain large sections of buggy legacy code deep within the bowels of the system, which refuses to die
- The R&D team members are now so far removed from the production environment that they are ignorant as to how the software they are writing functions or performs, once it eventually goes live
- The operations team members are now so far removed from the development process that they are ignorant to what's being delivered and how it's being developed
- There are many corporate hoops to jump through and process hurdles to overcome before software changes can go anywhere near the production servers
- Quality is starting to suffer as last-minute changes and frantic bug fixes are being applied to fit into release cycles
- Technical debt amassed during the fast and loose days is starting to cause major issues
- More and more R&D resources are being applied to assist in releases, which is impacting the development of new features
- Deployments are causing prolonged production downtime—both planned and unplanned
- Deadlines are being missed, stakeholders are being let down, and trust is being eroded
- The once-glowing reputation is being tarnished

The main problem here, however, is that this attrition has been happening very slowly over a number of months and not everyone has noticed—they're all too busy trying to deliver.

Let's now revisit the process flow for delivering software and see what's changed since last we looked—it's not a pretty picture.

Software-delivery process flow Version 2.0

As you can see from the following diagram, things have become very complicated for the ACME team. What was simple and elegant has become complex, convoluted, and highly inefficient. The number of steps and barriers has increased, making it extremely difficult to get software delivered. In fact, it's increasingly difficult to get anything done. The following figure gives you an overview of the ACME Version 2.0 software-delivery process:

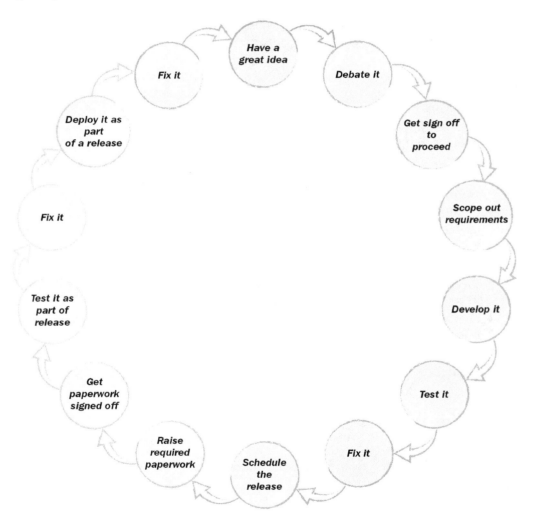

Overview of ACME Version 2.0 software-delivery process

This far-from-simple process is something that large software businesses will recognize. Looking again from a CD and DevOps perspective, this process is far from ideal as there are now many barriers between those delivering software and those supporting it.

If I'm honest, the process as depicted is actually missing some additional detail in relation to the change-management hoops that can add more complexity, effort, and pain. Let's add this detail and look again:

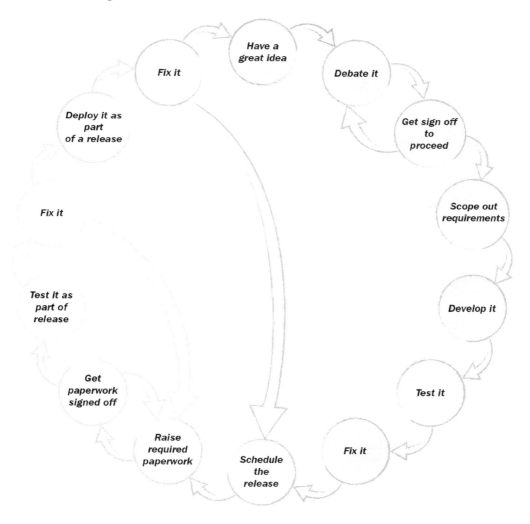

More realistic overview of ACME Version 2.0 software-delivery process

As you can see, things are far from ideal. What was efficient and effective is now the exact opposite. More importantly, the dialogue, quality of the communication, and trust between all of those involved in delivering changes is at best fragmented and pretty much non-existent at worst. What used to be a five-minute chat over a coffee is now a 20-page email thread, meetings, and Skype chats. The ex-ACME engineering team members are less like colleagues and more like entrenched combatants.

Not only is the process long-winded, but the chances of a single change getting all the way through the process without issue is very slim—most of the time, changes have to go around the loop a number of times before they can be classed as shippable; for example, a defect found within any part of the process may push the change all the way back to the beginning of the process.

I mention dialogue, quality of the communication, and trust for a very specific reason—most of the things you read about and hear in relation to CD and DevOps seem to imply that some new tooling and best-of-breed architectural approaches will give you what you need. While this can help, it can also massively hinder—especially when trying to bring these changes on board whilst a business is going through organizational changes and/or growth. In the ACME example, too much was changing too quickly for everyone to understand what was going on and where the journey would end. This inevitably lead to human nature kicking in and people building up barriers and silos to add some stability within the chaos.

If you were to take all of this into account, from an outsider's perspective, the process(es) ACME systems uses to deliver software is now, for all intents and purposes, broken.

OK, so this may be a little over the top, but it just goes to highlight how having a relative chasm between those involved in the delivery of changes—especially the R&D team members (who are tasked with delivering much-needed changes and features) and the operations team members (who are tasked with supporting the live environment into which the changes will be applied)—can completely derail things.

An outsider's perspective from the inside

As was previously stated, not everyone noticed the attrition within the organization—luckily, a few observant souls did. A small number of the ACME team's members were aware things are not great and decided to step back and look at things from an outsider's perspective. They then started to see the issues within the overall process as clear as day and became determined to expose these issues for all to see. In addition, they decided to sort the issues out—there was just the small problem of how to do this while everyone was going at full pelt to get software delivered at all costs in their own silos with their own problems.

At first, they invested a vast amount of personal time into investigating and building rough and ready tools, including build and test automation, **Continuous Integration (CI)**, a continuous-deployment pipeline, and system-monitoring solutions. The intention was to automate as many parts of the broken process as possible to reduce the pain. They also applied energies evangelizing within their technically-focused peer groups. Although their ideas and suggestions were welcomed by the majority, there was not the appetite to adopt these new-fangled tools—everyone was far too busy trying to ship software within the broken process. They needed another way.

They decided that they needed some assistance, so they sought out a like-minded manager with influence within the wider business who could help them get some much-needed traction. After much cajoling, discussions, and pleading, the manager agreed to help them to obtain budget to form a small team focusing on advancing the CD and DevOps tooling. The newly-formed team's members spent a few months identifying and breaking down the immediate and most painful issues, and built, installed, and implemented tooling to remove some of the pain—to ease the adoption, many of the tools are bespoke to fit into the existing processes.

This went some way to address the broken process but the reality is that the tools did not have the impact they envisaged. In fact, the tools themselves needed to be altered so much to fit the existing process that they started to become unreliable and too complex, so much so that those who were originally behind the approach started to question the validity of their decisions.

Ultimately, there is a much bigger issue that tooling cannot address—the culture of the organization itself, the behaviors of those within it, and the many disjointed methods of communication between the disconnected silos that had formed over the years. It became obvious that all the tools and tea in China will not bring pain relief; something more drastic was needed.

The team's members refocused and soon realized that it's not the tools that need to change to fit the process, but the process and ways of working that needs to change. If this was addressed, the tools could simply be taken off the shelf—so to speak—and used without extensive modification. The team's members have to drastically change their direction, become less technology-focused, and act more like agents for business change. They then highlighted this now-obvious fact to as many people as they can up and down the organization while the influential manager worked to obtain backing from the senior leadership to implement far-reaching business change. Luckily, their reputation and standing within the organization was such that getting backing was easy.

We're now going on to the third stage of the evolution, where things start to come back together and the ACME team regains their ability to deliver quality software when it is needed.

ACME systems evolution phase 3.0

Now that the CD and DevOps team has official backing from high up, its members start to address the broken culture and behaviors, and develop ways to overcome and/or remove the barriers. They are no longer simply a technical team; they are a catalyst for business change.

The remit is clear—do whatever is needed to streamline the process of software delivery and make it seamless and repeatable. In essence, implement what we now commonly refer to as CD and DevOps.

The first thing they do is to go out and talk with as many people across the business as possible to ensure they are also aware of the broken process and its root causes. Simply put, if someone is actively involved in the decision-making process of getting software from conception to consumer, or involved in supporting it when it's live, they are a chat target. This not only gathers useful information, but also gives the team the opportunity to evangelize and form a wider network of like-minded individuals.

The team has a vision, a purpose, that its members passionately believe in what needs to be done, and they have the energy and drive to do it.

Over the next few months, they embark on (among other things):

- Running various in-depth sessions to understand and map out the end-to-end product-delivery process
- Refining and simplifying the tooling based upon continuous feedback from those using it—where applicable, replacing in-house built solutions with off-the-shelf ones
- Addressing the complexity of managing dependencies and the order of deployment
- Engaging experts in the field of CD and DevOps to independently assess the progress being made (or not, as the case may be)
- Arranging offsite CD and DevOps training and encouraging both R&D and Ops team members to attend the training together (it's amazing how much DevOps collaboration stems from a chat in the hotel bar)
- Reducing the many handover and decision-making points throughout the software-release process
- Removing the barriers to allow developers to safely deploy their own software to the production platform
- Working with other business functions to gain trust and help them to refine and streamline their processes
- Removing the us-and-them attitudes and behaviors, and reinforcing trust-based relationships
- Working with R&D and operations teams to experiment with different agile methodologies, such as Kanban, scrum, and lean
- Openly and transparently sharing information and data around deliveries and progress being made across all areas of the business
- Replacing the need for complex performance-testing with the ability for developers to closely monitor their own software running in the production environment
- Removing the need for downtime to release changes
- Evangelizing across all areas of the business to share and sell the overall vision and value of CD and DevOps

This is by no means a walk in the park and it takes determination, steadfast focus, patience, and, above all, time to produce quantifiable, positive results, however after some months, the vision and benefits start to be realized. Now the process of building and delivering software has transformed to the extent that a code change can be built, fully tested, and deployed to the production platform in minutes many times per day—all at the press of a button and initiated and monitored by the developer who made the change, all with no downtime and little/no impact on the customers. The stakeholders have a trusted and reliable way of delivering value to their customers, the R&D team has the tooling and empowerment to deliver value as and when it is needed, and the Ops team has a stable and reliable platform that it can support and optimize.

Let's look again at the software-delivery process flow to see what results have been realized.

Software-delivery process flow version 3.0

As you can see from the diagram, the process looks much healthier. It's not as simple as Version 1.0, but it is efficient, reliable, and repeatable. Some much-needed checks and balances have been retained from Version 2.0 and optimized to enhance rather than impede the overall process:

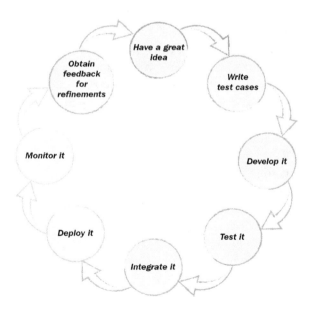

Overview of ACME 3.0 software-delivery process

This more elegant and well-oiled process is something that a mature yet modern software business will recognize. The barriers between those delivering the software and those that support it are there to ensure there is a degree of control and quality assurance, but both sides benefit from and embrace them.

This highly efficient process has freed up valuable R&D and operations resources so that they can focus on what they are best at—developing and delivering new high-quality features, and ensuring that the production platform is healthy and customers are delighted.

The ACME systems team has got back its mojo and is moving forward with a newfound confidence and drive. It now has the best of both worlds, and there's nothing stopping it.

ACME systems beyond Version 3.0

The ACME systems team's members have come through their challenges stronger and leaner but their story doesn't end there. As with any successful business, they don't rest on their laurels but decide to expand into new markets and opportunities—namely, to build and deliver mobile-optimized clients to work with and complement their core web-based propositions.

With all they have learned throughout their evolution, they know they have an optimal way of working to allow them to deliver quality products that customers want, when they want them, and they know how to deliver quickly, reliably, and incrementally. However, the complexities of delivering features to a hosted web-based platform are not the same as the complexities of delivering features to an end consumer's mobile device—they are comparable but not the same. For example, the process of delivering code to production servers many times per day is under the control of the ACME team, whereas they have little or no control over how their mobile clients are delivered to end customers, nor if and when the end customer will install the latest and greatest version from the various app stores onto which the mobile client is published. In addition to this, the production platform onto which the mobile client will be installed is pretty much an unknown in terms of spec, performance, and storage.

All is not lost, though—far from it. The members of the ACME systems team have learned a vast amount throughout their evolutionary journey, and decide to approach this new challenge as they had done previously. They know they can build, test, and deliver software with consistent quality. They know how to deliver change incrementally with little or no impact. They know how to support customers and monitor and react quickly to change. They know their culture is mature and that the wider organization can work as one to overcome shared challenges.

As the new venture progresses, they also discover another side-effect of their newly rekindled success: the amount of traffic and transactions start to grow very quickly. They therefore need to scale out their platform and they need to do it as soon as possible. Rather than rely on their own datacenters, they decide to move their entire platform to a globally-distributed cloud-based solution. This brings with it new challenges: the infrastructure is completely different, the provisioning tools are new, the tools used to build and deliver software are incompatible with the existing ACME tools. Again, the ACME systems team take this in stride and forge ahead with confidence using the highly collaborative ways of working, techniques, and approaches that are now part of their DNA.

 Would ACME systems Version 1.0 business have been able to take on these new challenges and succeeded? It's possible, but the results would have been mixed, the risks that much greater, and the quality that much lower. It's pretty obvious that ACME systems Version 2.0 business would have had major struggles, and by the time the products had hit the market, they would have been out of date and fighting for market share with the quicker and leaner competition.

Let's look at what this all means from a holistic point of view.

The evolution in a nutshell

Throughout this chapter, we have been following the evolution of ACME systems: where they started, the growing pains that came from success, how they discovered that rapid growth brings with it negatives as well as positives, how they overcame their near extinction by adopting CD and DevOps, and how they regained their mojo and confidence to move forward. All of this can be represented by the following simple diagram:

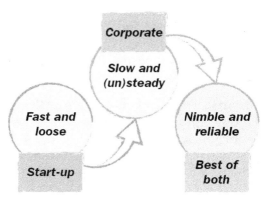

Overview of ACME systems evolution

What they also learned—somewhat late in the evolution—was that CD, and DevOps-adoption has little to do with technical tools and everything to do with how people work together. Without the changes to the culture and behaviors of everyone involved in the end-to-end delivery process, it is almost impossible to realize and maximize the benefits that a successful adoption of CD and DevOps brings. It could be said that if they knew this simple, yet mostly overlooked, fact from day one, then the adoption would have happened sooner and the business would have been far stronger far sooner. Hopefully, this will provide some food for thought for you as you move through the rest of the book.

Where am I on the evolutionary scale?

At the beginning of this chapter, I stated that the effectiveness of adopting CD and DevOps is very much dependent on where a business sits on the evolutionary scale. We've been through ACME's evolution and the phases it went through. Please take into account that ACME is fictional and its story is pretty simplistic. A real-world business is not simple—far from it—and it is pretty difficult to ascertain where a given business sits on the CD and DevOps evolutionary scale. Without this information, it's hard to understand how receptive, responsive, and open to adoption a business actually is.

With that said, there are some simple ways of getting a clearer idea. For example, the following list of questions can help you get a rough idea. Looking at your business, ask yourself the following:

	Option #1	Option #2	Option #3
Does your business favor process over people?	Process	People	We don't have any processes worth mentioning.
Do immovable deadlines in project plans take precedence over delivering quality solutions incrementally?	Yes, meeting deadlines is the only thing that matters.	We have the flexibility to make small changes, and re-plan to ensure quality doesn't suffer.	We do whatever is needed to keep the customer happy.
Are your projects run with fixed timescales, fixed resource, and fixed scope, or is there flexibility?	Yes, and this is all agreed up front, signed off, and intricately planned.	No, we have flexibility in at least one of these areas.	We do whatever is needed to keep the customer happy.

	Option #1	Option #2	Option #3
Do your developers have access to the production environment?	No, why would we trust developers to not screw things up?	All developers have secure read-only access to the live environments and all configuration via specific tools.	Yes, they have full access to do whatever is needed.
Is failure scorned upon or used as something to learn from?	Failure is failure and there are no excuses—heads will roll.	We ensure failure will have a small impact and learn from our mistakes.	Failure means no more business and we're all out of a job.
Who is on-call for out-of-hours production issues?	The T1 help desk, with the T2 operations support and T3 applications support teams backing them up.	We normally have a point of contact on call who can reach out to anyone they need.	Everyone within software engineering
Are you able to ship code when it is ready or do you have to wait for a scheduled release?	The release team schedule and agree on the delivery into production via the CAB and transition team based upon the agreed program plan.	We trust our engineers to ship code using our deployment tools when they are confident it is ready and doesn't compromise overall quality.	Our engineers normally FTP code to the production servers when it's finished compiling.
Does your senior leadership understand the complexities and challenges of delivering software?	They don't know in detail, but there are many reports compiled and generated by the PMO which are regularly reviewed during project-review meetings.	They all have access to tools which give visibility of the various projects and metrics representing progress.	They don't have the time or inclination to understand this—they expect stuff gets done.
Do the engineering teams have an understanding of how the business is doing from a commercial perspective?	All of the top-level financial information is compiled and published by the CFO to the company intranet every 6-12 months.	They all have access to the tools that give visibility of the current KPIs and metrics representing progress.	They don't, but as long as they get paid, that should be enough.

Does the engineering team have access to customer feedback?	This is normally collected and vetted by the customer service team and raised as defect or enhancement requests.	Customer feedback is captured via specialist tools and available to all.	Yes, this normally relates to defects and bugs that need fixing.

 If you were to apply these to the ACME business at certain points through their evolution, you would find that the Version 1.0 business would mostly answer 3, the version 2.0 business would mostly answer 1, and the highly-evolved version of the business would mostly answer 2.

The preceding is simply an example that gives you and insight into how you can—at a very holistic viewpoint—ascertain how mature the business is and where it sits within the CD and DevOps evolutionary scale. You will no doubt have some additional, complimentary, or more relevant questions you could use. However, if you follow a similar format, you will be able to get a feel for where things sit, and more importantly, what areas need the most focus. You should widen the net as much as possible to get a view from as many parts of your business as possible—that way, you won't come across surprises when you decide to take the plunge.

Summary

The ACME systems evolution story is not atypical of the many software businesses out there today. No doubt, you will recognize and relate to some of the traits and challenges detailed in the ACME journey, and you should now be able to plot where your business (or your client's/partner's business) currently sits within the CD and DevOps evolutionary scale. You also got a holistic view of what CD and DevOps is and what it isn't.

We'll now move from storytelling mode and start to look in more detail at some of the practical aspects of adopting CD and DevOps, starting with how you identify the underlying problems that can (and do) stifle the delivery of quality software.

In Chapter 2, *Understanding Your Current Pain Points*, we'll be looking into how you go about identifying the problems and issues within their **Software Delivery Life Cycle (SDLC)** and highlight some tools, techniques, and approaches to surface said problems and issues so that they can be fixed.

2
Understanding Your Current Pain Points

In `Chapter 1`, *The Evolution of Software Delivery*, you were introduced to ACME systems and given an insight into how it realized that there were problems with its software delivery process (severely impacting its ability to meet the expectations of its customers and deliver value to them), how it identified and addressed these problems, evolved, and after some hard work, determination, and time, adopted CD and DevOps ways of working to overcome them.

The story based upon a fictional business is pretty simplistic and linear to make it easier for you the reader to follow. Real life is never that simple, but there are a number of key points that were raised during the storytelling that do apply to real-life businesses. The most important of these for any business considering—or actively pursuing—the adoption of CD and/or DevOps is that there has to be a reason for said adoption. CD and DevOps, like any solution, can help you solve a problem—or set of problems—but you need to truly understand and quantify the problem(s) beforehand; otherwise, you'll never know for sure whether the solution has helped.

Just as ACME systems did, you need to take the time and make the effort to, as the well-used agile term states, inspect before you can adapt.

Your first reaction to this may be that you don't have any problems and that everything is working well and everyone involved with your software delivery process is highly effective, engaged, and motivated. If that is indeed true, then one of the following has happened:

- You have achieved software delivery utopia and as such don't need to read any further beyond this point
- You are in denial
- You do not fully understand how efficient and streamlined software delivery can (should) actually be

It's more likely that you have a workable process for delivering software but there are certain areas within the overall process—maybe certain teams or individuals—that slow things down. This is most probably not intentional; maybe there are certain rules and regulations that need to be adhered to, maybe there are certain quality gates that are needed, maybe no one has ever questioned why certain things have to be done in a certain way and everyone carries on regardless, or maybe no one has highlighted how important releasing software actually is.

Something else to take into account is the fact that different people within your organization will see (or not see) a given problem in different ways. Let's go back to ACME for a moment and examine the views of three personas (Stan the manager, Devina the developer, and Oscar the ops guy) in relation to having the software releases wholly controlled by the operations team:

I don't see this arrangement as being a problem. This is the way it's always been and seems the most logical way to do things. It was set in place by the IT operations director and I don't want to rock the boat with him.

The release process is someone else's problem and I will do the bear minimum in preparation for it — I'm far too busy writing software.

I dread each release. Every release is the same — it never goes smoothly and I spend many long hours getting the thing to work and days afterward clearing up the mess.

As you can see, different people will have wildly different views depending on what part they play in the overall process. Again, for ease of understanding, this example only features three personas—in reality there will be many more people who will all have their own slightly different viewpoint; consider how a project manager, release manager, tech writer, SecOps, or even a CEO would see this specific scenario.

For the sake of argument, let's assume that you do indeed have some problems releasing your software with ease and want to understand what the root cause is—or most likely the root causes are—so that you can make the overall process more efficient, effective, and streamlined. As stated, before you **can** adapt you **need** to inspect—this is the fundamental premise of most agile methodologies. The following chapter will surface some of the approaches and techniques that will help in this.

Throughout this chapter we will explore the following topics:

- How to identify potential issues and problems within your software delivery process
- How to surface them without resorting to the blame-game
- How it can sometimes be tough to be honest and open, but that doing so provides the best results
- How different people within your organization will see the same problem(s) in different ways

Before we start looking into how to inspect, I would like to go off on a slight tangent and talk about a large (normally) gray mammal.

Elephant in the room

Some of us have a very real and worrying ailment that blights our working lives, elephant in the room blindness—or to give it its medical name, Pachyderm in situ vision impairedness. Those inflicted are aware of a big problem or issue that is in their way, impeding their progress, efficiency, and willingness to engage and draining their morale. What do these poor souls normally do? They normally choose to either simply accept it or worse still, ignore it—depending on the size of the problem. Those that don't bury their heads in the sand, so to speak, then find ingenious ways to work around, circumvent, or avoid said problem by making very localized changes to how they work. Sometimes, at the detriment to others. In fact, they normally invest a lot of effort, time, and money in building these ingenious solutions and then convince themselves and their leadership that this is the best thing to do.

To stretch this metaphor a little more—please bear with me, there is a point to this—I would like to turn to the world of art. The artist Banksy exhibited a piece of living artwork as part of his 2006 Barely Legal exhibition in Los Angeles. This living artwork was in the form of an adult Indian elephant standing in a makeshift living room with floral print on the walls. The elephant was also *painted* head to toe with the same floral pattern. The piece was entitled—as luck would have it—elephant in the room. It seems ludicrous at first and you can clearly see that there is a massive 12,000 lb. elephant standing there; while it has been painted to blend in with its surroundings, it is still a massive elephant stood there in plain sight. This brings me to my point, the problems and issues within a software delivery process are just like the elephant and it is just as ludicrous that we simply ignore—or accept without question—their existence.

 Just like real life, the software delivery process elephant in the room is not hard to spot. It's normally sitting/standing/lurking where everyone can see. You just need to be willing to look, know how to look, and what to look for. Once you've mastered this, exposing it's existence is far easier.

Through the remainder of this chapter, we'll go through some ways to help highlight the existence of the elephant in the room and, more importantly, how to ensure as many people as possible can also see it and realize that it's not something to be avoided, worked around, or ignored.

Before you start removing the figurative floral pattern from the figurative elephant, there's still some legwork you need to do.

Defining the rules

With any examination, expose, investigation, or inspection there will be, to some degree, dirt that will need to be dug up—figuratively speaking. This is inevitable and should not be taken lightly or treated flippantly. The sort of questions that will be asked will include the following:

- Why are things done in certain ways?
- Who came up with this process in the first place?
- Who makes the priority decisions to do one thing over another and what right to they have to make the decision?
- When exactly are these decisions made?
- Who owns the overall product delivery process?
- Who owns the various steps within the process?
- Has anyone previously questioned the process? If so, what happened?

- Does anyone actually know how the process works end to end?
- Why can't the management see the obvious issues and why don't they listen to us?

These types of questions may well make some people very uncomfortable and may bring to light facts that produce emotive responses or emotional reactions—especially from those that may have originally had a hand in designing and/or implementing the very process that you are putting under scrutiny. Even if they can see and understand that the process they nurtured is broken, they still may have an emotional attachment to it—especially if they have been involved for a long time. You need to be mindful that these self-same people may be needed to help replace and/or refine the process, so tread carefully.

To keep things on a purely professional level, you should map out some ground rules that clearly define what the investigation is for and what its goal is. These need to be clear, concise, and easy for everyone involved to understand and worded in a positive way. The sorts of things you should be looking at are as follows:

- We're trying to understand how the end to end process as it stands came to be
- We need to understand what business/legislative/legal constraints there are
- We need to see how the many and varied process link together to form the end to end process
- We need to verify if our process(es) actually work for us and the wider business
- We want to surface issues and problems so that everyone can see them and help fix them
- We want to make things better

To further ensure you minimize the emotional reactions, you should define some rules of engagement so that everyone involved understands where the line is and when it is about to be crossed. Again, keeping these rules simple, concise, and using positive language will help everyone understand and remember them. Good examples would include the following:

- No naming and shaming
- No personal attacks or witch hunting
- This is not a post mortem
- There are no right or wrong answers
- No detail is too trivial
- Stick to facts over fiction
- Leave egos at the door

Retrospection can be a powerful tool to gain a greater understanding of what can be improved, but if used incorrectly it can cause more trouble than good—you can shoot yourself in the foot many, many times if you approach this without some foresight. You need to make sure you know what you are letting yourself in for, before you embark on this sort of activity.

Let's now consider who you will need to be involved with and who will add the most value. Hopefully, this will be one and the same, but it's not always that simple or obvious

Including (almost) everyone

What you need is information and insight from individuals who can actively contribute, are engaged, are ideally open to change (or at least would like to see things change for the better) and understand and agree to the aforementioned rules. These engaged contributors should come from all parts of the business—if they are involved in product creation and delivery, they should be considered. You will need a broad set of information and data to move forward, therefore you need to get a broad set of engaged contributors involved.

To ensure you can identify as many people as possible, you will need to establish a good network across the organization or at the very least access to those who already have one—especially if your organization is sizable as it's not practical to identify and be on speaking terms with everyone. You will normally find that individuals who have been around for a good while normally have a well-formed and mature internal network you can tap into.

 Individuals who work in product support, business analysis, product management, sales and marketing, or project management are good people to seek out as they will spend most of their working lives forming relationships and networks with various people around the organization.

You should proactively engage with these individuals and explain what you're trying to do—remember the aforementioned positively worded goals and rules of engagement—and ask them to help build up your list. If you can also add them to the engaged contributors list then that will speed things up as they can do some of the evangelizing and leg work for you.

As the title of this section implies, although you will have the best intentions to include everyone involved in or affected by the software delivery process, this is not be realistic nor practical—especially in large organizations—so if you can get almost everyone involved, that should suffice.

As you start compiling the list of participants—which for a large organization can be quite daunting, demanding and not without effort on your part—you will no doubt find that there will be some degree of natural selection as you start to ask people to contribute; some may say they're too busy, some won't want to be involved for reasons they don't want to disclose, some may simply not care enough either way.

Identifying key people

While compiling the list of engaged contributors, you should also identify the key people within the overall process. These key people may not be obvious at first; however, asking the same simple questions of a number of different people from different parts of the business during your network building will give you some strong indications as to how key the individuals are. Examples of these simple questions would be as follows:

- Who do you feel should I ensure I invite to this?
- Who do you normally talk to if there's a problem?
- Who knows how this all works?
- Who normally makes changes to the process?

There is also a very strong possibility that many of this key people will be the ones who say they are too busy. The fact that they are too busy may be directly attributed to the fact that the process they are working in is broken, but they don't have time to stop and realize this. I would highly recommend that you take a little more time to ensure that those key people who fit into this category are encouraged, cajoled, and convinced to take part. For example, you'll need be very flexible in terms of aligning to their availability—this may mean changing your plans at short notice just to get 15 minutes with them; however, I would encourage you to do this as disengaged contributors can easily become active detractors later down the line.

If certain individuals are key, it sometimes helps to let them know this, as an ego boost can sometimes help win them over. Also, playing the "If you don't take this opportunity to sort things out for the better, someone else might and it might be worse" card sometimes works.

You will no doubt also come across individuals who are very (sometimes overly) eager to be involved simply because they have an axe to grind or need a soapbox to proclaim their personal opinion. These individuals aren't that obvious to spot, however with a few well-placed questions their intentions become more obvious—especially when their responses seem biased and include words and/or phrases such as blame, fault, them, or not my problem. If these individuals want to be involved then that's fine, but you need to be mindful of the fact that such people can potentially derail the process—which again may be why they want to be involved. One word of warning; do not simply dismiss these individuals out of hand as they may have valuable observations to bring forward and dismissing them may foster further negativity and make them very vocal active detractors. You should however ensure these individuals agree to be engaged contributors and understand the ground rules you have set. During the next stage, you will no doubt need to keep an eye on them—much like the naughty children of the class—so that disruption and negativity are kept in check. That said, you may be surprised at how much value they bring to the process.

Too many cooks

As you build your list of engaged contributors you may well encounter a positive problem—you simply have too many people who want to be involved. In some respects, this is a good thing—over-subscription is a nice problem to have as you will be able to capture more valuable data—however this can cause problems—but things can get disorganized and noisy very quickly if you don't manage this part of the process.

If you do have over-subscription, rather than dropping people from the list, you should consider running multiple sessions. We'll cover the format of the session(s) in more detail later but suffice to say they can turn out to be very interactive with a high degree of active participation. As such, I would advise you try and keep the numbers for each session down to a manageable level, otherwise you will end up with too many voices and opinions generating too much noise and too many discussions going off at tangents to each other. You should also ensure that each session has an even mix of individuals from different parts of the business (for example, don't just run a developers session followed by an operations session followed by a project managers session—mix things up) as you want input from a broad spectrum.

A rule of thumb would be that 20-30 participants as more than enough for each session—unless you're a very experienced facilitator, you will struggle to keep things orderly and focused.

You will also encounter a physical challenge whereby you need to be in two or three places at once—unless you have mastered the art of cloning or astral projection, that's simply not possible. You should therefore run the sessions sequentially rather than concurrently thus giving yourself a gap to rest and compile the data captured. If this isn't possible, then you should consider enlisting one or more co-facilitators you feel have the same goals, drives, and passion you do in relation to revealing the elephant. A word of warning here: you all need to be very aligned in your approach; otherwise, you may skew the data.

 If you do end up running multiple sessions, ensure that each participant only attends one of the sessions—especially those of an axe-grinding persuasion. You want to ensure everyone has an equal voice.

To all intents and purposes the preceding equates to this: you need to engage and include as many different people as possible who are actively involved in the process of defining, building, testing, shipping, and supporting software within your organization. The wider the net is cast the more relevant the information and data you will catch, so to speak.

Not only is the way in which the investigation is to be conducted and who is involved very important, it is also vitally important that you ensure the environment is set up correctly to allow for those attending to be open, transparent, and more importantly honest—this will also encourage appropriate behaviors to surface. We'll be looking into behaviors in more detail later, but for now let's concentrate on the aforementioned three key areas.

Openness, transparency, and honesty

To truly get to the bottom of a given problem, you need to gather as much information and data about it as possible, so that you can collectively analyze and agree the best way to overcome or address it—you need to know how big the elephant truly is before you can expose it and remove it. The natural reaction of most senior management types—especially those in the higher MBA educated echelons—will be to then enlist a costly business change consultancy agency to run a closed-session top-level investigation with a handpicked select few from middle management to take part to produce a management report.

Although this well-trodden approach may provide some information and data, I would argue that it will not give you or the business what you need. In addition, during these types of investigations the environment is normally such that attendees will feel watched and intimidated therefore will not feel free to be honest and disclose pertinent pieces of information—just in case this adds a black mark to their record and/or career. Because of this, basic human nature will kick in and things will be missed, individuals may simply forget an important detail, or worse still some of the information may be misinterpreted or simply taken it out of context. All in all, closed-session investigations are a hotbed for distrust, non-disclosure, disengagement, blinkered points of view, and secrecy.

Secrets hiding the truth

As previously mentioned, to realistically get the level of information and engagement required, you need to create an open and transparent environment in which positive behaviors can flourish. An environment where trust, honesty, disclosure, and constructive dialogue are encouraged and commonplace. This does not mean you have to work within a glass house and have every conversation in public and every decision made by committee. What is needed is **a distinct lack of secrets**.

Let me clarify what I mean by using an example: Bernie is the CEO of a small but successful software business. Over the last few months, more and more customers have started to complain about broken promises and obviously rushed and buggy releases. She is also hearing that employees are not happy and productivity is down. She considers the following:

- Begrudgingly admit that there may be a few problems that need addressing and instruct the VP of engineering to handpick a team of people he trusts to compile a list of solutions to present back to the board within the week. The VP will under orders to not disclose or discuss this with anyone outside of the closed group.
- Commission an external consultancy to run a top-level closes-session investigation.
- Invite every employee to an all day workshop and ask everybody to provide open and honest feedback about the issues they face day to day. She will then get her leadership team together and spend a few weeks openly working through all of the feedback. A follow-up workshop will then be arranged to honestly discuss and debate the various problems raised and options available.

I think it's plain to see the difference, and which of these approaches would bear fruit and which would wither and die.

This all may sound unrealistically simple but without openness, honesty, and transparency, people will remain guarded and you will not get all of the facts you need—the word "facts" is used intentionally. You need an environment where anyone and everyone feels that they can speak their minds and more importantly, contribute. One other thing you need to take into account is collaboration.

Location, location, location

Ideally, you should plan to run your investigation(s) collocated (so that everyone is in the same physical location) as this allows for greater human interaction, building of rapport—which is essential for building trust—and the general ebb and flow of conversation in what can be highly interactive exercises.

 You may want to consider running these sessions on neutral ground (for example, a conference room in a local hotel or a shared office complex) which not only puts people at ease but provides some focus away from the office and its day to day distractions.

Realistically, you may well have remote teams or individuals who you need to be involved. Some may work from home or another office or in another country. If this is the case, you'll need to be a little more creative in how you approach things as you'll need to make things as seamless as possible. As stated previously, the ideal situation is to have everyone you need in the same place. Depending on the numbers of individuals involved and where they normally physically reside will determine the best approach to take—for example, as follows:

- If the majority of the engaged contributors are collocated in one office, then consider bringing the remote team(s) or individuals to them—budget permitting
- If the majority of the engaged contributors are based in a remote location, then consider taking the the local team(s) or individuals to them—again, budget permitting
- If neither of these are viable, then consider using a reliable and high quality video conferencing solution (voice conferencing just isn't good enough for what you'll be doing) along with some real time collaboration software

If you are forced to run the session(s) across two or more locations, then you may also need take into account challenges around time zones and come up with workable options (that is, don't expect your Boston-based team to remotely attend a workshop at 5:00 EST just because it's easier for the UK team). There will have to be some creative planning around this.

As you can see, before you embark on the challenge of exposing the elephant in the room, there is some pre-work preparation you need to do.

Throughout this chapter, you have been introduced to terms such as "investigation", "elephant exposure", and "retrospection". In relation to your software delivery process, these all mean pretty much the same thing: gathering information and data on how the process works end to end so that you can highlight the issues, which can then be rectified. We'll now move on to some of the ways you can gather this information and data, but before we do, let's clear a few things up.

It's all happy-clappy management waffle – isn't it?

Some of you of a technical ilk may be reading this chapter wondering who it's targeted at and thinking "Surely, this is all soft skill people management self-help waffle and doesn't really apply to me". In some respects, this is very true; any good manager or leader worth their salt should at least know how to approach this type of activity, but you have to take into account the very real fact—an ineffectual process has a greater impact on those within it than those who are perceived to be running it. Put simply, if as an engineer your effectiveness, moral, and enjoyment of your role is impacted by a process that you feel is broken and needs changing, then you have as much right and responsibility to help change it for the better as anyone else. In my experience, the best engineers are those who can examine, understand, and solve complex problems—be they technical in nature or not. In addition, who better to have on board while trying to find out the problems with a process than those directly involved in it and affected by it?

If you're a software engineer or an operations engineer, or a project manager or a build and release engineer, or a QA engineer or anyone else involved in delivering software, and you're stuck in a process that slows you down and impacts your ability to effectively do your job, then I would strongly encourage you to get involved with investigating and help to highlight the problems (there will be many and some may not be as obvious to you as you first think). Yes is can be daunting and yes if you're employed to analyze requirements or design systems or cut code or look after the infrastructure then you'll be asking yourself why you should get involved in what equates to business analysis. It's simple really; if you don't do anything then someone else might, and it may get worse.

If you're a manager or leader, then I encourage you to lead by example and get involved. More importantly, you should proactively encourage all members of your team(s) to get involved as well—even if it means taking them away from their day jobs for a relatively short period of time. As stated previously, they are the individuals who are living within the process day to day and by implication know the process very intimately—far better than you I would wager. As a leader, some team members may need your help, some may need encouragement, some may need training or coaching, some may need empowerment, and some may need all of these. In the long run, it will be worth it.

Not only should you encourage the troops to be actively involved, you should also use your influence and encourage your peer group to do the same. On the face of it, this may seem easy to achieve but it can be quite a challenge, especially where other managers start putting roadblocks in your way. The sorts of challenges you going to up against will include the following:

- Convincing them it is a good and worthwhile thing to do
- Getting them to agree to allow many of their team to stop doing their day jobs for a few hours so that they can participate
- Getting them to agree to listen and to not drive the agenda
- Getting them to be open and honest within a wider peer group
- Ensuring that they allow subordinates to be open and honest without fear of retribution
- Getting them to trust you

As you can imagine, you may well be involved in many different kinds of delicate conversations with many people, roles, and egos across the business. As I mentioned previously, in relation to convincing the key people to get involved, you should again consider using some simple human psychology to appeal to their better natures. It won't be easy, but the perseverance will be worth it in the long run.

Now that that's cleared up, let's move on to the fun part—exposing the elephant.

The great elephant disclosure

Let's presume at this point that you have overcome all of the challenges of getting people in the same location (physically and/or virtually), you have obtained buy-in from the various management teams, have agreed some downtime, and have a safe environment set up in a neutral venue. You're almost ready to embark on the elephant disclosure—almost. What you now need to do is actually pull everyone together and run the workshop(s) to capture the data you need.

To make things a little less daunting it may help to consider your overall end to end process as four distinct stages:

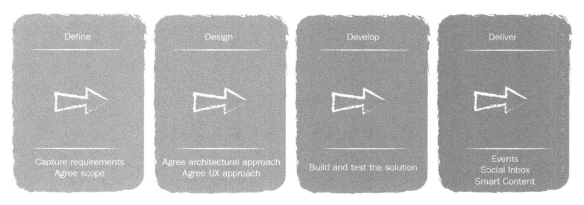

Four distinct phases of a typical end to end software delivery process

Breaking the overall process into these smaller stages can assist in mapping out the flow and structure of the workshop(s) you'll be facilitating. For example, if you decide to run an all-day workshop you can break this down into multiple sessions, each focusing on a specific stage, then bring everything together at the end. An example workshop agenda would look something like this:

Times	Agenda item
08:00 - 08:30	Introductions, setting goal and rules of engagement for the day
08:30 - 10:00	Session #1 focussing on the definition stage
10:00 - 10:15	Break
10:15 - 11:45	Session #2 focussing on the design stage
11:45 - 13:15	Session #3 focussed on the development stage
13:15 - 13:45	Lunch
13:45 - 15:15	Session #4 focussed on the delivery stage
15:15 - 15:30	Break
15:30 - 17:00	Session #5 bringing everything together
17:00 - 17:15	Next steps and wrap up

As you can see from this, these types of workshops can turn into a very long day—especially with a large group of people—so it's vitally important you are very organized and keep things on track throughout. Just trying to wing it will not give you the results you need. Some may consider compressing the overall time taken by removing the various breaks, however these breaks are very valuable as they allow for rapport building and guard dropping and also allow for the participant's brain to inwardly digest the information being disclosed and discussed.

Scheduling such workshops across multiple sites and/or time zones can be extremely complex and challenging, which is why running collocated workshops are preferable.

It is possible to run these types of workshops over two days, however I would recommend that you don't leave too large a gap between them otherwise focus will be lost and participants—especially those key people you identified—may get dragged into day to day problems. If you need to split the workshop, I would recommend that you schedule the day one workshop to finish late in the day and start day two first thing the following morning.

To ensure things go as smoothly as possible—considering the challenges you'll have keeping everyone focused and on track—I would recommend you keep things as simple and obvious as possible, not only for your sake but also for the participants. To this end, you'll need to prepare two things:

- You'll need the staple tool-set of any agile practitioner/facilitator: some big blank walls covered in paper, some large whiteboards, some flip charts, some sticky notes, various colored pens, and various colored stickers, some space, plenty of snacks, and a little bit of patience
- You'll need to pick a tried and tested agile technique that provides the format for the workshop itself

With regards to point #2, this is where I would have loved to provide pages of detailed explanation on the many varied and proven techniques and exercises with wonderful names such as StoStaKee, the Starfish, and the Sailboat, however this would make a book in itself.

 Before you send out invites to the workshop(s), you should ensure all concerned are aware of the format—as you'll be asking them to trawl back through their memories they may want to bring some pre-prepared notes along with them so plenty of notice will speed things up.

Let's move on from planning to doing.

Tools and techniques to expose the obvious

As stated, there are many agile tools and techniques available to you, however for the sake of space I'll include reference to these within the Appendix A, *Some Useful Information*, and we'll focus on two in particular that have proven to be highly effective over the years; those being timeline and value stream mapping.

Timeline

The timeline retrospective technique is an agile tool to look back over a specific period of time and capture key data points and information to help drive forward positive changes. These data points normally relate to specific events/challenges (such as a project kick-off or a budget cut after a quarterly review or a power cut that took all the production servers offline) but also can surface regular patterns of behavior, communication break-down, bad planning, and inefficient processes.

As you will be looking back over a period of time and surfacing details of things that happened (or didn't as the case may be), it's always a good idea to narrow down what you will be examining. From experience, you should consider a specific large and complex project or a business initiative or a specific release—I'm sure you'll also have some other ideas. As you are trying to expose problems and issues within your delivery process, I would not recommend picking something that went swimmingly well at this stage as you might not learn as much as you could—that can come later down the line to ensure any changes made have had a positive impact. Whatever you pick should be the focus for the workshop(s).

The format of a timeline retrospective is quite simple:

- You define and agree the timeline (that is, start date—end date) and draw that horizontally along a wide wall (or rather on the paper covering the wall).
- You then break this down into smaller periods of time (that is, months or weeks) and mark those points along the timeline.
- Next, you get all participants to write out sticky notes related to notable events that they remember during the period in question and ask them to add these to the timeline on the wall (if you have remote members taking part ask someone within the room to act as proxy for them). There is no limit to the number of notes—encourage participants to keep going as long as possible.
- As this goes on you will start to see groups of similar event notes forming—you should encourage the participants to start grouping these together. Some of these specific event notes may occur more than once throughout the timeline indicating a pervasive problem.
- If there are no more event notes to add you should then instruct the group to mark the notes with colors (either stickers or with a marker) indicating how they feel about the event—green for glad, blue for sad, or red for mad.

Throughout these, you should be actively encouraging open and honest discussion throughout the participants—maybe picking on specific event notes and asking questions such as "Is there any more detail to add?" or "Did anyone else notice this?" or "Did this happen more than once?"

You will now have a highly visual representation of what events happened over the timeline and how these events made people feel. You can then facilitate an open and honest group discussion applying some focus on those events that provoked the most emotions. During this discussion, some solutions may be put forward to resolve the pains—these should be noted for later use but hold off agreeing on an action plan for the moment.

The following depicts an example output from a timeline workshop representing a rather painful project and should give you some ideas of what you should end up with:

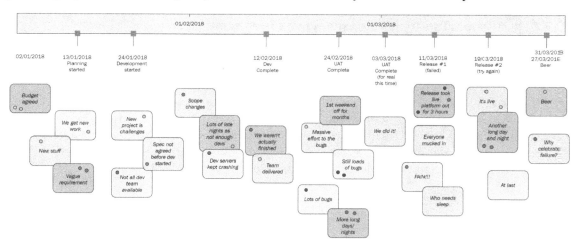

An example timeline board

Another proven and well-documented technique is value stream mapping.

Value stream mapping

This lean technique derives from—as quite a few agile methodologies and tools do—manufacturing and it has been around, in one guise or another, for many years. As with any lean methodology/tool/technique, value stream mapping revolves around a value versus waste model. In essence, a value stream map is a way to breakdown a product delivery process into a series of steps and handover points; it can also be used to help calculate efficiency rates if that's useful to you. The overall map can be laid out and analyzed to see where bottlenecks or delays occur within the flow; in other words, which steps are not adding value. The key metric used within value stream mapping is the lead time (for example, how long before the original idea starts making hard cash for the business).

 There are lots of resources and reference materials available to detail how to pull together a value stream map and there are a good number of specialists in this area should you need some assistance.

kTo effectively create a value stream map, you will need a number of people across all areas of the business who have a very clear and, preferably hands on, understanding of each stage of the product delivery process—sometimes referred to as the product life cycle. If you have done your legwork effectively, you should have those individuals in the workshop. Ideally, a value stream map should represent a business process; however, this may be too daunting and convoluted at first. To keep things simple, it may be more beneficial to pick a recent example project and/or release and break that down.

As an example, let's go through the flow of a single feature request delivered by the ACME systems Version 2.0 business (before they saw the light):

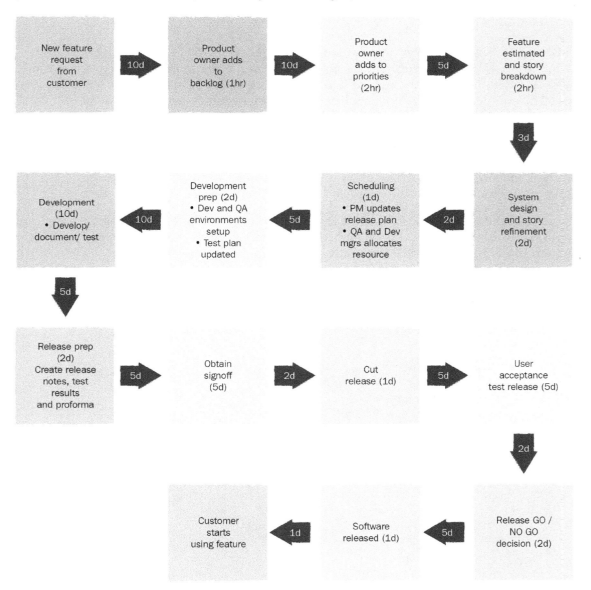

Each box represents a step within the overall process. The duration value within each box represents the working time (that is, how long it takes to go through each step). The duration value in each arrow represents the wait time between each step (that is, how long it took between each step).

This is a very simplistic overview but it does highlight how much time it can take to get even the most simplistic requirement out of the door. It also highlights how much waste there is in the process. Every step has a cost, every delay has a cost, and every mistake has a cost. The only real value you get is when the customer actually uses the software.

On the face of it, generating this type of map would be quite simple but it can also be quite a challenge. This simplistic diagram is created in real-time with input from many different areas of the business. There will be lots of open and honest dialogue and debate as facts are verified, memories jogged, dates and times corroborated, examples clarified, and agreements reached across the board as to what actually happens.

If you prefer to use the standard value stream mapping terminology and iconography, you could take the sticky notes version and convert it into something like the following, which again represents the flow of feature requests through the business:

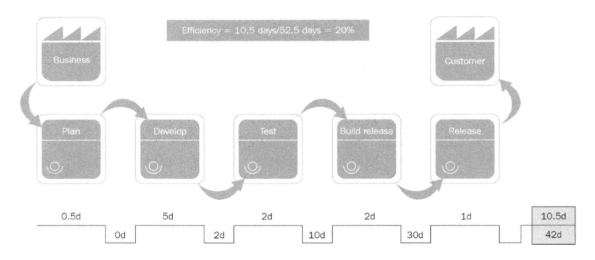

This diagram also includes the efficiency (which is based upon the amount of time value is being added versus dead time within the flow)

The most valuable output from this particular technique is that you can spot the obvious areas of waste. These are the parts of the overall process that are slowing down and impeding your overall ability to deliver. With this information, you can now focus on these problem areas and start to look at options that will make them less wasteful and more valuable to the overall process.

As previously stated, there are many other techniques you can use to provide similar data, some of which will be included in the Appendix A, *Some Useful Information*.

Summary

Throughout this chapter, you have been given an insight into the following aspects: how to expose problems within your product delivery process (what we're calling the elephant in the room), the challenges and benefits of using collaborative and engaging approaches to identify these problems, and some effective tools and techniques to help you break down the problems into easily identifiable chunks of work.

Now, you know how to obtain valuable information and data about your problem(s) and have some much-needed actions to work with. You also now know how to inspect. Let's presume these problems revolve around the waste created through long release cycles and a siloed organization. That being the case, you have a very clear objective that will almost certainly address the problems and deliver what the entire business needs. All you now need to do is pull together a plan of attack to implement it. In other words, you now need to adapt. Which is handy as that's what we'll be covering very soon.

Before we do that, I want to delve a little further into the human side of CD and DevOps and highlight two areas that are pivotal to the success or failure of adoption; those being culture and behaviors. In the next chapter, we'll take a deep dive into how culture and behaviors can impact the CD and DevOps adoption—both positively and negatively, and why ignoring this is not a good idea.

3

Culture and Behaviors are the Cornerstones to Success

In Chapter 2, *Understanding Your Current Pain Points,* we learned that asking people to be open and honest is not that easy, unless you take the time to set the environment up to allow for it. The environment had to be such that a culture of honest disclosure could take place. On top of this, you had to ensure that every participant agreed to behave according to the flexible rules and processes set out.

We will now take this experience and expand upon it to ensure the environment, culture, and behaviors throughout the organization are set up to allow for—what can be—potentially massive change. The sorts of things we'll be covering throughout this chapter are the following:

- Why culture is so important
- How your working environment can impact your culture
- How culture and behaviors affect your progress and success
- Encouraging innovation at a grass-roots level
- Fostering a sense of accountability across all areas of your organization
- Removing blame from the working environment
- Embracing and learning from failure
- Building trust
- Rewarding success in the right way
- Instilling a sense that change is good
- How good PR can help

Throughout this chapter, we'll also be looking at what this means to the three personas you were previously introduced to:

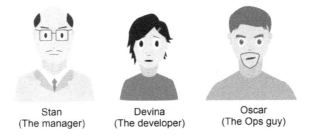

Stan
(The manager)

Devina
(The developer)

Oscar
(The Ops guy)

In addition, we'll include a new persona who runs the show from an IT perspective:

- Victoria the veep

Victoria
(The Veep)

It should be noted that I am by no means an expert in the human sciences nor do I have a PhD in psychology. What follows is learning I have gathered through observation, experience, and collaboration with experts in this field.

Let's start by clarifying why culture is so important to the successful adoption of CD and DevOps.

All roads lead to culture

There are many people in the tech industry—some very influential—who believe that the adoption of CD and/or DevOps simply amounts to implementing some technical tools and then making slight tweaks to existing heavyweight processes to potentially allow software to be released every few weeks/months.

Worse still, some see this as a *bona fide* reason to set up a new DevOps team inside the existing organization that—all things considered—spend their time building and implementing tools and processes that make little or no difference to successful delivery of quality software.

If you believe these views to be correct, then you are simply wrong at best and delusional at worst. Just to reiterate, CD and DevOps are—put very simply—agile ways of working. The DevOps tools are just that—tools. When we say ways of working, we're not simply talking standard operation procedures or HR policies here, we're talking about the default way in which people work, think, and behave.

Just like any other efficient and effective ways of working, CD and DevOps are only as good as the culture and environment in which people work and the behaviors they exhibit. All of which play a massive part in the success or failure of adoption of any change:

THE CONVERGENCE OF MANY ROADS

The convergence of many roads

When we talk about culture, this mainly refers to corporate and organizational culture rather than geographical, geo-political, or social group culture. That said, these can also have some bearing on how people behave, therefore you should be cognizant of this. For example, if you were to consider a culture that values and respects social hierarchy over individual views and opinions, then those self-same individuals may see openness and honesty as an unnatural or alien concept—or at the very least, may feel uncomfortable with the approach. This can also lead to individuals verbally accepting change simply because someone above them has asked (or instructed) then to do so—not because they personally believe in it.

Although you should be mindful of people's cultural values and motivations, you should not let this dictate or define your approach—you should simply accommodate them along the way.

The sorts of cultural and environmental aspects that are not conducive to successful adoption of CD or DevOps include the following:

- Barriers or power struggles between teams
- Silos across your organization
- Ineffective lines of communication
- Rigid, old-school hierarchies
- Strong embedded beliefs that how things have always been done is best
- Dysfunctional leadership
- The business is resistant to change
- Avoidance of learning from failure
- Command and control

Attempting to implement CD or DevOps in an environment where these are prevalent, without addressing the underlying and overarching cultural issues that sustain them, will ultimately lead to failure.

You may be reading this and thinking that you may have worked in (or work in) a business that has adopted CD or DevOps and be thinking that some/all of the preceding points do apply but on the whole things seem to be working well. The key phrase here is *seem to be*, which, if you were to apply it to other everyday scenarios, you wouldn't accept as readily:

- I checked the brakes on your car and things seem to be working
- I pulled together a fix for the DDOS defect that could expose personal details of 3 million active users and things seem to be working
- I investigated the reported payroll system issues and things seem to be working
- We've constantly lost 10% of our customer base over the last three quarters, but since the recent organizational changes and headcount reductions, things seem to be working

As you can see, perception can be a powerfully misleading thing and can set a false sense of security. If you were to change *seem to be* with *are* in the previous examples, you will notice the way in which you perceive the statements would be very different.

If you then apply this rule to your thinking in relation to your organization's CD and DevOps adoption, you may struggle to apply *are* within the statement as freely because the culture and behaviors of people involved are not as they should be. To effectively change *seem to be* to *are*, you need a positive and progressive culture to work in.

Defining culture

Culture is a very nebulous thing and can be difficult to visualize, understand, and define. This becomes more difficult when applied to a positive and progressive culture; however, the following diagram may go some way to visualizing what this means in relation to CD and DevOps adoption—some of this we'll cover in more detail throughout this chapter:

THE CULTURAL INTERCONNECTEDNESS OF ALL THINGS CD AND DEVOPS

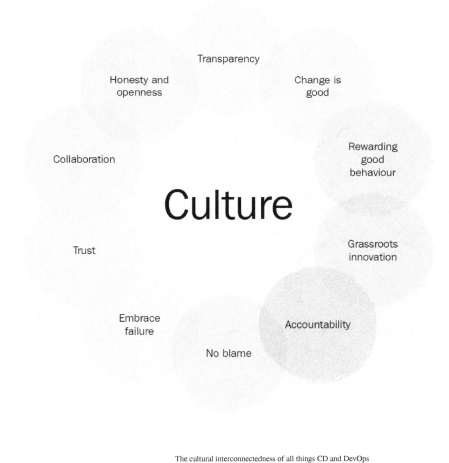

The cultural interconnectedness of all things CD and DevOps

In the previous diagram, you'll see that culture is central to enabling, encouraging, influencing, reinforcing, and sustaining positive behaviors. These positive behaviors will need to become the norm if you are to ensure your adoption succeeds. Some may believe that the opposite is true; however, the reality is that culture is so central that all of the work, effort, and best intentions in relation to establishing and sustaining positive behaviors can be thwarted almost overnight by a dysfunctional and poisonous culture. That isn't to say that you can't work from the outside in with enough sustained and consistent effort; however, from experience, I know this can be very long-winded, difficult, and fragile—it just takes one bad decision or event to undo months of work. Ultimately, you need to focus on the culture.

To put it another way, try to imagine your organization as an apple tree that needs strong and healthy roots to allow for the buds and blossom to form—if the roots (or culture) are unhealthy, the tree *seems to be* surviving but it will never bear fruit (or positive behaviors):

THE TREE OF CULTURE

The tree of culture

What has this got to do with CD and DevOps adoption? To truly benefit from adopting CD and DevOps, you need positive behaviors to be prevalent, encouraged, and embedded so that they become the norm. For this to truly happen, you need the culture to be positive and progressive. You may have witnessed some of these positive behaviors being exhibited while exposing the elephant in the room, so this shouldn't be an alien concept.

But what about the environment? Again, going back to the horticultural analogy, for healthy roots (culture) to grow and remain healthy, you need fertile and enriched soil (environment).

The following diagram represents the relationship between the environment, the culture, and the behaviors—all of which need to be aligned and healthy for the adoption of CD and DevOps to truly work:

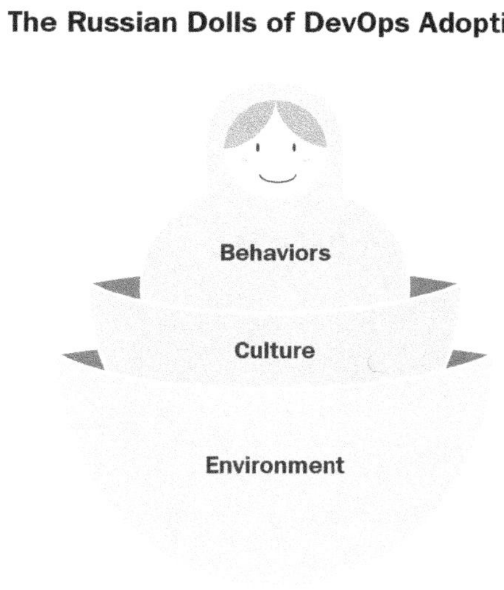

The Russian Dolls of DevOps Adoption

Behaviors

Culture

Environment

The Russian dolls of DevOps adoption

If this sounds familiar, then that's for a good reason. During the elephant exposure, you had already planted the seeds by setting up the environment—albeit in safe greenhouse conditions—to allow for positive behaviors to surface. The culture—even if it was for a short time—was generally positive and progressive. Due to this, you managed to expose the problems within your organization, thereby proving that with some effort and an aligned approach, you can produce results that otherwise would not have been realized. What you need to do is nurture this seedling and encourage it to grow, which can be harder to do than you think.

For all intents and purposes, true and successful adoption of CD and DevOps can be a pretty big change, and to some organizations it can be quite revolutionary. Throughout history, when it comes to cultural revolution, the acceptance and adoption normally resonates better with the general populace or those on the shop floor than the higher echelons. In terms of the tech industry, it's normally the engineers, testers, and other team members who are the ones to grasp and accept the concepts and benefits of CD and DevOps and will ultimately benefit the most when it's adopted.

That's all well and good; however, the reality is that the power to make decisive change is normally in the hands of those individuals higher up the corporate/social food chain. It is therefore crucially important that your leadership has a clear understanding and appreciation of the benefits CD and DevOps can bring, and more importantly, how the environment, culture, and behaviors can massively help or hinder the successful adoption. We'll cover this in more detail later in the chapter.

As mentioned, behaviors can have an influence on and be influenced by the environment and culture. There are a few other factors that share this symbiotic relationship. The key ones are processes, communications, and tools and techniques, as depicted in the following diagram:

More Russian Dolls of DevOps Adoption

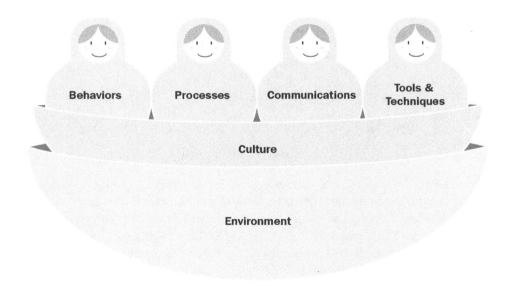

More Russian dolls of DevOps adoption

Let's briefly look into each of these.

Processes

As you will have noticed during the elephant exposure, one of the many problems most businesses suffer from are the processes that operate within them—many of which will be complex, convoluted, and deeply rooted. Now consider having to retain these processes while adopting CD and DevOps—as you can imagine, this would be far from an ideal approach.

For the adoption to be successful, you will need processes that are streamlined, efficient, and effective. They also need to complement and reinforce the positive culture, environment, and behaviors. For example, let's consider a typical example of an existing heavyweight process for getting a single-line code change through to a production environment:

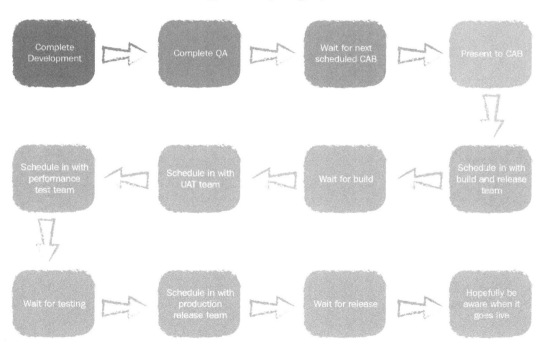

A typical heavyweight process

OK, so this may be slightly over the top; however, it's not unusual—especially in large organizations and/corporates that strictly follow frameworks such as ITIL or similar. If you also consider that this represents the happy path version of the process, it's not hard to imagine the loops and hoops you would have to go through should any problems or defects be found during the various steps (normally, this will mean starting back at square one). All in all, this kind of process would not be conducive to the adoption of CD and DevOps nor would it be closely aligned to a positive culture, environment, and behaviors.

Now let's compare this to a typical CD and DevOps process for shipping a single-line code change:

Simple CD equivalent process

Simple CD equivalent process

Again, this is an over-simplified representation; however, when compared to the previous example, you can see the sort of process changes you'll need to implement. Not only is the latter process streamlined and optimized when compared to the former, but it also helps to encourage positive behaviors, such as collaboration and a sense of ownership.

As you can imagine, making radical and impactful changes such as these can be nigh on impossible without having a culture and environment that would support it.

Communications

Communication is another key factor for the successful adoption of CD and DevOps. We'll be covering communication in more detail later in the book; however, let's have a look at why it is so key.

As is the case with any change, getting CD and DevOps accepted and adopted will need a considerable amount of PR, conversation, evangelism, discussion, and information- and knowledge-sharing. This will amount to lots of communication (by lots, I mean a vast amount). As was the case during the elephant exposure, the culture and environment needs to be such that communication between all involved can to be free-flowing, openly encouraged, and, above all, consistent.

 In terms of the messaging of CD and DevOps adoption, this needs to be targeted to the audience to ensure it is understood. As such, you will need to ensure that the communication is tailored to ensure that all concerned have a clear idea of what CD and DevOps is about, in terms they understand and can relate to.

As previously noted, there may be individuals whose social and cultural beliefs are not truly aligned to the open and honest culture and behaviors that are required for a successful adoption of CD and DevOps. You should therefore take time to ensure communication is tailored to accommodate these individuals.

Tools and techniques

When we talk about tools and techniques, we're not referring exclusively to technical tools, what I'm referring to here is agile tools and techniques that will help the adoption of CD and DevOps—sometimes referred to as engineering best practices. As previously mentioned, a vast number of the CD and DevOps specialist businesses that have come into being in the last decade specialize in technical tools targeting CD and DevOps (mainly DevOps, to be honest); however, there's not a vast amount of adoption of said tools outside of the traditional (Dev)Ops realm. This could be attributed to the specialist knowledge required to master the tools—something developers don't normally have the time/inclination to understand. The opposite is also true of tools and techniques favored by Dev teams but not prevalent within their Ops peers, such as the adoption of scrum, strict version-control, and test-first development.

Some development tool vendors have realized this and built technical tooling to allow for developers to seamlessly interact with so-called DevOps tools and Ops to seamlessly use engineering best practices traditionally targeted at developers. It does have to be said that, at the time of writing, this is still far from the norm.

Going back to environment and culture, consider this: even if developers did have access to so - called DevOps tools, unless the environment and culture is such that they can freely use them (for example, they are freely able to automatically ship code changes to a given environment using a DevOps pipeline), there doesn't seem much point in them having these tools as they can't actually do anything of value with them.

To allow CD and DevOps adoption to thrive, the culture and environment in which both Devs and Ops work should allow for seamless collaboration and interaction. Along with this, the tools and techniques used to deliver software changes should be chosen by and used across both specialisms (for example, Devs should know how to use tools such as Octopus deploy, and Ops should know how to use tool such as Visual Studio).

In relation to techniques, one massive win for CD and DevOps is the configuration-as-code approach. We'll go into this in more detail later, but suffice it to say that without an environment and culture that encourages collaboration, there's a strong possibility that such a game-changing technique will not come to fruition.

Let's see what our personas can do to help:

Good approach	Not-so-good approach
Victoria (the veep) and her peers can lead by example; even simple things such as being seen to take an interest in the environment and culture, and exhibiting positive behaviors will help. If changes are required, they can be executive sponsors so that everyone takes it seriously.	Victoria (the veep) ignores what is going on below her (or takes no interest), ignores the requests for help, and continues to exhibit a command-and-control culture.
Stan (the manager) should been seen to exhibit positive behaviors and encourage his peer group to do the same. He can research some best practice approaches and mentor his team(s) to adopt those that are relevant and make time for them to refine how they work.	Stan (the manager) does nothing to help improve and reinforce positive behaviors nor shows any inclination toward adopting or accepting modern agile techniques.
Devina (the developer) and Oscar (the Ops guy) can work together, exhibit positive behaviors, and encourage their peers to do the same. They can also encourage their peers to work with their managers and highlight areas for improvement in terms of environment and the culture.	Devina (the developer) and Oscar (the Ops guy) insist on working apart, only communicating when needed, and avoid collaboration wherever possible.

Thus far, we've been looking at the various parts you'll need for a successful CD and DevOps adoption. Let's now start digging into specific details, starting at the top with the environment.

An open, honest, and safe environment

Apart from sounding like something taken directly out of a management training manual, what does having an open, honest, and safe environment actually mean? In relation to CD and DevOps adoption, this means that anyone and everyone involved in your product-delivery process is willing, encouraged, and able to openly comment on and discuss ideas, issues, concerns, and problems, without the fear of ridicule or retribution—especially from those in leadership positions.

As you found during the elephant exposure stage, allowing for open discussions and honest appraisals of how things are done within the organization and the product-delivery process brings to the surface details and facts that otherwise would have been missed or stayed hidden. You need to persist the environment where the distinct lack of secrets culture and behavior is prevalent and maintained.

 If there is a time delay between the elephant exposure and adoption, then you will have more work to do to rekindle the initial euphoria, as most will have fallen back into their day jobs and ways of working. Therefore, you should seriously consider keeping the time delay to a minimum.

On the face of it, this all sounds like common sense, but unfortunately, this way of working is not encouraged, or worse still, is actively discouraged in some working environments—especially in corporate business. If you find yourself in this situation, then you have some additional challenges to overcome simply due to the fact that these edicts are normally defined and enforced through the HR and management guidelines, which in turn define the policies under which the business operates. You therefore can't simply break or bend these rules at will. We'll cover this in more detail later in the book, but suffice it to say that you need to tread very carefully and ensure you lead by example in terms of your behaviors.

Let's break down these concepts in more detail.

Openness and honesty

Openness and honesty are key factors to ensure that the implementation of CD and DevOps is successful. Without these behaviors in place, it's going to be very difficult to break down barriers and implement the much-needed changes throughout your organization. You already engaged the majority of the business during the elephant disclosure to obtain honest feedback about the current situation. You now need to ensure that you continue this dialogue with all concerned. Everyone involved in the product-delivery process, from developers and testers through change and release controllers to product owners and senior managers, must have a forum they can use to share their thoughts, suggestions, observations, worries, and news.

The most effective way to do this, as was the case previously, is via face-to-face human interaction, be this in person or virtually via video-conference systems (remember that video is preferable to voice as this allows for greater human interaction). There is one potential drawback to this approach—getting everyone in the same place at the same time can be difficult. We'll look at some ways to overcome physical environment challenges later; if face-to-face is not wholly viable most/all of the time, there is a rich and mature market in collaboration tools such as Slack, Flowdock, Yammer, or MsTeams (to name but a few), all of which provide you with real-time interpersonal interaction.

One thing to be mindful of when considering such collaboration tools—as most tools are public-internet-hosted **Platform as a Service (PaaS)** or **Software as a Service (SaaS)** offerings—is how their usage adheres to the IT security policy within your business. You should engage with your SecOps team and, if possible, get them on board with the implementation—thereby extending the CD and DevOps approach and community.

 Despite the long-held belief, email is not an effective collaboration tool and should not be considered as such.

Whatever approach you choose, it is advisable that you set up some form of etiquette or guidelines so that everyone knows what is acceptable and what is not. Normally, common sense will prevail; however, with openness and honesty come responsibility and maturity—some may forget this, so a gentle reminder can always help. On the flip side, what should not prevail is a heavy-handed policing or moderation of the content as this will actively discourage openness and honesty and ultimately make the solution(s) redundant. You should review existing policies and engage with your HR team to see whether they can help.

Going back to the main theme of openness and honesty, let's look at what this means in terms of the previously introduced personas:

Good approach	Not-so-good approach
Victoria (the veep) should openly share plans and information (within reason) with her department (ideally in person or via webinar) and openly ask for feedback.	Victoria (the veep) doesn't make the effort to communicate with her department and keeps all plans and information held back until the eleventh-hour faceless email is sent out.
Stan (the manager) should opening and regularly share plans and information (within reason) with his team(s) and ask for feedback. If collaborative tools are implemented, Stan and his peers should be actively using them and encourage their team(s) to do so as well.	Stan (the manager) emulates Victoria's behaviors and keep things secret and hidden from his team(s). Information is normally shared via email. Collaborative tools are seen as something only the teams use.
Devina (the developer) and Oscar (the Ops guy) proactively communicate in person—physically or via video conference — as much as possible and not just when problems occur. Use of collaboration tools over email should be the norm and they should encourage their peer group to do the same.	Devina (the developer) and Oscar (the Ops guy) continue to work in silos and only communicate when issues occur—normally via email. Information is shared on a need-to-know basis.

As you can see, it's far easier to fall into the not-so-good approach; however, the extra effort required to stay on the good approach path is far more beneficial as it will encourage open and honest dialogue.

It's all well and good to ask and encourage others to be open and honest, but you should also practice what you preach. As you go through the adoption of CD and DevOps, it is extremely important that you have regular open, honest, and truthful feedback from all concerned in terms of what is working with the implementation and, more importantly, what is not. Again, the simplest and most effective way is face-to-face human interaction; simply walk around and ask people. If this is not wholly viable, you should consider sort of lightweight survey solutions (such as Survey Monkey or similar) to capture feedback. The word *lightweight* is important here as no one will provide feedback on a regular basis if they have a 10-page questionnaire to fill out every few weeks.

If you follow or use an agile methodology and run regular retrospectives, ask those running these sessions to forward any feedback related to your implementation or, better still, join the session yourself and observe.

You're hopefully getting an idea of what open and honest dialogue is all about, but there is another very important thing you will need to cater for: courageous dialogue. Let's now review what it is, why it's important, and how it comes into the equation.

Courageous dialogue

There will be times when someone lower down the food chain will have an opinion or a view on how those above them help or hinder the product-delivery process.

You may also have individuals whose views are at odds with specific parts of the business, or indeed certain teams or individuals. It takes guts and courage for an individual to speak up about something like this, especially within a corporate environment. If we're honest, most would shy away from this approach for fear of retribution in one form or another.

For these people to speak up, they need to be sure that what they say (within reason, of course) is not taken as a black mark on their record or held against them in other ways. To this end, you should consider setting up a dialogue de-militarized zone (or DDMZ for short), where they can freely share their ideas, views, and opinions—where they can point out the emperor's new clothes.

You should work with the leadership team and HR department to ensure that there is a forum for this type of very important and valuable dialogue. The content might not be enlightening, but if you have a good number of people saying the same thing, then there is a good chance that something needs to be addressed.

If setting up a DDMZ is not applicable, at the very least, you should look to implement some sort of amnesty or a way for anonymous feedback to be collected—something as simple as a suggestion box or an online survey may suffice. It should be noted that as the culture and environment mature, the need for such measures should abate.

One important thing to also consider in terms of courageous dialogue is the quiet ones. Let me elaborate: generally speaking, there are two distinct types of personality traits: individuals who are introverted and those who are extroverted.

This is a very generalist and overly simplistic statement—in reality, there are many personality traits—however, for simplicity's sake, let's stick with the two.

The extroverts are the ones who are not afraid to interact, talk, and discuss their views and feelings in public. For extroverts, open, honest, and courageous dialogue isn't something they would normally shy away from. Introverts, on the other hand, when faced with conflict (potential or otherwise), will more often than not simply close down or just go with the flow. You, therefore, need to be very mindful of this fact and ensure everyone has the opportunity to contribute and voice their opinions. It might seem like additional work, but from experience, it will be worth it as the contributions from the introverts are normally well-considered and enlightening.

 If you have difficulty spotting the different types, then here's one easy tip: extroverts talk to make their brains work, whereas introverts use their brains to make their mouths work.

Let's be very open, honest, and courageous about how easy it will be to implement and embed these sorts of behaviors into normal ways of working: it is not. It will be challenging, complex, time-consuming, and, at times, extremely frustrating. However, if you persevere, and things start to work (and they will), you'll find it's a very effective way to work. You will find that once openness and honesty are embedded into the normal ways of working, things really start coming together.

Let's summarize what we've covered so far:

Do	Don't
• Allow freedom of expression • Encourage anyone and everyone to have their say (within reason) • Be patient with the quiet ones as it will take a bit longer for them to open up • Ensure management and HR understand why openness and honesty are essential • Get management to actively contribute and lead by example • Have a distinct lack of secrets	• Have a closed and secretive environment and culture • Ignore or dismiss people's opinions and views • Use open and honest feedback in a negative or nefarious way • Be impatient • Ignore do as I say not as I do attitudes

Let's look at what our personas can do to help:

Good approach	Not-so-good approach
Victoria (the veep) officially sponsors the creation of a DDMZ and encourages her department to communicate openly (within reason) on areas that matter to them. She also works with her HR peers to ensure actions are taken based upon feedback given.	Victoria (the veep) sees open and honest communication and dialogue as a way to spot and target the troublemakers who should be removed from the organization.
Stan (the manager) should reinforce Victoria's message and actions, and lead by example. When feedback from his team(s) is given in confidence, it should remain so.	Stan (the manager) plays lip service to any feedback provided and continues to act in such a way as to improve his career progression.
Devina (the developer) and Oscar (the Ops guy) take the opportunities given to be open and honest with each other, their peers, and managers. When surveys are sent out to allow for open and honest feedback, they take the time to complete them and provide truthful information.	Devina (the developer) and Oscar (the Ops guy) are afraid to say what they really feel for fear of repercussions to their career prospects.

What might not be obvious is the fact that the physical environment is something that can and does cause further complications when looking at encouraging open and honest dialogue and behaviors. We'll now look at this.

The physical environment

Some of you might be lucky enough to work in nice, airy, open-plan offices with plenty of opportunities to wander around for a chat and line-of-sight visibility of people you collaborate with. The reality is that most of us are not so lucky and have teams physically separated by office walls, flights of stairs, the dreaded cubicles of doom, or even time zones. At this point, let's hypothesize that the office space is not open-plan and there are some physical barriers.

There are a few things you can look at to remove some of these barriers:

- Keep the office doors open or, if possible, remove them altogether.
- Set aside an area for communal gatherings (normally in the vicinity of the coffee machine) with comfortable seating, such as sofas or bean bags, where people can chill out and chat.
- Have regular (at least weekly) sessions where everyone gathers (normally in the vicinity of coffee and free doughnuts, cakes, cookies, pastries, or whatever would entice people away from their desks) to chat and chill out.
- Get a foosball or table-tennis table; it's amazing how much ice is broken by having a friendly bit of competition within the office.
- If you use scrum methodology (or similar) and have separate teams locked away in offices, each holding their daily stand-up in private, hold a daily scrum of scrums (or stand-up of stand-ups) and have one person from each team attend it. Better still, mix things up and have members of each scrum team attend other team's stand-ups.
- Have teams hold their daily stand-ups away from the normal team area.
- See whether some of the partition walls can be removed.
- If you have cubicles, remove them, all of them. I personally think that they are the work of the devil and produce more of a negative environment than having physical walls separating teams.
- See whether an office move-around is possible to get people working closer together, or at the very least, mix things up.
- Where possible, replace desktop PCs with laptops—it's easier to be able to sit next to someone you are working with if you can take your workstation with you without needing a trolley to shift it.
- Stop relying on email for communications and encourage people to talk—have discussions, mutually agree, and follow up with an email, if need be.

These are, of course, merely suggestions based upon a very broad assumption of your environment and my experience in different organizations. You will no doubt have better ideas. The end game here is to remove the barriers, be they virtual or physical, which could stifle the successful adoption of CD and DevOps.

Let's see what our personas can do to help:

Good approach	Not-so-good approach
Victoria (the veep) listens to what those below her are saying and works with her fellow senior leaders to help facilitate any changes required to the physical environment—securing budget if needed.	Victoria (the veep) looks out from her plush office and suggests people stop moaning and just get on with their work as she orders new cubes for the additional developers she's budgeted for.
Stan (the manager) works within his peer group to convince those above of the importance of changes to the physical environment. Trying this alone, especially when money needs to be spent, might be challenging, so having many management voices saying the same thing will add weight. He also considers spending time working in the office space with his team(s)—a few hours per week may suffice.	Stan (the manager) looks out from his slightly-less-plush office and orders some blinds so that he doesn't have to look at the teams that are all crammed into the office space.
Devina (the developer) and Oscar (the Ops guy) work together to make small changes and run experiments, for example, to be seen to have face-to-face discussions, rather than via email, or take over an area of the office and sit together.	Devina (the developer) and Oscar (the Ops guy) insist on continuing to work in separate parts of the office, communicate via email, and don't mention anything to their leadership team about the working conditions.

We'll now move on from the seemingly simple subject of openness and honesty to the seemingly simple area of collaboration.

Encouraging and embracing collaboration

As you set out on your journey to adopt CD and DevOps, you will no doubt be working with the assumption that everyone involved wants to play ball and collaborate.

A large part of the business actively contributed to the elephant exposure exercise to capture and highlight the shortcomings of the incumbent business processes and ways of working, and did so in a very collaborative way. Surely, they would want to continue in this vein?

At first, this might be true—assuming there has not been an aforementioned delay; however, as time goes on, people will start to fall back into their natural siloed positions. This is especially true if there is a lull in the CD and DevOps adoption activity—you might be busy building/implementing technical tools or applying focus to certain areas of an existing process that are most painful. Either way, old habits will sneak back in if you're not careful.

It is, therefore, important that you keep collaborative ways of working at the forefront of people's minds and encourage everyone to work in these ways as the default mode of operation. The challenge is to make this an easy decision for all concerned. In essence, what you need is for people to believe and feel that working collaboratively is easier to do than not. When people believe and feel this, it becomes habitual and commonplace.

Luckily, there are many proven ways to encourage collaboration, but whatever you choose, you need to keep things lightweight and ensure that those you are encouraging don't feel that this way of working is being forced upon them; some reverse-psychology to make them feel it's their idea would help here. Here are some simple examples:

- Encourage everyone to use your online collaborative forum/messaging/chat solution as the first port of call instead of email when face-to-face communication isn't viable—even incentivize its use with leader boards and prizes at first to get some buy-in.
- If the norm is for problems to be discussed at a weekly departmental meeting, rather than having a five-minute discussion at someone's desk, then cancel the departmental meeting, instead encourage people to get up and walk and talk (or use the aforementioned collaboration tools).
- If the norm within the office is headphones on and heads down (which encourages isolation and stifles good, old-fashioned human-to-human discussion), look for ways to change this behavior so it isn't the norm. If people like to listen to music while working, you can consider something radical, such as a jukebox or some networked speakers. You could also consider agreements of when headphones on and heads down is viable (for example, only in the afternoon). In addition, if people need quiet time/space, see whether you can change the physical environment to allow for it.
- Even if you don't follow a scrum methodology, use the daily stand-up technique across the board—you can even mix it up across teams and encourage people to move around the stand-ups and listen in.

- Install some magnetic whiteboards around the office space, which will encourage people to get up, mix, and be creative while explaining problems, showing progress, or simply having fun and doodling. If you have set up a communal chill-out area, have a whiteboard installed there as well—this will encourage collaboration.
- Ensure you mingle and keep open discussions with all teams—you never know, you might hear something that another person has also been discussing, and you can act as the CD and DevOps matchmaker.

Once collaboration starts to take hold, you must continue to keep your eyes and ears open to ensure you get an early indication of when things slip back. If you have built up a network of like-minded individuals, make sure you utilize it to find out what's happening on the ground and take early action if you hear a siloed approach sneaking back in.

You should also be mindful of the fact that collaboration can also be impacted—both positively and negatively—by the physical environment. For example, if teams are spread out across different buildings or even floors in the same building, collaboration can be severely hampered. Some of the previous techniques may not be wholly possible/viable—especially when close physical proximity is required—however, being creative with technical collaboration tools should be encouraged to fill the gaps.

Let's again see what our personas can do to help:

- Collaboration is not the exclusive realm of engineers. Managers and senior leaders can and should collaborate and—more importantly—be seen to do so. Stan (the manager) can use some of the previous techniques and the technical collaboration tools.
- To be honest, most senior leaders would not normally consider using the aforementioned collaborative techniques and tools on a day-to-day basis; however, Victoria (the veep) should at least have an appreciation for them and evangelize throughout her peer group. Budgeting for the cost of technical tools would also help.
- Devina (the developer) and Oscar (the Ops guy) should practice what they preach, evangelize, and be highly visible when collaborating (ideally within the team/office area rather than hidden in meeting rooms). Even simple things, such as encouraging developers and operations engineers to go to the same pub at lunchtime on a Friday, can make a difference.

As collaboration becomes embedded within the organization, you will see many changes come to life. At first, these will be quite subtle, but if you look closely, you'll soon start to see them: more general conversations at people's desks, more "I'm trying to solve a problem but not sure of the best way to approach it, anyone fancy a chat over coffee to look at the options?" in the online chat room, and more background noise as people talk or share the joke of the day.

Some subtle (or sometimes not-so-subtle) PR might help, for example, posters around the office, coffee mugs, or even prizes for the most collaborative team; anything to keep collaboration in sight and mind.

Let's leave collaboration for now and together move on to innovation and accountability.

Fostering innovation and accountability at a grass-roots level

If you're lucky enough to work (or have worked) within a modern technology-based business, you should be used to having innovation as an important and valued input for your product backlog and overall roadmap. Innovation is something that can be very powerful when it comes to implementing CD and DevOps, especially when this innovation comes from the grass-roots level.

Many of the world's most successful and most-used products have come from innovation, so you should help build a culture throughout the business where innovation is recognized as a good and worthwhile thing rather than a risky way of advancing a product. Most engineers thrive, or at least enjoy, innovation, and truth be told, this was most probably one of the major drives for them choosing to become engineers—this and the fine wine, fast cars, and international jet-setter lifestyle (OK, this might be stretching things a bit too far).

This isn't to say that they can all go off and do what they want; there are still products to deliver and support. What you need to do is allow some room for investigation and experimentation—rekindle the R in R&D. Innovation is not just in the realm of software; there might be different ways of working, or product-delivery methodologies that come to light, that you can and should be considering.

 Innovation is not restricted to products and tools; agile techniques, such as **Test-Driven Development** (**TDD**), scrum, XP, and Kanban, all started out as innovative ideas before gaining wider adoption.

Despite normal convention, innovation is not the exclusive right of solutions and systems architects; anyone and everyone should be given the opportunity to innovate and contribute new ideas and concepts. There are many ways to encourage this kind of activity (competitions, workshops, and so on), but you need to keep it simple so that you get a good coverage across the business. One simple idea is to have a regular innovation forum or get-together, which allows anyone and everyone to put forward, and, if possible, prototype, an idea or concept.

Innovation can increase risk, new things always do; therefore, the engineering teams must understand that with the freedom they are given to make decisions and choices comes responsibility, ownership, and accountability for the new stuff they come up with, produce, and/or implement. They cannot simply implement shiny new toys, tools, processes, and software and hand them off to someone else to support. The **Somebody Else's Problem** (**SEP**) or throw-it-over-the-wall approaches will no longer work.

A good example of this is the ACME systems plan to allow developers to deploy code directly to production. On the face of it, this is very much what CD and DevOps is all about, but one simple question caused the plan to falter. The question was, who is going to hold the pager? Or, to bring this into the 21st century, are the developers going to be on-call when things go wrong out of hours? Ultimately, you need everyone involved in the process of delivering and supporting software to have the same strong sense of accountability so that the question need not be asked.

So, how can these values and behaviors be instilled in your organization? Let's see what our personas can do to help:

Good approach	Not-so-good approach
Victoria (the veep) should invest some time investigating and reviewing how innovation has transformed the way successful businesses operate and increased revenue and profits.	Victoria (the veep) ignores the importance of innovation in modern business and sticks to the old approach of delivering to the spec and nothing more.
Stan (the manager) should actively allow time for his team members to try things out or experiment, be this by setting aside some notional 10% time or simply encouraging them to put forward their ideas and suggestions for product or productivity advancement.	Stan (the manager) ignores the importance of innovation and forces his team(s) to focus on the delivery of product features over everything else.
Devina (the developer) and Oscar (the Ops guy) should actively pursue this agenda as part of discussions with their managers during one-to-ones or team meetings. To help things along, using some spare time on an idea, and then presenting it back, might be a good thing as it shows commitment and that you're serious. Working together collaboratively will also add credence.	Devina (the developer) and Oscar (the Ops guy) should simply keep their heads down and do what they are told, even if it goes against modern engineering best practices.

As your adoption of CD and DevOps matures, you will find that innovation and accountability become commonplace as the engineering teams (both software and operations) will have more capacity to focus on new ways of doing things and improving the solutions they provide to the business. This isn't just related to new and shiny things; you'll find that there is renewed energy to revisit the technical debt of old to refine and advance the overall platform.

Believe it or not, sometimes things will go wrong. We'll now look at how things that don't go so well should be dealt with, and why a culture of blame is not a good thing to have.

The blame game

Encouraging a fail-fast way of working is a critical element to good agile engineering practice; it is all well and good to say this, but this has to become a real part of the way your business works—as they say, actions speak louder than words. If, for example, we have a manager who thinks that pointing the finger and singling people out when things go wrong is a good motivational technique, it's going to be very difficult to create an environment where people are willing to put themselves out there and try new things. A culture of blame can quickly erode all of the good work done to foster a culture of openness, honesty, collaboration, innovation, and accountability.

Ideally, you should have a working environment where when mistakes happen (we're only human and mistakes will happen), instead of the individual(s) being jumped upon from on high, they are encouraged to learn from the mistake, take measures to make sure it doesn't happen again, and move on. No big song and dance. Not only this, but they should also be actively encouraged to share their experiences and findings with others, which enforces all the other positive ways of working we covered so far.

Blame slowly, learn quickly

In a commercial business, it might sound strange and be seen as giving out the wrong message (for example, you might seem to be ignoring or encouraging failure), but if lessons are being learned, and mistakes are being addressed quickly out in the open, then a culture of diligence and quality will be encouraged. Blaming individuals for a problem that they quickly rectify is not conducive to a good way of working. Praising them for spotting and fixing the issue might seem wrong to some, but it does reinforce good behaviors.

The following illustration shows the possible impact of a blame slowly, learn quickly culture:

Learning vs Blame over time

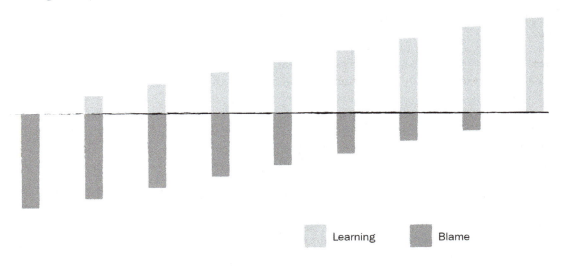

As blame diminishes, learning will grow as people will no longer feel that they have to keep looking over their shoulders and only stick to what they know or are told to do

As blame diminishes, learning will grow as people will no longer feel that they have to keep looking over their shoulders and only stick to what they know or are told to do.

 If managers are no longer preoccupied with the small issues, they can focus on the individuals who create issues but don't fix them or take accountability.

As you can understand, this culture change is not going to be easy for some, especially for the managers who have built up the reputation of being Mr. or Mrs. Shouty. Sometimes they will adapt, and other times they might simply step out of the way of progress—as the groundswell gains momentum. They will have little choice but to do one or the other.

Let's again summarize this:

Dos	Don'ts
Accepting accidents will happen	Pointing fingers
Encouraging a fail fast, learn quickly culture	Calling out an individual's failings
Encouraging accountability	Blaming before all of the facts are known
Encouraging the open and honest sharing of lessons learned	Halting progress
Not making a big deal out of issues	
Focusing on individuals who don't exhibit good behaviors	

Removing the threat and culture of blame from the engineers' working life will mean that they are more engaged, willing to be more open and honest about mistakes, and more likely to want to fix a given problem quickly.

Let's see what our personas can do to help:

Good approach	Not-so-good approach
Victoria (the veep) actively pursues a blame-free culture where mistakes are seen as just that, as long as people proactively learn from them. Her language and communication style reflect this as well.	Victoria (the veep) sees a mistake as a disciplinary offence and instills a sense of fear within her department that whenever a problem occurs, the person at fault will be found.
Stan (the manager) ensures that time is given to learning and training—especially when mistakes occur due to knowledge/skills gaps. His language and approach to understanding the root cause of problems is open and avoids use of the term *blame*.	Stan (the manager) mirrors and agrees with Victoria's approach. To emphasize this, he will pick out faults and ensure those responsible are identified and called out.
Devina (the developer) and Oscar (the Ops guy) are not afraid to admit when there is a gap in their collective knowledge/skillset and highlight this to their manager(s). When a mistake is made, they freely admit their part in it and are proactively involved in learning how to stop it happening again.	Devina (the developer) and Oscar (the Ops guy) work hard to distance themselves from any issues found and stick to doing what they are told rather than use their skills and experience to find creative was to solve problems—which can carry risk.

Of course, there is a large element of trust required on all sides to make this work effectively.

Building trust-based relationships across organizational boundaries

Now, I will freely admit that this does sound like something that has been taken directly from an HR or management training manual; however, trust is something that is very powerful. We all understand what it is and how it can benefit us. We also understand how difficult things can be with a complete lack of it. If you have a personal relationship with someone, and you trust them, the relationship is likely to be open, honest, and a long and fruitful one. Building trust is extremely difficult; you don't simply trust a colleague because you have been told to do so—life doesn't work this way. Trust is earned over time through peoples' actions. Trust within a working environment is also a very hard thing to build. There are many different reasons for this (insecurity, ambition, reputation, personalities, and so on), so you need to tread carefully. You also need to be patient as it's not going to happen overnight.

Building trust between traditional development and operations teams can be even harder. There is normally a level or an undercurrent of distrust between these two areas of the business:

- The developers don't trust that the operations team know how the platform actually works or how to effectively investigate issues when they occur
- The operations team don't trust that the developers won't bring the entire platform down by implementing dodgy code

This level of distrust can be deeply ingrained and is evident up and down the two sides of the business. These types of attitudes, behaviors, and the culture they create are all too negative. It's hard enough to get software developed, shipped, and stable without playing silly games with who does what and who doesn't. If you have an environment like this, the business needs to grow up and act its age. There is no silver bullet to forge a good trust-based relationship between two or more factions; however, the following techniques have proven to be effective:

- If you arrange for some off-site CD or DevOps training, ensure that you get a mix of software and operations engineers to attend and ensure they are in the same hotel. You will be amazed by how many collaborative working relationships start in the hotel bar.
- If there are workshops or conferences you are looking at attending (for example, DevOpsDays), make sure there's a mix of Devs and Ops in attendance and a hotel bar.

- If you are a manager, be very mindful of what promises and/or commitments you make and ensure you either deliver against them or you are very open and honest as to why you didn't/couldn't. If you are an engineer, act in exactly the same way.
- If you have set up an innovation forum (as mentioned previously), encourage all sides to attend and contribute.
- Discourage us and them discussions and behaviors.
- If it's viable, try to organize job swaps or secondments across the software and operational engineering teams (for example, get a software engineer to work in operations for a month, and vice versa). This can also include management roles.

Let's see what our personas can do to help:

Good approach	Not-so-good approach
Victoria (the veep) encourages her management team (Stan and his counterpart within the Ops team) to work closely together and, more importantly, to be seen to work closely together. She also approves a budget for cross-team events, training, and team-building activities.	Victoria (the veep) ignores the fissure between the Dev and Ops team (and their management) and maintains the strict separation between Dev and Ops in terms of ways of working and priorities. She also refuses to fund joint events, training, and team-building activities, and encourages open conflict.
Stan (the manager) is seen to be collaborating with his counterparts within Ops team and encourages his team(s) to ignore organizational boundaries to get the job done. He also encourages his team to mix with the Ops teams in social settings.	Stan (the manager) actively ignores or is seen to avoid collaborating with his counterparts within Ops and insists his team(s) are constrained to stay within the organizational boundaries. Fraternizing with the Ops team(s) is something he frowns upon and hostility is seen as the norm.
Devina (the developer) and Oscar (the Ops guy) ignore the organizational and hierarchical boundaries at work and simply work together to solve problems, mirroring the actions of their leadership.	Devina (the developer) and Oscar (the Ops guy) mirror the actions of their leadership and avoid every opportunity for cross-team collaboration.

We'll now move from trust to rewards and incentives.

Rewarding good behaviors and success

How many of us have worked with or been part of a business that throws a big post-release party to celebrate the fact that, against all odds, you managed to get the release out of the door? On the face of it, this is good business practice and Management 101; after all, most project managers are trained to include an end-of-project party task and budget in their project plans. This is not a bad thing if everything that was asked for has been delivered on time to the highest quality. Let's try rewording the question.

How many of us have worked with or in a business that throws a big post-release party to celebrate the fact that, against all odds, you managed to deliver most of what was asked for and only took the live platform offline for three hours while they tried to sort out some bugs that had not been found in testing?

If the answer to the question is quite a few, but it was a hard slog, and we earned it, then you are a fool to yourself. Rewarding this type of behavior is 100% the wrong thing to do. The businesses that deliver what customers want, and do it quickly, are the ones that succeed.

If you want to be a business that succeeds, you need to stop giving out the wrong message. We did say that it was OK to fail as long as you learn from it quickly; we didn't, however, mention rewarding failure to deliver. You should be rewarding everyone when they deliver what is needed when (or before) it is needed. The word *everyone* is quite important here as a reward should not be targeted at an individual as this can cause more trouble than it's worth. You want to instill a sense of collaboration and DevOps ways of working, so make the reward a group reward, such as a party or a day out.

The odd few

OK, so there might be the odd few who will put in extra effort when times get sticky, and rewarding those individuals is not a bad thing; however, this should not be the norm. If engineering teams (software and operational) are consistently being told to work long days, long nights, and weekends, then there is something wrong with the priority of the work. If, however, they decide to apply some extra effort to overcome some long-outstanding technical debt or implement some labor-saving tools to speed things up, then this is completely different, and you should be looking at specific rewards for these specific good behaviors.

At the end of the day, you want to reward individuals or teams for doing something amazing that is above and beyond the call of duty, rather than simply successfully releasing software. As CD and DevOps ways of working become embedded, you will notice that you don't actually have what you would previously have called releases anymore (they are happening too quickly to notice each one), and therefore, you need to look at other ways to give rewards. For example, you can look at throwing a party when a business milestone is hit (such as when you reach the next millionth customer), when a new product successfully launches, or simply because it's sunny outside and the bosses want to say thank you.

CD and DevOps will change the way the business operates, and this fact needs to be recognized across all areas. As such, the way you reward people needs to change to instill the good behaviors previously mentioned (openness and honesty, innovation, accountability, and so on). This can be quite a shift for some businesses, and some might even need to implement new reward systems, solutions, or processes to cater for this.

One of the standard ways of rewarding people is via some kind of bonus or incentive scheme. This will also need to change, but first you need to recognize how the current system might foster the wrong behaviors and can stifle your implementation of CD and DevOps.

Recognizing how Dev and Ops teams are incentivized can have an impact

There is a simple and obvious fact that some people might not instantly realize, but it is something that is very real and very widespread throughout the entire IT industry. This fact is that development teams are incentivized to deliver change, whereas operations teams are incentivized to ensure stability and system uptime, thus discouraging change. The following diagram highlights this:

Incentivizing developers to deliver more quickly is at odds with incentivizing operations teams with keeping things stable and safe

There's no simple answer, but there are some examples you can look at to ease the pain:

Incentive	Pros	Cons
Having the same incentives across both Dev and Ops.	If you are incentivizing to allow for continuous change, you will increase the potential for having CD and DevOps becoming the norm as everyone involved will focus on the same goal.	There is more risk as people might think that changing things quickly is more important than quality and system uptime.
Including each side of the DevOps partnership in each other's incentive schemes.	If some of the bonus of the software-engineering team is dependent on live platform stability, then they'll think twice before taking a risk. If some of the operations-engineering team's bonus is dependent on enabling CD, they will think twice before blocking changes just for the sake of it.	If the percentage of the swap is small, it might be ignored as the focus will remain on getting the majority of the bonus, which will still encourage the old behaviors.
Replacing the current incentive scheme with one that focuses on good behaviors and encourages a DevOps culture.	This has the potential to remove conflict between the engineering teams (Dev and Ops) and would encourage them to focus on what is important: delivering products customers want and need.	The reality is that it will be quite difficult to get a full agreement, and get it in place quickly, especially in a corporate environment. This doesn't mean it's not something worth pursuing.

Whatever you do with regard to incentivizing and rewarding people, you need to instill a sense of positivity around change, while at the same time ensuring risk is reduced.

Embracing change and reducing risk

In the same vein as fostering innovation and accountability at a grass-roots level, you need to work across the wider organization to ensure they accept the fact that change is a good thing and not something to be feared.

It is true to say that changing anything on the production platform—be it a new piece of technology, a bug fix to a 15-year old code base, an upgrade to an operating system, or a replacement storage array—can increase the risk of the platform, or parts thereof, failing. The only way to truly eliminate this risk is to change nothing, or simply switch everything off and lock it away, which is neither practical nor realistic. What is needed is a way to manage, reduce, and accept the risk.

Implementing CD and DevOps will do just that. You have small incremental changes, transparency of what's going on, the team that built the change and the team that will support it working hand in hand, a sense of ownership and accountability from the individual(s) who actually wrote the code, and a focused willingness to succeed.

The major challenge here is getting everyone in the business to understand and embrace this as the day-to-day way of working. The most effective way to do this is to prove it.

Changing people's perceptions with pudding

Getting the grass roots to understand this concept should be quite simple when compared to other parts of the business that are, by their very nature, risk-averse.

I'm thinking here of the QA teams, senior managers, project and program managers, and so on. There are a few ways to convince them that risks are being controlled, but the best way is via using the proof of the pudding methodology:

1. Pick a small change and ensure that it is well-publicized around the business
2. Engage the wider business, focusing on the risk-averse, and ensure they are aware; also invite them to observe and contribute (team stand-ups, planning meetings, and so on)
3. Ensure that the engineers working on the change are also aware that there is a heightened sense of observation for the change
4. As the change is progressing, get the engineering teams involved to post regular blog entries detailing what they are doing, including stats and figures (code coverage, test-pass rate, and so on)
5. As the release goes through the various environments to production, capture as many stats and measurements as possible and publish them
6. When all is done, pull all this into a blog post and a post-release report, then present them

You might be thinking that this is a vast amount of work, and to be honest, it is if you follow the preceding steps for each and every change you make. What it does do is serve a purpose: it proves to the business that change is good, and risks can be controlled and managed. I recommend you follow these steps a few times to build trust and confidence—you can always refine later down the line. Another positive you will find is that it will foster a culture of diligence at a grass-roots level; if they are very aware that the business is keeping an eye on things, especially when things go wrong, then they will think twice before doing something silly.

 It should be noted that even though these steps will generate additional work, this is nothing compared to how some organizations currently function; changes are fully documented, and risks assessed, progress meetings are held, the project progress is publicized, and every meticulous detail is captured and documented. Is it any wonder that delivering software can be painful?

As with anything in life, if you make a small change, the risk is vastly reduced. If you repeat the process many times, the risk is all but removed and habits are formed. To follow this thread, if infrequent releases contain a large amount of change, the risk is large. Make it small and frequent, and the risk goes away. It's quite simple when you look at it this way.

As part of the proof of the pudding example, there was a lot of publicizing and blog-posting going on. This should not be seen as an overhead, but a necessary part of CD and DevOps adoption. Being highly visible is key to breaking down barriers and ensuring anyone and everyone is aware of what is going on.

Being transparent

As we previously covered, being secretive about what you do and how you do it is not conducive to building an open, honest, and trust-based working environment or culture. If anyone and everyone can see what is going on, there should be no surprises. What we're looking for is a culture, and ways of working where change is good and frequent, individuals work together on common goals, the wider business trusts the product-delivery teams to deliver what is needed when it is needed, and the operations teams know what is coming. If there is a high degree of visibility across the entire process, anyone and everyone can see this happening, and more importantly, how effective it is.

You should look at the option of installing large screens around the office to display stats, facts, and figures. You might well have something like this set up already, but I suspect these screens display very technical information-system stats, CPU graphs, alerts, and so on. I also suspect that most of these reside in the technical team areas (development, operations, and so on). This is not a bad thing, it's just very specialized, and those of a nontechnical nature might ignore them or most likely don't even know that they exist. See whether you can move some of the screens to communal areas of the office or try to find some budget to buy new ones.

You should also complement this highly technical information with very simple, easy-to-read-and-understand data related to your CD and DevOps process. You should be looking at displaying the following kinds of information:

- Number of releases this day, week, month, and year against the number yesterday, last week, last month, and last year
- The release queue and progress of the current release going through the process and who initiated it
- Production system availability (current and historical)
- If you use an online scrum/Kanban board (such as Jira, Rally, or Trello), consider having this data displayed to show your backlog, work in progress, and work completed, along with related stats such as velocity and burndown
- The latest business information, such as share price, active user numbers, and the number of outstanding customer care tickets

The last point is very important. You should publish, display, and advertise complementary information and data that is business-relevant, rather than simply focusing on technical facts and figures. This will help to heighten engagement and awareness outside of the technical teams. Having this information visible as you progress through your adoption and implementation of CD and DevOps will also provide proof that things are improving.

Summary

We covered quite a lot of ground in terms of the human side of implementing CD and DevOps throughout this chapter. Hopefully, it has been impressed upon you that the culture in which you operate dictates the success of CD and DevOps. When it comes to collaboration, you will find that trust, honesty, and openness are powerful tools that allow individuals to take responsibility for their actions. Rewarding good behaviors and removing blame will also help drive adoption.

At this point, you should have a plan and some insight into the importance of culture and behaviors when implementing CD and DevOps. In Chapter 4, *Planning for Success*, we'll look at some practical things that will help as you drive forward.

4
Planning for Success

Throughout Chapter 2, *Understanding Your Current Pain Points*, you were introduced to the tools and techniques to identify the problems you may well have with your overall product delivery process. We referred to this as the elephant in the room as it is something that is not hard to spot, just very easy to ignore.

We then drilled down a little further during Chapter 3, *Culture and Behaviors are the Cornerstones to Success*, to highlight (and in some ways reinforce) the fact that the culture and environment within which the teams working on and delivering changes operate has a massive impact on behaviors. This in turn impacts how they work and the quality of what they deliver.

We will now take these learnings and apply some focus on the various methods, approaches, techniques, and tools you can use to turn this into something that you can implement to overcome the challenges—a plan of attack to implement CD and DevOps, if you will.

Throughout this chapter you will be introduced to the following:

- Why defining a goal and vision for your CD and DevOps adoption is very important
- Why it's important to ensure that everyone understands what it is all about and is au fait with the language and terminology used
- How to improve engagement and communication through the use of online collaborative solutions
- Making sure the business understands the breadth of the implementation of CD and DevOps
- Why effective PR, evangelism, courage, and determination are so important to the success of the project
- The costs, some obvious and some not so, that must be taken into account before you embark on your adventure

This plan of attack should not be taken lightly; just like the elephant exposure stage, there is quite a bit of groundwork you need to do to ensure the scope of the implementation is understood, accepted, and communicated.

Before we dive into the planning, let's have a look at the types of problems that you will no doubt be dealing with.

Some common problems

During your elephant exposure, you will have surfaced some problems with how you are currently delivering software. You will also start to consider the problems within your culture, environment, and the behaviors being exhibited.

The presumption here is that the problems identified are the commonplace issues related to most software delivery processes within most businesses around the globe. These will include some of the following:

- Waste from having too many handover and decision points in the process
- Waste due to unnecessary wait time between steps
- Many software changes are packaged up into large, complex big bang releases
- Large and infrequent releases breed an environment for escaped defects and bugs and mistrust between those delivering change and those supporting it
- Releases are seen as something to dread rather than a positive opportunity for change
- Most of the team(s) are disengaged or there is low morale (or both)
- Communication between key teams is fragmented, stilted, and sometimes non-existent
- Software changes are not trusted until they have been tested many, many times. Even then, go-live is not without issue
- Over-complex dependencies within the software design, which makes testing and releasing very challenging
- There is duplication of tasks and activity throughout the process

It would be ludicrous to say that simply creating a plan will solve all of the problems and issues—after all, some of the problems and issues may actually be due misaligned plans—however, without a plan it's going to be very hard to at least make a dent. Successful adoption of CD and DevOps can be hard enough as it is, so having a unified and understood approach will drastically improve your chances.

As with any plan or project, there needs to be an end goal and a vision of how to get there.

Setting and communicating goals and vision

A goal and vision for any project is important as it ensures all concerned know what is expected and for those working on the project understand where it, and they, are heading. It may sound quite simple, but it is not always obvious. In addition to setting the goal and vision, it is just as important what you communicate and how you do it. Do either incorrectly, and you are in danger of losing buy-in, support and engagement from the business. As pointed out in `Chapter 3`, *Culture and Behaviors are the Cornerstones to Success*, the environment, culture, and default behaviors exhibited throughout the organization can help or hinder CD and DevOps adoption, so you need to be mindful of this when formulating the goal, vision, and communication approach.

These challenges can become very polarized when dealing with senior management. For example, they may believe that simply fixing a few of the issues highlighted during the elephant exposure will be enough to overcome every problem that the business has taken the time and effort to lay bare for all to see—as soon as you start to hear terms such as low-hanging fruit you should start to worry. A simple rule of thumb that has helped many business changes over the years is that you have to be crystal clear what you plan to achieve, and crystal clear who you are communicating this to.

When it comes to adopting CD and DevOps, this can be quite challenging as the deliverables and benefits are not always easy or obvious for the un-initiated to understand or envision. It may also be difficult to fully quantify as some of the benefits you obtain from the adoption are not wholly tangible—it can be quite hard to measure increases in team collaboration and happiness. Some leaders may align their decisions to **Return On Investment** (**ROI**) models and only consider applying budget to such things where the return is very obvious and quantifiable. Again, this can be very hard to directly convert the advantages adopting CD and DevOps will give into a pure monetary value.

The best advice is to follow the **keep it simple stupid** (**KISS**) approach. You have a list of issues, which the wider business has provided for you, and what they want is something (anything) that will make their lives easier and allow them to do the jobs they were hired and are paid to do. I would also suggest that the majority would also like to have the opportunity to add value to the business, the customers and their self-worth. Regarding the list of issues, if truth be told, you most probably have more things on the list than you can effectively deliver. This should be seen as a good thing as you have some wriggle room when it comes to prioritization of the work.

Your challenge is to pull together a goal and vision, that will resonate with all of the stakeholders, employees and the wider business and ensure it is something that can add business value. More importantly, you need to ensure that the goal and vision can be delivered. This will need quite a bit of effort, thought, and planning, but it is doable. To give you some ideas, let's go back to ACME systems to see how they approached this.

When ACME systems were planning the adoption of CD and DevOps, it pooled together its ideas and came up with a goal for the project. This was pretty simple and self explanatory; to be able to release working code to production 10 times per day. It further simplified this to deliver value 10 times per day, which formed a nice simple tag line that everyone could understand (almost everyone, but we'll come to that soon) and formed the basis of its vision and communication strategy.

Yes, this was an ambitious goal but the company knew with some hard work, courage, determination, and the right people involved, it was possible to achieve.

Setting your goal may be just as easy. You have a good understanding of the business problems that need to be overcome, you know which teams are involved, and you have a good idea of what will resonate with the stakeholders. This may sound nice and simple, but it's true to say that with a blank whiteboard and a pen you will be able to fill most of the space up with example goals. Canvas opinion from people whose judgment you trust; if they think your proposed goal is way off the mark, it might just be so. If you're lucky enough to have PR or marketing people available, canvas their opinions; this is after all something they are pretty good at. Pulling together a top-level communication plan may also help to focus the message for the target audience(s).

Let's go back to the ACME systems again and see how it approached communication. They had a goal (deliver value 10 times per day) and needed to set out the vision. This vision included a wide variety of deliverables that it believed would solve a majority of the problems highlighted during their elephant exposure. These deliverables were both technical and non-technical in nature but above all were easy to understand, explain, and could all be clearly communicated. These deliverables were listed out, broken down and ranked to give an indication as to what would be addressed in what order. Those of you who are au fait with agile ways of working will recognize this as a prioritized feature backlog.

To reinforce this, it then worked on the business justification that would resonate with the stakeholders and business leadership. They did this by reviewing the list of problems and identifying those that directly related to cost—or more importantly wastage. The examples it focused on related to excessive repetitive manual test runs, repeated meetings attended by (expensive) senior leadership and cost of downtime for releases. To complement this, it also pulled together facts and figures relating to escaped defects and number of hotfixes required to address them.

The next step was to document and present the goal and vision to the decision makers in the business and the influential stakeholders to gain agreement that what was being proposed would address the problems and issues captured during the elephant exposure. This presentation was directed to as wide an audience as possible—not just the leadership—with many sessions booked over many days to allow as many people to be involved as possible. The preferred outcome was to gain agreement from those that had been involved in the original exercise to expose the elephant in the room to fully understand, get behind, and accept the proposed approach.

After much discussion, presenting, cajoling, and some time the goal and vision were agreed across the organization. With the vision agreed, it then went about breaking down the highest priority items of the vision (read, highest priority features) into requirements (read stories), which could be worked on and more importantly delivered.

The next step was to bring together a team of like-minded individuals to assist in the delivery—be that from a technical tooling perspective or education, coaching, and advisory capacity to help the wider team succeed in its goal.

To ensure transparency and ease of access to the goal and vision, the ACME systems team's members needed to ensure that all data, information, and plans were made available for all to see. To this end, they fully utilized all internal communication and project repository and reporting tools available to them: internal wikis, blogs, websites, intranets, and forums.

If you don't have tools such as these available to you, it shouldn't be a vast amount of effort to get one set up using open source solutions. There are even online solutions that are secure enough to keep company secrets safe. Having this level of transparency and openness will help as you move forward with the execution of the plan. This is especially true of *social* solutions such as blogs and forums, where feedback can be given, and virtual discussions can take place.

Let's see what our personas can do to help:

Good approach	Not-so-good approach
Victoria (the veep) can continue her active involvement in the project and help her team to quantify the business case, socialize the goal, vision and business benefits within her peer group. Ideally, becoming project sponsor will add weight to the activity.	Victoria (the veep) distances herself from the activity as she's expended enough time and effort already. She also starts to openly question the validity of the goal, vision, and project as there is no obvious ROI.
Stan (the manager) continues his active involvement to ensure that the goal and vision are realistic, achievable and messaged correctly. He could also call upon peers within marketing to help with targeting the message. As Victoria has done, he can help socialize the goal and vision throughout his peer group. If he has scrum masters or agile coaches available, he should get them assigned to assist in formulating the backlog.	Stan (the manager) mirrors the behaviors of his boss (Victoria) and openly questions the need for a goal and/or vision. He also encourages his team(s) to ignore this and simply get on with it.
Devina (the developer) and Oscar (the Ops guy) can and should remain actively engaged in the project and pull together as much background data as possible to.	Devina (the developer) and Oscar (the Ops guy) keep their heads down and simply do as they are told.

It all sounds pretty simple when it's put down into a few paragraphs and to be honest it could be with the right environment and the right people involved. It's just a case of ensuring you and they have a good grasp of what the business and stakeholders want, how to summarize this into an easily understandable goal that people can relate to and get behind. It's the case of aligning the vision to drive things in the right direction. The key here is "easily understandable", which can sometimes be a challenge, especially when you consider how complex it can become communicating across many business areas (and possibly many time zones and cultures) who each have their own take on the terminology and vocabulary that may be used. This brings us nicely on to how you should communicate and ensure everyone involved understands what is happening.

Standardizing vocabulary and language

One small and wholly avoidable thing that can scupper any project is the misinterpretation or confusion of what the deliverables are. This may sound a little alarming, but projects can fail simply because one person expects something, but another person misunderstands or misinterprets and delivers something else. It's not normally down to ignorance; it's normally due to both sides interpreting the same thing in different ways.

For example, let's look at something relatively innocuous; the word release. To a project manager or a release manager, this could represent a bundle of software changes, which need to be tested and put live within a schedule or program of work. This will normally entail detailed project plans, close coordination with all departments inside and outside of the product delivery function and lots of meetings, paperwork, and late nights. To a developer working in an agile way, a *release* could be a one-line code change, which could go live soon after they have completed coding and ran the automate tests. As you can see, one simple word can be perceived as something that will take a considerable amount of work by one member of a product delivery team member and perceived as something simple that just happens on a daily basis. These perceptions can cause lots of unforeseen and wasteful problems.

There can also be a bit of a problem when you start to examine all of the different words, terminology, and TLAs (three-letter acronyms) that we all use within product delivery and IT as a whole. We therefore need to be mindful of the target audiences we are communicating to and with to ensure they easily understand the message they are given Again, the KISS method works well here. You don't necessarily have to go down to the lowest common denominator; that may be very hard to do (you could end up writing an entire book) and could make matters worse. Try to strike a balance. If some of the target audience don't easily understand, then get someone who does understand to talk with them and explain; this will help bridge the gaps and also form good working relationships.

Another suggestion to help bridge the gap is to pull together a glossary of terms that everyone can refer to. The following is a simple example:

Term	What it is	What it is not
Continuous delivery	A method of delivering fully working and tested software in small increments to the production platform, thus providing customer value quickly	A very complex method of delivering huge chunks of code every few weeks or months
DevOps	A way of working that encourages the development and operations teams to work together in a highly collaborative way towards the same goal	A way to get developers to take on operational tasks and vice versa
CD	See continuous delivery	
Continuous integration	A method of finding software issues as early as possible within the development cycle and ensuring all parts of the overall platform talk to each other correctly	Something to be ignored or bypassed because it takes effort
CI	See continuous integration	
Definition done	A change to the platform (software, hardware, infrastructure, and so on) is live and being used by customers	Something that has been notionally signed off as something that should work when it eventually goes live
DOD	See definition done	
Release	A single code drop to a given environment (testing, staging, production, and so on)	A huge bundle of changes that are handed over to someone else to sort out
Deploy	The act of pushing a release into a given environment	Something the operations team does

If you have an internal communication/collaboration tool such as a wiki or intranet or blog or forum, then that would be a good place to share this as others can update it over time as more buzzwords and TLAs are introduced.

The rule of thumb here is to ensure whatever vocabulary, language, or terminology you standardize on, you must stick to it and be consistent—chopping and changing at a whim can should be avoided. For example, if you choose to use the term CD and DevOps you should stick with it through all forms of communication, written and verbal. It then becomes ingrained and others will use it day to day, which means conversations will be consistent and there is much less risk of misinterpretation and confusion—failure to do this can and will lead to bad decisions being made.

One other thing to take into account is industry standard terms vs those that your business are used to. For example, if everyone throughout your business feels a shudder of dread when the word *release* is mentioned then don't try and change the meaning to match an industry standard as some will still associate the negative connotation. Instead, try using alternative terms—such as delivery—which will not have the historical baggage. All in all, chose your words carefully as they'll be with you for a while.

Let's see what our personas can do to help:

Good approach	Not-so-good approach
Victoria (the veep) takes an active involvement in the language and vocabulary used within her organization and uses the agreed terms within all communication (written and verbal). She is also seen to be correcting her peers and members of the wider org when they revert to the what we used to use terms and language.	Victoria (the veep) ignores the relative importance of language and vocabulary used throughout her organization and lets incorrect terms and language slip with no challenge. In fact she still uses incorrect terms, language, and vocabulary herself.
Stan (the manager) mirrors the behavior of his boss (Victoria) and at times corrects her which she slips up. Stan should also actively encourage his team(s) to compile, refine, and utilize the standard notation in all communications.	Stan (the manager) mirrors the behavior of his boss (Victoria).
Devina (the developer) and Oscar (the Ops guy) also mirror the behaviors of their bosses and encourage their peers to do the same.	Devina (the developer) and Oscar (the Ops guy) simply ignore whatever is going on and carry on using the terms, language, and vocabulary they have always used.

Let's move forward with the presumption that you now have a goal, a vision, a high-level backlog, a standard way of communicating, and you're ready to roll. Almost. The execution of the vision is not something to be taken lightly. Whether you are a small software shop or a large corporate, you should treat the adoption and implementation of CD and DevOps with as much gravitas as you would any other project, which touches and impacts many parts of the business. For example, you wouldn't implement a new finance and payroll system into the business as if it were a small-scale skunkworks project. Any change that impacts the wider business takes collaboration, close coordination, and planning. The adoption of CD and DevOps is not trivial and therefore should be seen in the same light.

A business change project in its own right

Classing the implementation and adoption of CD and DevOps as a business change project may seem a bit dry but that's exactly what it is; you are changing the way business operates, for the better. Not something to be taken lightly at all. If you have ever been involved in business change projects, you will understand how far-reaching they can be.

There's a high probability that the wider business may not understand this as well as you do. They have been involved in the investigation and have verified the findings and seen what you intend to do to address the issues raised. What they may not understand fully is the implication of implementing and adopting CD and DevOps—in terms of the business, it can be a life changing event. A little later in the book, we'll go through some of the hurdles you will face during the implementation, but if you have a heads-up from the start you're in a much better position to leap over the hurdles.

Suffice to say that you should ensure you get the business to recognize that the project will be something that will impact quite a few people, albeit in a positive way. The way certain parts of the business currently operate, the processes they have in place, the ways of working, and skillsets required will need to change. We not just talking about product development here either; adopting CD and DevOps will change the way the business thinks, plans, decides, and the speed at which it operates.

For example, let's assume that sales, marketing, product and program management teams are currently working on a three- to six-month cycle to take features to the market. If the CD and DevOps adoption goes to plan, the cycle will become much shorter, whereby a feature may be available in days or weeks:

A typical multi-month software delivery cycle:

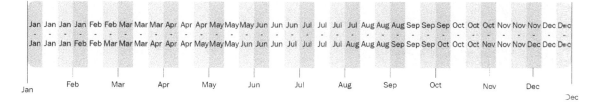

A typical agile software delivery cycle

The aforementioned teams will need to work at a different cadence and will have to speed up and streamline their processes, planning, and communication. They will also need to refine their go to market approach to ensure clients don't get shocked by getting features before they are ready to take them on.

From experience, the adoption of CD and DevOps and the consistent increased speed of delivery also brings some unexpected and very positive benefits—that being a renewed level of trust throughout the business that when the product delivery and operations team commit to deliver something they actually deliver it—time and time again. On the face of it, that's a good thing, however if downstream teams such as sales and marketing are used to feature deliveries being consistently delayed, they will have no doubt been factored into their plans, therefore having features delivered on time may actually take them by surprise.

It also means the whole end to end process can be streamlined as the traditional plan B, C and D—normally put into place if (when) things go wrong—is no longer required. The way features are delivered will drastically change, and the rest of the business needs to accept this and be ready for it.

When you start to consider the (positive) impacts adoption of CD and DevOps can and will have on the wider business, you can start to appreciate how careful you should approach it. If you have access to a program management team specializing in business change, then you would be wise to engage them so that they can help provide the overarching plan.

It should be noted that changes will not happen overnight, but history shows that businesses that truly adopt CD and DevOps are normally transformed in a matter of months (depending on size of the organization of course), so it's always best to have a plan to get ahead of the curve as things will creep up on you pretty fast.

Going back to the skunkworks example, you should be mindful that the adoption of CD and DevOps will initially be seen by the wider business as just that—some skunkworks project that the development and operations team need to implement to overcome their inefficiencies. What the business needs to appreciate is that the adoption of CD and DevOps is far bigger than that. The sooner they realize, the better. We'll now focus on that subject.

Dev + Ops + Org

In the early stages of the adoption, the wider business will most probably believe that the impact of CD and DevOps—as the name suggests—will be localized to the development and operations teams. The following pretty standard diagram depicts the size of this bubble as the wider business will see it:

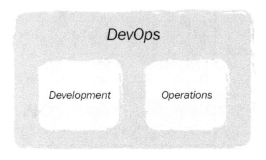

What the business sees at the early stages

At first, this may not be too far from the truth and you will no doubt start small so that you can get to grips with the subtleties and to find your feet, as it were. This is fire; however, once you get some momentum—which will not take long—things will start to change very quickly and if people aren't ready, or at least aware, you may hit some barriers, obstacles and pain points that could slow things down or even stop the adoption in its tracks.

As previously stated, the adoption of CD and DevOps is a business change project which—as the name implies—will impact the business itself, not just the techies. The business must therefore accept that the impact will be far reaching as depicted in this wider and more realistic bubble:

DevOps

| Marketing | Planning | Development | Operations | Sales | HR | Finance | Logistics | Procurement and M&A |

What the business should be seeing as representative of the areas that will be impacted and involved

If you think back to when the elephant in the room was exposed in `Chapter 2`, *Understanding Your Current Pain Points*, you'll recall that the wider, the wider business functions were involved in the activity of investigating, understanding, and highlighting the issues within the end to end business process. That being the case, they should not simply walk away from the hard bit and should stay engaged and actively involved in addressing and changing the ways of working to realize the benefits and eradicate the problems surfaced.

I don't want to sound like a stuck record, but adoption of CD and DevOps is not simply related the product delivery teams—the impacts and changes will be wide-reaching, therefore you need to ensure the wider business keep involved.

I think I've labored the point enough, so let's move forward with the presumption that the business is in agreement regarding the wide-reaching nature of the implementation and (almost) everyone is fully behind the project. The next challenge is deciding to form a dedicated team to drive forward the implementation of the goal and vision, and eventual CD and DevOps adoption.

The pros and cons of a dedicated team

There are several schools of thought in relation to whether or not to have a dedicated and committed team overseeing the adoption of CD and DevOps. One school sees this as a necessary and logical move as only those with an interest in or experience/knowledge of CD and DevOps will actually understand the value of both/either and know (or at least have a pretty good idea) how it should be adopted. This is very true, however there are drawbacks—which we'll cover shortly. The other school suggests that this is a bad idea as it's not really that far removed from any other business change project, therefore can be managed through close collaboration and coordination without specialist knowledge. In truth, both schools are correct and also incorrect at the same time.

What it boils down to is this: if a dedicated team can get the adoption moving quickly, efficiently, and effectively then go for it, as long as they don't end up doing everything themselves in isolation and are therefore seen as the CD and DevOps team who just implement technical things and don't need/work with anyone else. As I've stated previously, just having a CD and/or DevOps team in your organization does not mean you have adopted CD and DevOps, it's far more complex than that. Like any successful business change project, a dedicated team should be there to help steer, guide, mentor, and coach the like-minded individuals (not just Dev and Ops) involved to collaborate and contribute while at the same time actively contributing themselves and focused on moving the adoption along. The sometimes overused business bingo term here is enablers or agents for change.

If you prefer to forgo a dedicated team and simply run the adoption as a business change project bringing in skills and individuals as when required, then you should at least need have someone(s) heavily involved who has a knowledge and/or experience of what CD and DevOps adoption actually means and can ensure the goal and vision are realized—without that, things may go off the rails somewhat. Something to also consider is whether or not the same sense of ownership and close collaboration will come out of a collection of individuals who occasionally work together vs a dedicated team who share a common goal and vision.

It really is your call, however my recommendation is to join the form a dedicated CD and DevOps adoption team school. You will need to ensure that the team is not wholly technical in experience/background, are willing and able and capable of working across the wider business, and more importantly have the ultimate goal of making themselves redundant. I don't mean they will lose their jobs, what I mean is that the dedicated team should be transient and once the CD and DevOps adoption has taken hold the team can be disbanded with little/no fuss and go back to their day jobs.

From past experience, the simplest way to decide on an approach is to go back to basics and list out the pros and cons as they apply to you and your business. Let's presume for ease of reading and page count that at this point you have decided to form a dedicated team—what's next?

As with any highly collaborative project, collocation of the team members is always preferable, however, not always possible. If you have geographically diverse (or dispersed) teams, then you need to ensure the you have members of the dedicated CD and DevOps adoption team in each location as they will need to be close to hand and in the same time zone as the people they are steering, guiding, mentoring, and coaching. They also need to work very closely together on a day to day basis—I would suggest you follow the tips and suggestions highlighted within `Chapter 3`, *Culture and Behaviors are the Cornerstones to Success*, in relation to collaboration and the physical environment.

When we say dedicated, it means just that. The main day to day role of the team members will be to focus on doing whatever is needed to successfully implement the previously agreed goal. Now, it's not unusual to recruit or buy in a dedicated team from outside of the business but this isn't always a wise move as these individuals won't have the business domain knowledge or have an established connection to the wider business. That said, bringing in outside experts and/or individuals with experience in CD and DevOps adoption can help as long as they complement the core dedicated team. Again, this is really something you need to consider based upon your business needs, resource constraints, and budget.

Whatever you decide, you need to be mindful that you will be taking a number of key people out of the business and away from their day jobs for a considerable amount of time to focus solely on the implementation and adoption of CD and DevOps.

As soon as this is highlighted, I can pretty much guarantee that you will get some areas of the business take a big step back in terms of engagement—especially those areas which manage the very people you want to second onto your dedicated team. This is understandable as they will most probably be the subject matter experts in their area and are therefore pivotal to their existing team/functional area.

It is down to you to cajole, beg, bargain, and barter to get the people you need. To be honest, it shouldn't be too difficult as you have quite a large amount of ammunition to use—the same information and data you worked so hard to compile and which the business itself agreed was causing pain. If you used the value stream mapping exercise you should also be able to pinpoint the pain areas with accuracy. Let's take a typical discussion between you and the head of testing and QA—let's call him Chucky:

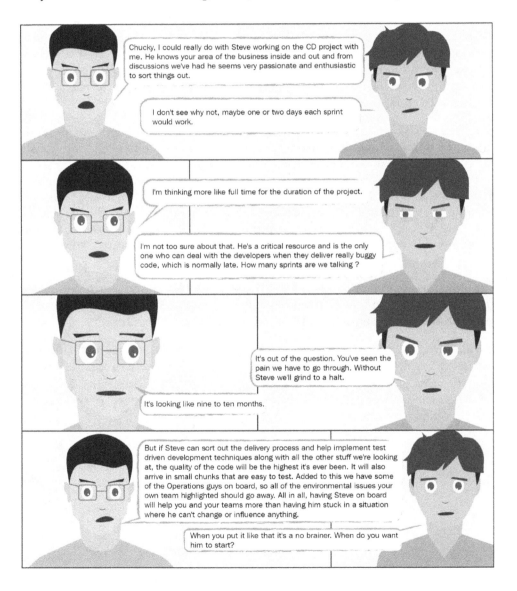

I admit it might not go exactly along those lines but hopefully you can see the point. You have been given a clear insight into what pains the business and have been asked to remove said pains. The business needs to realize that this will not come without some cost and that they need to provide you with what you need to get the job done.

In relation to the setup of the dedicated CD and DevOps adoption team, that really depends on the way in which your business is set up. A typical business would normally have something like development, QA, operations, and change management teams involved in the software release process; therefore, you should include someone from each area. To make things as agile as possible, add a Scrum Master and a product owner and top it all off with a Senior Manager (someone who can act as the project sponsor and represent the team at a higher level), and you'll end up with something as shown in the following diagram:

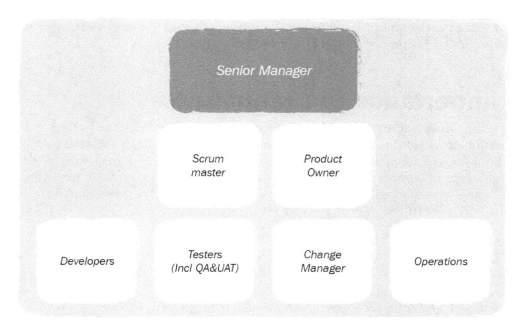

An example team setup

Now, that's all well and good but doesn't this simply look like a typical IT project team? In a word, yes. However, this is mainly due to the skills and experience within this area. CD and DevOps are historically derived from IT folks, and as such you don't tend to get many sales executives or accountants having a working understanding of CD and/or DevOps (unless they have read this book of course).

As previously mentioned, you should be proactively engaging with areas of the business that will be impacted, however you need to decide on who should be actively involved and who should be classed as stakeholders. The rule of thumb here should be if someone is actively involved and contributing on a day to day basis, they should be included in the dedicated team. If they have an interest or need to be consulted regularly, they should be stakeholders.

 One tool that would really help you here is RACI which allows you to define who is Responsible, Accountable, Consulted, and Informed—there's plenty of information available on RACI so I suggest you do some homework.

Just to reiterate, a dedicated team must be made up of more than just Devs and Ops if they are to have credibility across the wider business.

Now that you have the art of persuasion and positive influencing under your belt, you and your newly formed team need to learn the art of evangelism.

The importance of evangelism

To evangelize across an entire business all of the time is going to take some effort and some determination. It will also take some energy. Actually, that's wrong; it will take a lot of energy. Your target audience is wide and far-reaching, from senior management to the shop floor, so it will take up quite an amount of time for you and your team to get the message across. Before we go into the details of what to say to who, when, and how, let's get the ground rules sorted:

- If you are to be convincing when evangelizing to others the virtues of CD and DevOps adoption, you and your newly formed team need to truly believe in it—if you don't, then how can you expect others to?
- You, the team, and whoever is involved in the project, must practice what you preach and set a good example for others to follow. For instance, if you build/implement some tools as part of the project, make sure you build and deploy them using the exact same techniques and tools you are evangelizing about.
- Many (most) people will not get it at first, so you and the team will have to be very, very patient. You may have to explain the same thing to the same person more than once. Use these kinds of individuals as a yard stick; if they start to understand what CD and DevOps adoption is then there's a pretty good chance your message is hitting home.

- Remember your target audience and tailor your message accordingly. Developers would want to hear technical stuff, which is new and shiny; system operators would want to hear words such as *stability* and *predictability*; and management types would want to hear about efficiencies, optimized processes, and risk reduction. Do not use one message for all.
- As you evangelize and sing the praises of CD and DevOps adoption, ensure you are measuring the impact of your message—the rule of thumb is if you see their eyes glaze over, your message is not hitting home, so change it.
- Some people will simply not want to know or listen, and it may not be worth focusing your efforts to make them (we'll be covering some of this in a `Chapter 3`, *Culture and Behaviors are the Cornerstones to Success*). If you can win them around, then kudos to you and the team but don't feel dejected by one or two laggards.
- Keep it relevant and consistent. You have a standardized language, a goal, and a vision so use them.
- Don't simply make stuff up. Just stick to what can be delivered as part of your goal and vision; no more, no less. If there are new ideas and suggestions get them added to the backlog for prioritization.
- Don't, on any account, give up.

What it boils down to is you and the team will need to talk the talk and walk the walk. There will be quite a bit of networking going on so be prepared for lots and lots of discussion. As your network grows so will your opportunities to evangelize. Do not shy away from these opportunities, and make sure you are using them to build good working relationships across the business as you're going to need these later on. Evangelizing is rewarding and if you really believe that CD and DevOps is the best thing since sliced bread you will find that having opportunities to simply talk about it with others is like a busman's holiday.

Evangelism is basically PR so if you have PR people available (or better still as part of the team) you should also investigate getting simple things together like a logo or some freebies (such as badges, mugs, mouse mats, and so on) to hand out. This may seem a little superfluous, but as with any PR you want to ensure you get the message across and have it embedded into the environment and people's psyches.

Up until this point, I may have painted things in a somewhat rosy glow. Adopting CD and Dev Ops is no picnic in the park. There's quite a big hill to climb for all concerned. As long as everyone involved is aware of this and has the courage and determination to succeed, things should go well.

The courage and determination required throughout the organization

Courage and determination may seem like strong words to use, but they are the correct words. There will be many challenges, some you are aware of some you are not, that will try to impede the progress, so determination is required to ensure this keeps moving in the right direction. Courage is needed as some of these challenges will require you, the team, and the wider business to make difficult decisions, which could result in actions being taken from which there is no going back. I'll refer to ACME systems Version 2.0 for a good example of this.

In the early days of their adoption of CD and DevOps, they started with a small subset of their platform as the candidates for releasing using the new deployment toolset and ways of working. Unfortunately, at the same time there was a lot of noise being generated around the business as another release (using the old *package everything up and push out as one huge deployment* method) was not going well. The business asked everyone to focus on getting the release out at all costs, including halting the CD trials. This didn't go down too well with the team. However, after a rather courageous discussion between the senior manager of the ACME CD and DevOps adoption team and his peers, it was agreed that resource could be allocated if there was universal agreement that this would be the last of the big bang releases, and that all future releases would use the new CD pipeline process going forward. The agreement was forthcoming, and so ended the era of the big bang release and the new era of CD and DevOps dawned. After the last of the big bang releases was eventually completed, the entire development and operations teams were determined to get CD up and running as soon as possible.

They had been through enough pain and needed another way or rather *a better way*. They persevered for a few months until the first release, using the new tooling and ways of working, went to the production environment, then the next, and so on. At this point, there was no turning back as too much had changed.

As you can no doubt appreciate, it took courage from all parts of the business to make this decision. There was no plan B and if it hadn't worked they had no way to release their software. Knowing this fact, the business was determined to get the new CD and DevOps ways of working embedded and established.

This could be classed as an extreme case, but nonetheless it goes to show that courage and determination are sometimes very much needed; if there's a will there's a way.

Before we move away from the planning stage, there are still a couple of things you should be aware of as you prepare to embark on your new adventure: where to seek help and ensuring you and the wider business are aware of the costs involved with implementing and adopting CD and DevOps. We'll cover costs first.

Understanding the cost

Implementing CD and DevOps will ultimately save the business quite a lot of money; that is a very simple and obvious fact. The effort required to release software will be dramatically reduced, the resources required will be miniscule when compared to large *big bang* releases, the time to market will be vastly reduced, the quality will be vastly increased, and the cost of doing business (that is, volume of bug fixes required, support for system downtime, fines for not meeting SLAs, and so on) will be negligible. That said, implementing CD and DevOps does not come for free. There are costs involved and the business needs to be aware.

Let's break these down:

- A dedicated team assigned to the CD and DevOps project
- Changes to business process documentation and/or business process maps
- Changes to standard operating procedures
- Changes to hosting (on the assumption there is a move to virtual/cloud infrastructure)
- Tweaks to change management systems to allow for quicker and more lightweight operations
- Internal PR and marketing materials
- Enlisting the help from external specialists
- Things may slow down at the start as new ways of working become the norm

These costs should not be extortionate; however, they are costs that need to be taken into account and planned for. As with any project—especially one as far reaching as CD and DevOps adoption—there will always be certain costs. If the business is aware of this from the outset, then the chance of it scuppering the project later down the line can be minimized.

There may be some costs that are indirectly caused by the project. You may have some people who cannot accept the changes and simply decide to move on; there will be costs to replace them (or not, as the case may be). As previously stated at the beginning of the transition from big bang releases, you may well slow down to get quicker. If you have contractual deadlines to meet during this period, it may be prudent to renegotiate them.

Those actively involved in the CD and DevOps adoption will know your business better than anyone—especially after the elephant exposure—so you may have better ideas related to costs. Just make sure you do not ignore them.

Let's now focus on where you can get help and advice should you need it.

Seeking advice from others

Before you take the plunge and change the entire way your business operates, it may be a good idea to do some research and/or reach out to others who meet one of the following descriptions:

- Have been through this transition a few times and have the battle scars to prove it
- Are in the same boat as you
- Specialize in wide-reaching agile business change
- Are recognized as experts in the field of both CD and DevOps

There is an ever-growing number of people around the globe who have experience in implementing (and even defining) CD and DevOps. Some are experts in the field and focus on this as their full-time jobs; some are simply members of the growing community who have seen the light and selflessly want to help others realize the benefits they have witnessed and experienced.

To reiterate, implementing CD and DevOps is no picnic and sometimes being at the forefront can be a lonely place. Do not feel like you should struggle alone. There are some valuable reference materials available (this book being one of those I would hope) and more importantly there are a good number of communities—online and face to face meet-ups—that you can join to help you. You never know, your story and input may be an inspiration for others, so in true CD and DevOps style, break down the barriers and enjoy open and honest dialogue. I'll include a list of some of the reference materials and contacts in `Appendix A`, *Some Useful Info*.

Summary

So, what have we covered in this chapter? We have learned that without defining our goal and vision, it's pretty difficult to clarify and communicate what CD and DevOps adoption will mean, and what business value they will bring. Staying with communication, we have learned that without having a common standard in relation to terms, language, and vocabulary, it will be difficult to collaborate across the organization. In terms of who is impacted by CD and DevOps, we have covered the fact that this is a wide-reaching business change and not localized to the traditional IT organization. Just like any business change, CD and DevOps adoption will not be free; there will be cost (some obvious, some not so obvious) and you need to take that into account. Lastly, you are not alone; there are a large number of people, teams, and businesses around the globe who have already been through this adoption and came out the other side in a much better position.

Let's assume at this point that you have followed this advice and now have a team, a plan, executive backing and sponsorship, defined ways to communicate, some budget, and some support from battle-weary experts. You're now ready to move to the next stage—implementing the goal and vision, which is what we'll be covering in the next couple of chapters. We'll start by looking at some of the proven approaches, tools, and techniques that will help you move forward.

5
Approaches, Tools, and Techniques

The last chapter focused on getting a goal, vision, and dedicated team together (or not, as the case may be) to help with the implementation and adoption of CD and DevOps within your business. Over the next couple of chapters, we will go through the steps of executing the plan to ultimately deliver the goal you have defined.

Throughout Chapter 3, *Culture and Behaviors are the Cornerstones to Success*, we focused on the human side of what needs to be in place for CD and DevOps adoption. Chapter 4, *Planning for Success*, then looked at how to build the plan and some of the building blocks that need to be put into place to make the adoption successful. We will now apply focus on the technical side of the execution—the tools, techniques, approaches, and processes you and the team should be looking to implement and/or refine as part of the plan.

There will be quite a lot of things to cover and take in, some of which you will need, some of which you may already have in place, and some of which you may want to consider implementing later down the line. I would recommend you read through everything, just in case there are some small chunks of wisdom or information that you can adapt or adopt to better fit your requirements.

Quite a bit of this chapter is focused on software engineering (that is, the Dev side of the DevOps partnership), and more CD than DevOps, but bear with me as some of the points covered are as relevant to system operations as they are to software engineering—this is, after all, what DevOps is really all about.

It is worth pointing out that the tools and processes mentioned are not mutually exclusive—it is not a case of all or nothing; you just need to pick what works for you. That said, there is a logical order and dependency to some of the things covered over the next chapter or two, but it's down to you to decide what is viable.

One other very important thing to take into account is that there are a plethora of other books, websites, blogs, and such that go into far more detail than I will. I will endeavor to provide a flavor and overview of what you'll need to drive the CD and DevOps adoption forward. It's down to you and the team to dig a little deeper.

Throughout this chapter, I'll be referring to tools and/or software solutions that you should consider to reduce the burden and ease the CD and DevOps adoption. As with any investment, I would recommend that you don't just chose the first one that appears in your favorite search engine or the one that an existing vendor is pushing. The CD and DevOps tooling market is very competitive; therefore, you should have more than one or two options. Understand what problem you need to solve based upon your specific needs and apply due diligence to the selection. If you need to trial a few different tools, you should do so. The effectiveness of your CD and DevOps adoption may rely upon these tools, so choose carefully.

Now that's out of the way, let's start with some engineering best practices.

Engineering best practices

For those of you who are not software engineers, nor from a software engineering background, your knowledge and/or interest in how software is developed may be extremely minimal. Why, I hear you ask, do I need to know how a developer does their job? Surely, developers know this stuff better than I do? I doubt I even understand 10 percent of it anyway!

To some extent, this is very true; developers do (and should) know their stuff, and having you stick your nose in might not be welcome. However, it does help if you at least have an understanding or appreciation of how software is created, as it can help to identify where potential issues could reside.

Let's put it another way: I have an understanding and appreciation of how an internal combustion engine is put together and how it works, but I am no mechanic—far from it, in fact. However, I do know enough to be able to question why a mechanic has replaced my entire exhaust system and rear axle when I took my car in for a fuel-injector problem—in fact, I think I would vigorously question why.

It is the same with software development and the process that surrounds it. If you're not technical in the slightest and haven't done your homework to understand how software should be written, you leave yourself open to decisions being made by (or at the very least, noise emitting from) individuals who prefer to deflect by using technobabble rather than be open, honest, and willing and able to work with you. You will no doubt have come across such individuals during the elephant exposure, and I would wager that they have avoided getting involved with this pipe dream of shipping software quickly without everything going to pot—at least that's what they think. You and the team will need try to and work on the same level as them, so having some idea of what you're talking about will help with those discussions.

Let's start with the basics: CD is based upon a premise that quality software can be developed, built, tested, and shipped many times in quick succession (that's the continuous bit)—ideally, we're talking hours or days at the most. When you consider this list and apply it to a traditional waterfall-style development project, you'll no doubt have found that every step takes time and effort, and contains waste. You would also no doubt have found that it's the shipping part that is the most painful, costly, and risky. When applied to a modern agile development project, you'll normally find that the first three items on the list are more honed, efficient, and effective (although not without some waste and time lag—depending on the maturity of the team), whereas the shipping part is still painful and takes a vast amount of time and effort. We will focus on the shipping (or to be more accurate, the delivery) section later.

From this point forward, I'm going to assume you know what the differences between waterfall and agile development are (if not, I suggest you stop here and do some homework) and move swiftly on.

Let's go back to basics and cover some fundamentals in terms of modern agile software engineering:

- All code, config, and related metadata are stored in a modern source/version-control solution
- Small and complete code changes are committed to the source-control repository frequently
- Unit tests are included by default and sit with the source-code repository
- Refactoring code happens on a regular basis
- Code should not be overly complex and documented
- Branches are short-lived, and merges are frequent

- Automated tests sit alongside the code within the source-control repository and are run very frequently
- Pair programming, code reviews, or pull requests are used consistently
- Build and automated tests are orchestrated and controlled by a **Continuous Integration** (**CI**) solution
- Failing tests are not the end of the world; nor is having others find fault in your code

 I may have lost some of you, but before you skip this chapter, please read on a little more as I'll be going through some of these concepts soon.

The preceding list is pretty simplistic and, as stated previously, most software engineers who work on modern agile software development projects will see this as common sense and common practice.

The reference to modern agile software development is purposeful as there are still some (in some industries, that should read *many*) old-school code cutters who believe that they are exempt from this due to the fact that they have been delivering code without of all of this newfangled hipster stuff for many years without any issues. That may be true; however, there's next to no chance of successfully adopting CD and DevOps without changing the way that software is written and delivered. No doubt these individuals would have been in the disengaged contributors group during the elephant exposure.

What is more worrying is when these individuals are actively discouraging the software engineers who do wish to follow modern agile software engineering best practice from doing so. Whatever the situation, these old dogs will have to learn new tricks.

Ultimately, modern agile software engineering is based on the simple premise of finding software problems as early as possible. Without this approach, these software problems **will** be found later down the line, they **will** slow everything down, and they **will** negatively impact the adoption and the perception of how successful the adoption is.

To put it another way, if you are continuously developing small incremental changes, which are being built, integrated, and tested, the ease of continuous delivery will be vastly increased.

Let's see what our personas can do to help:

Good approach	Not-so-good approach
Victoria (the Veep) should not ignore this as simply "what developers do" and ensure she is aware of the effort needed to successfully embed best practice within the engineering teams and be willing to supply budget and executive sponsorship.	Victoria (the Veep) sees this as more expense which may well slow things down and / or a low priority skunkworks project off of the side of the main product delivery process
Stan (the manager) should ensure that relative importance is front and center with leadership, peer group and team(s) alike. He should also ensure the correct resources are assigned and aligned across the organization	Stan (the manager) ignores the benefits that engineering best practice will bring and sees adoption as additional workload that will distract the team(s)
Devina (the developer) and Oscar (the Ops guy) should spend time understanding and fully embrace engineering best practice and lead by example throughout their peer groups.	Devina (the developer) and Oscar (the Ops guy) keep their heads down and leave the leadership to argue about the merits of engineering best practice which they continue to struggle to deliver

For those of you whose eyes may have glazed over, or those of you who need a refresher, let's break these down a little further, starting with source-control.

Source-control

There are many different flavors, versions, and solutions available for source-control (sometimes referred to as SCM or version-control systems), both commercial (not free) and open source (free). Most of these tools can be self-hosted (if that's something you need to do), or offered as a **PaaS** model (which isn't free but still relatively cheap). Taking this into account, there are no excuses not to use source-control. None!

If **all** of your code is in source-control, it is versioned (that is, there is a history of every change that has been made from the year dot), it is available to anyone and everyone who has access to the source-control system, it is secure, and it is (should be) backed up so you won't lose any of it.

Some of the more modern solutions can actually help you control the full life cycle of software delivery via inbuilt tools, workflows, and triggers. This can save you a lot of time, complexity, and cost. However, you should not be swayed by this too much. What you need is a solution that best suits your organization and the ways of working (now and in the future), and helps you to deliver quality software continuously.

Some of you may have heard the urban myth that a source-control solution is only useful for software source code. Just like all urban myths, this had some truth way back in the mists of time, but is now bunk. Source-control should not be restricted to software source code. Anything that can, could, and will be changed should be versioned and stored in source-control. I've already mentioned a few examples, so let's expand on this:

- Unit tests
- Test cases
- Automated test scripts
- Software configuration/metadata
- SQL scripts/SPROCS
- Documentation
- Environmental configurations
- Server configuration
- Anything and everything than can be changed, edited, or saved

The normal bone of contention is environmental/server configurations and other collections of artifacts such as start-up scripts and network routing config, which some may see as exempt from source-control as this is in the land of Ops rather than Dev. However, as you're moving to DevOps, this no longer makes any sense and is not applicable. The rule of thumb should be: if it can be changed, it should be in source-control and versioned.

The DevOps community refers to the approach of representing a given environment via configuration files that can (should) be stored in source-control as configuration as code. It should be pointed out that this approach has grown from the open source community, and therefore some areas of this approach may not be wholly applicable initially—for example, administering Windows servers is more point-and-click than a set of configuration files that would be used to administer a Linux cluster. However, you can also administer Windows via PowerShell scripts, so there is an option. The bottom line is that you should strive toward having every element of a given environment/server/switch/router/firewall represented as configuration files that can (and should) be stored and versioned within your source-control system. That way, you can create an exact clone of a given environment at a given point in time with relative ease (something we'll come to soon).

One thing that may become a blocker is security and access to the contents of the source within the source-control solution. For example, if you're storing environmental configuration as code, you ideally don't want the development team having access to the production database connection strings or API tokens. There are proven and well-documented ways and means to do this (masking, encryption, restricting access to certain repositories, and so on), so it shouldn't be a blocker if you plan for it upfront.

 There are books and reference materials aplenty regarding source-control that cover this subject in much more depth and detail, so I will not dwell on it here. Suffice it to say, if you do not have a source-control solution, implement one. Now!

As you'll no doubt gather, a source-control solution is a very valuable tool for CD and DevOps adoption. Along with having a central place to securely store your source code, it's also important to apply the same approach to your binary objects and artifacts.

The binary repository

As the name implies, a binary repository is somewhere to store your binary objects and artifacts. Binary objects/artifacts are, in software engineering terms, the runnable software that is created when the source code is successfully compiled.

Binary repositories function in much the same way as a source-control solution, but, as you would expect, are better suited to storing binary objects. Some solutions also provide mechanisms to version, and even package up the binaries for later installation on a target environment.

We'll cover the importance of binary repositories later in the chapter. For now, let's move on to the valuable practice of keeping changes small and frequent.

Small, frequent, and simple changes

Keeping changes small means the impact of the change—sometimes referred to as the blast radius—should also be small, the risks reduced, and the opportunities for change increased. It sounds overly simplistic, but it is also very true. If you consider how many changes to software a typical software engineering team makes in a day and then extrapolate that out to the number of teams you have making said changes, you'll soon find that this adds up. If you then take this number and multiply it by the number of days between releases, you'll find the volume of changes is not insignificant— and nor is the risk of those changes.

In terms of risk, let's assume we have a team of five software engineers who, on average, make 10 code changes each per day—that's 50 changes. Let's assume we have 10 teams all doing the same—that's 500 code changes per day. Let's now assume we're releasing every 12 weeks (or 60 working days); we're now talking 30,000 changes that need to go live. Even if we have industry-leading test coverage—let's say 99.9% coverage—there's still a chance something nasty could slip through. In this case, that's 30 changes not covered. In simple terms, there's a risk that 30 defects may be created every 12 weeks. OK, this is a very simplistic approach, but hopefully it illustrates the point that clumping together a large number of code changes is far from ideal.

One thing that may not be obvious is what happens if a simple defect is spotted the day after a release that can be fixed by a single-line code change. If we follow the preceding example, that defect will stay in production for another 11 weeks and 6 days (assuming we don't have emergency patch releases available to us). The same is true of any change made on day one of the 12-week release cycle—including customer feature requests.

If we were to break this down into smaller more frequent releases—say, every two weeks—and apply the same numbers, we would be looking at something like the following:

*500 changes * 10 days = 5,000 changes released with a risk of five defects slipping through.*

Now, let's again assume that if one escaped defect is spotted and fixed the day after the release, then that change will be live in nine days. Again, if a customer feature request change was made on day one of the release cycle, it could be live in 10 days. I think you'll agree that sounds slightly better than the first example.

The following diagram goes some way to illustrate what this could look like:

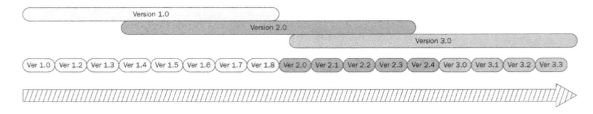

Large changes versus small incremental changes

Now, I will admit that the preceding example is very simplistic and may not reflect reality, and you might not currently have the luxury of shipping your code very frequently due to external factors (maybe your customers don't want—or can't accept—frequent releases, or your existing ops processes need time to allow for this); however, that is no excuse for not adopting the concepts now. If your software engineering teams become used to releasing in small and potentially shippable chunks, they form the habit of delivering continuously.

Another way of putting this is that once you have fully adopted CD and DevOps, they will have to work in this mode, so why not start getting used to it?

Continuously delivering small and frequent changes can also help in other areas; namely, reducing complexity, increasing code maintainability, and increasing quality. If an engineer only has to change a small amount of code then they have a far greater chance of refactoring the surrounding code to reduce complexity and overall maintainability of the codebase, including adding in additional unit tests. Another less obvious benefit of small and frequent changes is reducing the overhead of code reviews, pull requests, and merging, which can happen more frequently and become more of an everyday thing than a chore.

 This practice should not be restricted to software engineering; it is just as relevant to changes in the system operations area. For example, making a small, isolated tweak to the server configuration (such as memory allocation to a virtual server) is much safer and easier to control and monitor than making sweeping changes all at once. If you make small changes, you have a much better chance of seeing whether the change had an impact (positive or negative) on the overall operation of the platform.

Working with small, incremental changes is a very beneficial practice to follow. However, this is going to be pretty difficult to manage unless you have some tools to help automate the building of your software.

Automated builds

One of the common themes with CD and DevOps adoption is how automation is used. As mentioned previously, without some sort of automated tooling or solution, it will be very difficult to deliver on a frequent basis. You may be reading this and thinking, "Well, that's pretty obvious." However, even in this modern technological age there are software engineering teams who do everything manually using manual steps and/or handcrafted scripts—some of which may be older than the engineer running them. Luckily, this is very much a minority nowadays, although I'll cover some aspects of what automation is and why it's key to CD and DevOps adoption, just in case you're in the minority.

Every engineer that makes a change—be they a software or ops engineer—needs feedback as to whether a change they have made works (or not, as the case may be). The sooner they get this feedback, the sooner they can rectify any issues or move on to the next change. From a software engineering perspective, it is also very helpful to know whether the code they have written actually builds and/or compiles cleanly and consistently so that it can be tested.

This validation could be done via a manual process (or processes or scripts), but this can be cumbersome, inconsistent, prone to error, slow, and not always fully repeatable. Without consistency and repeatability, there's additional risk.

Implementing automation will help speed things up and keep things consistent, reliable, and repeatable, and, above, all provide confidence. If you are running the same steps over and over again and getting the same results, it's a strong bet that the process works and that you can trust it. It is therefore plausible that if you change one thing within your software, configuration, or environment, and the previously working process fails, there is a very good chance that the change has broken something.

There are plenty of tools available for building/compiling code—depending on the development language you are using—and all of them do pretty much the same thing: ensure the code is written correctly, the language syntax is as expected, ensure all external references are available, and—if all is as it should be—create a binary that can be run. This is overly simplistic, but hopefully conveys the point. There are a number of different ways to trigger this process: manually from the command line, manually via a script, or from within the developer's IDE itself. Whichever process you use, you should seriously consider automating the process so that you gain consistency and repeatability.

Another tool to consider including within the automation scripts/process is linting. Linting tools are there to help scan and check your source code for syntax issues. This can be a very useful addition as, if used before you build/compile code, it can vastly reduce the time taken to find issues—especially when you have quite a convoluted codebase, which means the build time is minutes rather than seconds. Again, there are plenty of options to consider, depending on the code language you're using.

Hopefully, you now have some insight into why automating the building of your software components is important. Let's now focus on test-automation.

Test-automation

A traditional software-delivery process will normally include an element of testing. However, depending on the organization and age of the software, running the test cases themselves is normally a manual process. That being said, test-automation has been around for a while—for as long as agile software development. However, it's not as prevalent as one would hope. I should point out that testing approaches and the automation of such is a massive subject, and I will not be covering everything here. If you need more information, I suggest you do some research and pick up some good books on the subject. What we'll cover here is pretty basic, but should give you enough information to understand how test-automation fits into CD and DevOps adoption.

There are principally three types of tests:

- Unit tests are normally written in the coding language of the software and are used to exercise *code* and *logic paths* within the code base itself. They do not normally align to any particular use case or area of functionality.
- Integration tests traditionally exercise the way in which one part of the software system/platform interacts with another (for example, to ensure the login page calls the authentication service correctly).
- End-to-end tests are normally focused on the real-world use cases that an end user would initiate (for example, when logged in successfully, the welcome page is presented and the text displayed is in the correct language).

This is an overly simplistic view, but hopefully elucidates the different types of tests.

In terms of tooling and technologies you can use to create, maintain, and run automated tests, there are a vast number of different flavors and solutions available, and the selection that best fits your needs can be hard to make. At a basic level, these tools pretty much do the same thing: they orchestrate the running of test scripts and capture the results. The choice of test-automation tooling is something you should not rush into, and my recommendation would be to give this as much thought as you did selecting the development language you use.

 You will at times hear the word framework being used—especially when researching how to include unit tests. These are basically predefined approaches that are (mostly) industry standards. This means that the tools themselves may be different, but the standards they adhere to are similar.

When choosing a tool, try to consider future-proofing in terms of the testing language used for creating and maintaining the tests themselves. Standardizing on something such as Cucumber would be a good start, and this is something quite a few tools all use. It helps should you wish to adopt a **TDD** and/or **BDD** approach for your integration and end-to-end testing.

Ultimately, what you need is to work toward what is widely referred to as "inverting the testing triangle." In essence, traditional testing approaches mostly rely on manually-executed tests, with automated and unit tests being less prevalent. For your CD and DevOps adoption to be successful, you need to change the ratio and vastly reduce the reliance on manual testing and increase automation. There are many documented reasons for this, but in relation to CD and DevOps, the main advantages are speed, reliability, repeatability, and consistency:

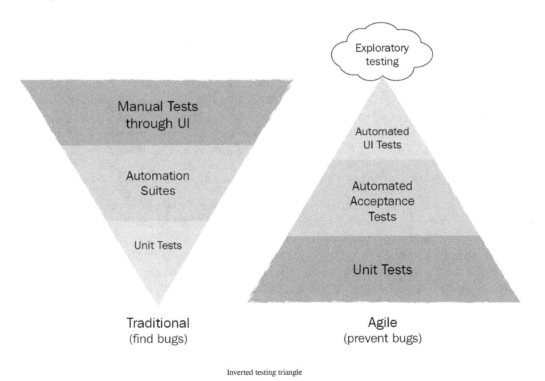

Inverted testing triangle

One thing you may notice in relation to the **Agile** triangle compared to the **Traditional** triangle is the relative size of the **Unit Tests** layer. This is the ideal situation to be in, as the more unit tests you have checking the code and logic flows within the code, the greater confidence you will have in the underlying code. This in turn should build greater confidence in higher-level tests. One less obvious advantage is cost—it's far cheaper to write unit tests than it is to write integration and/or full end-to-end tests.

Agile software engineering approaches, such as TDD and **eXtreme Programming** (**XP**), follow the premise that unit tests are always written and must pass before you progress to the next level of testing.

Staying with automated testing, there is one thing that does add confusion and can put people off: the fact that adopting test-automation can be very daunting— and that's putting it lightly. There are quite a few things to consider when you go down this route: How much of the codebase do you cover with tests? How do you replicate actual users and usage in the real world? Where do you start?

Unfortunately, there are no straightforward or generic answers. This becomes more challenging when you start to look at the reams of online materials, books, and information regarding this very subject. To make matters worse, some of it will be contradictory to others. The only advice I can give is to follow the keep-it-simple (KISS) approach. For example, you may want to start by mapping out some of the primary and most-executed use cases (for example, login/authentication, users navigating from a list to an item detail in a shopping cart, or users making a purchase), and trial a couple of tools by creating automated tests to cover those. As long as you gain the ability to run the tests and the results are consistent, reliable, and repeatable, you should be on the right path.

To use the KISS approach, even one automated test that validates some small part of the code base is better than nothing.

Once you have gained some confidence and trust in the overarching automated testing process, you can move onto the next use cases—or try another tool until you're happy.

I would also recommend the KISS approach for coverage—if you can cover 100% of the code base and use cases, then that's the figure you should chose. If you can't, then find the figure that is viable and increase it as you go along. What I mean by this is do not let the % decrease as new code and features are added. It may help to set a milestone date and realistic percentage goal so that a sense of urgency/focus isn't lost along the way.

There is another set of tools that can help with ascertaining your test coverage by inspecting/analyzing your codebase and source repository (which will, of course, include all of your automated tests) and providing useful information and dashboards for you to review. These can also give you a historical view so that you can measure increases (or decreases) in your coverage.

Another place to apply the KISS approach in is something that normally trips people up when adopting test-automation: the gnarly subject of test data. Test data can be a massive issue, and it can cause more problems than it solves—and quite a few arguments to boot. A good rule of thumb here would be to have the test data you need to run your test(s) created as part of the automated process and—more importantly—removed as a final step. I've seen far too many examples of this KISS approach not being followed, which means you will end up with stale data that may well become out of date quite quickly. This stale data can cause tests that previously ran without issue to start failing or, worse still, other people come along and base their tests on this very same data (which means you can't get rid of it even if you wanted to). It also compromises your ability to ensure your tests are consistent and repeatable.

Let's see what our personas can do to help:

Good approach	Not-so-good approach
Victoria (the Veep) should take an active interest in how test automation can vastly reduce overall cost and effectiveness of quality assurance and be willing to supply budget and executive sponsorship.	Victoria (the Veep) sees this as a head count / cost reduction solution and skimps on the budget to get the best deal rather than the best solutions which the team(s) need
Stan (the manager) should ensure that relative importance is front and center with leadership, peer group and team(s) alike. He should also ensure the most relevant resources are assigned and aligned across the organization.	Stan (the manager) doesn't bother to understand the advantages test automation brings - he sees this as post-development QA stuff and has no interest in it
Devina (the developer) and Oscar (the Ops guy) should spend time understanding, investigating and embracing test automation as a day to day activity that sits side by side with software development.	Devina (the developer) and Oscar (the Ops guy) ignore test automation as there's already a team testing software once it's built so what's the point?

One thing we have not covered thus far is the tooling that can run, manage, and control this automation. That is where continuous integration solutions come into play.

Continuous integration

Continuous integration, or CI as it's more commonly known, is a tried-and-tested method of ensuring the software asset that is being developed builds correctly and plays nicely with the rest of the codebase. The keyword here is *continuous*, which, as the name implies, is as frequent as possible (ideally on each commit and/or merge to the source-control system). The simplest way to look at a CI solution is to think of it as a tool to orchestrate your build and test-automation tools—the two things we've just covered.

Yet again there are, as you may have guessed, a vast number of mature CI solutions available, both commercial and open source, so there are no excuses for not selecting one and using CI.

As mentioned, CI solutions are a very basic-level, software solution that orchestrates the execution of your build and test-automation. The execution is controlled by what many refer to as *CI jobs*, which are invoked when certain events occur; for example, when code is committed to and/or merged to the source-control repository, or on a timed schedule, or when another automation tool triggers the CI, and so on. These jobs contain a list of activities (commonly referred to as *steps*) that need to be run in quick succession; for example, get the latest version of source from source-control, compile to an executable, deploy the binary to a test environment, get the automated tests from source-control, and run them.

If all is well, the CI job completes and reports a success. If it fails, it reports this fact and provides detailed feedback as to why it failed. Most tools also let you drill down into the failing step and see what went wrong. Each time you run a given CI job, a complete audit trail is written for you to go back and compare results and/or trends over time, as shown:

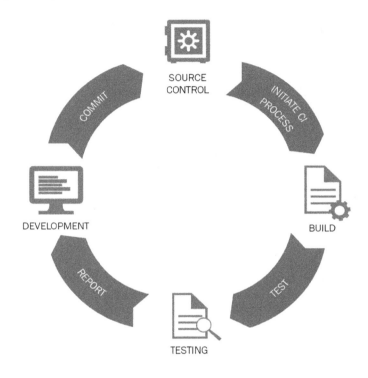

A typical CI process

CI tools can be quite powerful, and you can build in simple logic to control the process. For example, if all of the automated tests pass, you can then automatically move the executable (which could have the build version number baked in) to your binary repository, or if something fails, you could email the results to the engineering team. You can even build dashboards or information radiators so provide an instant and easy-to-understand visual representation of what's happening, and the results.

 CI solutions are a must for CD. If you are building and testing your software changes on a frequent basis, you can ship frequently.

The advantages of CI for traditional systems-operations changes are not as obvious, but they can help a great deal in terms of trying out changes without impacting the production platform. For example, let's presume that you have a CI solution that is running many overnight automated tests against an isolated test environment. The tests have been successfully passing (more commonly referred to as green) for a few days, so you are confident that everything is as it should be. You then make a server configuration change and re-run the CI suite, which then fails. The only change has been the server configuration; therefore, it must have had an adverse impact. This is a good example of the DevOps approach being applied.

Implementing CI is no small feat—especially if you have nothing in terms of automation to start with. However, CI is a very powerful tool and vastly reduces that overhead and risk of using manual methods for building and testing system changes. For all intents and purposes, trying to implement CD without CI is going to be a very hard slog, and therefore my recommendation would be to bite the bullet and implement CI.

Throughout this section, we have been talking about how to automate builds and tests to ensure the software can be validated and delivered. We also refer to results that, overall, should be positive—the automated build has to have completed and the automated tests need to have passed before they can progress to the next stage. In other words, if tests fail, that's a bad thing. On the whole, that is correct. However, failure can be a good thing, as long as the failures are found early in the process.

Fail fast and often

Failing fast and often may seem counter-intuitive, but it's a very good ethos to work to. If a defect is created but it is not spotted until it has gone live, the cost of rectifying said defect is high (it could be a completely new release), not to mention the impact it could have on your customers, reputation, and possibly your revenue. Finding defects early on is a must.

Agile engineering approaches such as **TDD** or **BDD** are based upon the principle of finding and catering for faults within software very early on in the process, the simple premise being that before code-development begins, tests are written to cover some/all of the use cases the software has to cater to—the proportion is normally referred to as coverage. As the code is being written, these tests can be run again and again as part of the CI process to spot gaps. If the test cases fail at this point, this is a good thing, as the only person impacted is the software engineer writing the code, rather than your customers.

This may sound strange—especially for the managers out there—but if defects are found early on, you should not make a big thing of it and you should not chastise people. Think back to what we learned about blame versus learning behaviors. What you want is to find the problem, figure out why it happened, fix it, learn from it, and move on.

One of the things that can sometimes scupper implementing engineering practices such as TDD is the size and complexity of the software platform itself. It may be a very daunting task to retrospectively implement a test suite for a software system that was not built around these principles. If this is the case, it may be wise to start small and build up.

We'll now move away from software building and test-automation and onto the challenges you will face when adopting CD and DevOps in relation to how your software system/platform is designed and architected.

Architectural approaches

The majority of businesses—despite what the tech press and jeans-and-t-shirt conference speakers would have you believe—are not running modern software architecture. The reality is that a vast number of software platforms and systems in the world on which we are reliant have evolved over many years, and some (most) are rather complex and cumbersome to maintain or advance. Even the young and hipster tech sector companies are running and maintaining what would be classed as *legacy* solutions and platforms that comprise a small number of large executables all built and tested together before getting delivered. That isn't to say CD and DevOps principles aren't being used or can't be adopted; it just means that it takes a little more work.

The immediate reaction may well be to spend vast amounts of time, effort, and money transforming your entire software platform to a new reference architecture model that will allow for seamless adoption of CD and DevOps. If you're lucky enough to have senior leadership who have fully bought into this and have deep pockets, then good luck. Most of us are not that lucky, and therefore need to be creative in our approach.

Something that is also a little daunting, if you were to research the best breed of reference architecture, is that you will find that there are many views (often differing) on what's the best approach. Not to mention the many and varied ways one would go about adopting and implementing said architecture. If you're lucky enough to have a high-flying visionary who knows instinctively what to do, you are off to a great start. In reality, what you will end up with is a target architecture and a plan to get there through what's referred to as legacy strangulation—that being an approach to systematically replace parts of the legacy platform with software components designed and built using a more modern approach and focused on particular functional (and non-functional) areas.

Although legacy solutions are a pain, they are not the end of the world when it comes to CD and DevOps adoption. Take into account the limitations that come from having to build, test, and ship the entire platform each time changes are made, and also the overall duration for this to complete, which can be many minutes (sometime hours) depending on the size and complexity of the platform itself.

This is where creativity comes into play. Let's assume that your *legacy* platform takes 30 minutes to build and another 90 mins for the automated test suite to complete. That's two hours to wait for *each* change you make and want to test. Scale that out to the number of engineers making changes. And that's what can only be described as unworkable. Most will overcome this by only triggering the CI job at certain times—for example, at the end of the working day—so that the time taken doesn't leach into the working day. This does help in some ways, but also adds the risk that an entire build could fail due to one simple mistake, defect, or typo, and then hold up all the other changes and engineers who want to move onto their next task.

You could overcome this by looking at some small tweaks to the process to make things (a little more) workable. For example:

- Split the testing suite into smaller, discrete test packs; for example, use a subset of the tests to run when the build completes (sometimes referred to as a smoke test) and a full set overnight
- Add more horsepower to your build and/or automated test servers
- Implement a clustered CI solution

- Parallelize the CI jobs (you'll need the additional horsepower/clustering)
- Alter the way the software is built so that only changes that have changed since the last build are built again (that is, only build deltas rather the entire platform every time)

Ultimately, you want to reduce the time taken to build, test, and ship your legacy software. The more you can achieve in this area, the more time you can buy yourself while you look at breaking down the legacy platform into smaller independent software components that can be independently built, tested, and shipped. Even the most integrated and closely-coupled software platform is made up of many small components all talking to each other.

If you take a step back and look at your legacy platform, you'll probably find you could actually split it (or at least most of it) into small, manageable chunks (shared libraries, different layers of technology, packaging solutions, and so on) that can be built and tested independently and quickly, and, more importantly, can be delivered frequently.

Component-based architecture

As previously mentioned, if you are lucky enough to have the opportunity to re-engineer your *legacy* platform—as did ACME systems—then you should take time to consider the best approach for your needs. Ideally, you should look at a technology or an architectural approach that allows the platform to be broken down into small, discrete modules or components that are loosely coupled. By this I mean that each component can be developed, built, tested, and shipped independently of all other components.

This approach has had many names over the years—web services architecture, **Service Orientated Architecture (SOA)**, or micro services architecture—but at a basic level they are pretty much the same thing: an architectural approach that allows loosely-coupled software components that are self-contained and coexist to provide functionality that would normally have been delivered as a complete monolithic platform shown as follows:

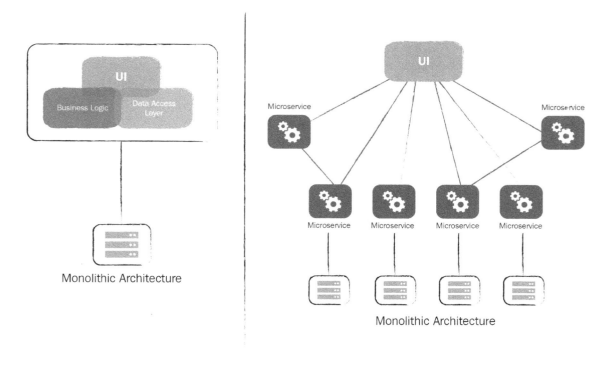

A typical architectural comparison

By going down this route, you have the advantage of small, discreet software components that can be developed and tested, and, more importantly, released independently. This goes a long way to realizing the benefits of CD.

Another advantage of this approach not directly attributable to CD or DevOps is cost saving. Not only does a component-based architecture allow for small and frequent changes to be released, it can also remove the need for large and costly IT infrastructure. For example, if you currently have one or two huge bits of code, you will have to have one or two hulking servers to run them. You then have one or two hulking DB servers and—to allow for Disaster Recovery—you'll have another set sitting and waiting. Just think how much that costs to acquire and keep running. With many small components, you can consider more cost-effective hosting approaches—something we'll look at later on.

There is a mountain of options and information available to determine the best approach for your current and future needs. Suffice to say, if you can move toward a component-based architecture, the pain and overhead of releasing will be a thing of the past.

One important thing to note here, should you adopt a component-based architecture (which you should do, by the way, just in case it wasn't clear), is how you release the components. There may be a temptation to use the same *clump it all into one big release* approach as used for the legacy platform, but that will simply lead to a world of pain and give you no advantage whatsoever. We'll be looking at CD tooling later, so please keep reading.

Let's have a look at another possible solution that may help with legacy strangulation and ease you toward the component-based architecture utopia.

Layers of abstraction

If you have quite complex dependencies throughout your platform, it may help to try and separate your software assets by using some form of abstraction. This technique should assist in removing, or at least reducing, hard dependencies within your platform, and will help move you toward a component-based architecture which, in turn, will give you the opportunity to adopt CD.

Let's say, for example, you have two software components that have to be deployed together, as they have been hardwired in such a way that deploying one without the other would cause a platform outage. Then you're going to struggle to follow the *small incremental changes* method—not to mention the fact that you will be hard-pressed to release without downtime.

There are plenty of mature and proven design patterns available that can give some good ways of achieving this, but at the very least, it is a good practice to remove close dependencies wherever possible so that you don't end up with clumps of assets that need to be deployed together.

One common area for close coupling is between software and databases. This means that a change to one may mean both need to be tested and shipped. Adding abstraction here could be as complex as adding a data-access layer proxy between the two, or as simple as using SQL views. Another problem area is UI and business logic code being bundled together, which again can be separated out by following a standard design pattern. Whatever the approach, the goal is the same: to be able to build, test, and ship software components independently.

Just to add to your homework, you should spend some time looking at and analyzing areas of the existing platform to find components that are closely coupled, and then see how you can add an abstraction layer to allow each to be worked on without impacting the other. You could also look at fast-moving versus slow-moving areas (for example, which software components are updated on a regular basis and which very rarely), as this may help you to pinpoint which components to separate first.

Never break your consumer

Your software platform will probably be complex and have quite a few dependencies—this is nothing to be ashamed of, and is quite normal. These dependencies can be classified as relationships between consumers and providers. The providers can be anything from shared libraries or core code modules to a database. The consumers will call/execute/send requests to the providers in a specific way as per some predefined interface spec (sometimes called a service contract).

A simple example would be a web page that utilizes a shared library to return content to render and display a user's address details. In this scenario, the web page is the consumer and the shared library is the provider. If the shared library originally returned four pieces of data but was changed to provide three, the consumer may not know how to handle this and may throw an error or, worse still, simply crash. You could, of course, add some defensive code, but in reality, this is just adding more complexity due to lazy change-management.

Most software platforms have many dependencies, which means it is sometimes very difficult to spot which *provider* has changed and is causing one of the many consumers to fail—especially when you consider that a consumer may also be a provider to another consumer higher up the stack (that is, a shared library, which consumes from a database and then *provides* said data to a web page, which then consumes it and provides that data to a JavaScript client, and so on).

To understand how prevalent this situation is, you'll need to do some impact analysis that will help you map this out. Be forewarned that unless you can map out your entire platform into one easy-to-understand format that is consistently up to date, it's going to be a difficult task. Luckily, there are many mature and established patterns that cover these sorts of problems, as well as tools that will help with the analysis.

What can also help is to establish some rules around how changes are approached going forward. In simple terms, if you are making a change to software, config, or a database which will be consumed by another part of the platform, it's the responsibility of the person making the change to validate that the change has not broken anything up/downstream. If you have CI and test-automation in place, then that can help spot issues early. However, simply adding some diligence to the code-review/pull-request process is cheap and easy, and can help cement good behaviors.

 Within the system operations area, the "never break your consumer" rule should also apply. For example, the software platform could be classed as a consumer of the server operating system (the provider); therefore, if you change or upgrade the operating system, you must ensure that there are no breaking changes that will cause the consumer to fail.

Sometimes breaking changes cannot be avoided (for example, the service contract between components has to change to accommodate new functionality). However, this should be the exception rather than the rule, and you should have a strategy planned to cater for this. An example strategy would be to accommodate side-by-side versioning, which will allow you to run more than one version of a software asset at the same time—something we'll cover later.

There may be times when the consumer/provider relationship fails as the person or team working on the provider is unaware of the relationship. This can be very true of providers within the system operations area. To overcome this, or at least minimize the risk, use open and honest peer-working practices.

Open and honest peer-working practices

There are many different agile software-delivery methodologies in use today, but all of them revolve around some form of highly-collaborative ways of working and free-flowing communication. Agile approaches such as **XP**, pairing, or a simple code-review process, all depend on engineers working closely together.

I cannot stress enough the importance of sharing your work with others. Even the best software engineers (or system admins) on the planet are human and they **will** make mistakes. If you think your code is precious and don't want to share it with anyone else, you **will** create defects and it **will** take longer to overcome small mistakes, which can cause hours of head-scratching, or worse, have an adverse impact on your customers.

If you are confident that your code is of the highest quality and can stand up to scrutiny, then do not hide it away—put your money where your mouth is and share your work. If you are not that confident, sharing with your peer group will help to build that confidence. One thing to point out here—in terms of software engineers—is that the peer group should not be exclusively made up of other software engineers; the operations team can (and should) also be included in this process. It may seem strange, as they may not be able to actually read your code (although you may be surprised how many system admins can read code), but they know how the live platform operates and may be able to provide some valuable input and/or ask some pertinent questions (for example, what the code will do if there's a network blip, how long-lived threads will be, or why connection-polling isn't being used). This also encourages the DevOps mindset and approach. The same rule should apply to changes made by the Ops team.

All things considered, the majority of the world's highest-quality software is built in a highly-collaborative way, so there are no excuses for you not to be doing the same. Some purists may scoff at this approach, but consider this: most of these types will most probably sing the praises of Linux-based operating systems, which, if they actually thought about it, is, like most open source software, written using highly-collaborative approaches that have been part of the development process from day one.

 Having an open, honest, and transparent peer-review process is as important within an Operations team as it is within a Development team. Changes made to any part of the platform run a risk, and having more than one pair of eyes to review will help reduce this risk. As with software code, there is no reason not to share system configuration changes.

One normally unforeseen advantage of working in this way is the fact that if your code (or configuration change) fails to get through peer review, the impact on the production system is negated. It's all about failing fast rather than waiting to put out something live to find it fails.

Let's assume you have seen the light and have decided to move to a loosely-coupled component-based architecture that has been written using best practices and you're ready to move to the next stage in your software engineering evolution.

Now you have everyone working together and playing nicely, we'll move on to the next challenge: how the expectations of the wider business need to be realigned in terms of release and feature delivery.

Incremental delivery of features

Earlier, we looked at breaking work down into small incremental chunks so that you can deliver and release quickly. You also need to consider how you deal with features. What I'm referring to here is the business-driven deliverables that turn into revenue. Typically, you'll have a year-long business plan that is represented by a number of key initiatives that need to be delivered within that year, and these are further broken down into a selection of features, which is what will be marketed and sold to customers. This is pretty normal in terms of business process.

 Please note that terms used within your business may differ and you may use terms such as epics, or themes, or goals, or MVP. In essence, we'll focus on the relationship between delivering a thing your business can make money from and the point in time when that thing becomes available to customers. To keep things simple, I'll refer to the thing as a feature and the point in time as a release.

How the adoption of CD and DevOps can impact this does depend on the current release cadence, but I would hazard a guess that you'll be looking at a cadence in months or quarters. Once CD and DevOps are embedded, you'll be looking at weeks, days, or hours between each release. This can only be a good thing, but let's take a moment to consider the wider impact:

- The wider business would currently be expecting a feature to be delivered in its entirety within a release cycle
- Business functions, such as sales, marketing, legal, and support, will have processes in place to cater for this
- You will be vastly reducing the release cycle and incrementally delivering changes

How should the wider business cater for this? When will the feature be ready? When should they start the wheels turning? What should they say to customers?

What you need to do is work with these business areas and come to an agreement in terms of how features can be incrementally delivered over a number of releases. There are a few approaches you should consider and discuss:

- Deliver the end-to-end experience in slices and build up the richness of the functionality over a number of releases until the feature is complete
- Focus on an area of functionality through to completion, then move onto to the next, then the next, until the feature is complete
- Incrementally build the feature over a number of releases but keep it hidden until it's completed

Something to consider is approaches such as the first and second could open up avenues such as alpha/beta releases, which means that you start to get customer feedback early on, whereas approaches such as the last one mean you don't get early feedback but the go-live is relatively painless (you've already shipped the code so go-live is really switch-it-on). Whatever approach you choose—and you will need to choose one—you need to ensure that those expecting "release equals feature delivery" are educated and their expectations are realigned.

We'll now move back into a more technical area: ensuring you are deploying the same software throughout your environments.

Using the same binary across all environments

Before a software asset can be used in a given environment, it has to have been built/compiled into an executable or a binary. This binary is important, as it is the version of the software that will be executed at runtime within your environments. Think of it as a snapshot in time. Some would say that the source code is more important than the binary object itself as the binary is simply a byproduct and can be recreated time and time again, although that's not strictly true.

You will not be running functional, regression, performance, or load tests against the source code. You will be doing so against the binary. It's therefore important that the resulting binary is treated with as much reverence as the source code from which it was created. This becomes more important if you're looking at side-by-side versioning and/or baking in versions during the CI process. For example, if your CI solution creates version 1.2.0.1 of the binary, then it's version 1.2.0.1 you should be using and testing.

The ideal, and recommended, approach is that the binary is only built once for a given release/deployment and that the self-same unchanged binary is used in **all** environments, including production. This may sound like common sense, but sometimes this is overlooked or simply cannot be done due to software design and/or tooling, or, more worryingly, it's not seen as important.

One example of tooling/software design limitations would come in the form of software tokens or config related to the environment (sometimes referred to as secrets). Let's take the credentials for a database server, for instance. Some would say that because this data is very sensitive—especially in higher environments such as production—it should be hidden away from all but a select few. One way around this is to *bake* this information into the binary itself at compile-time, which makes it secure. This is all well and good, but we only want to build it once, and therefore you would have to have the same credentials set up in all environments, including the completely open development environment—far from secure, I think you'll agree. Another drawback to this approach is the fact that someone could reverse-engineer the binary and get hold of the credentials without you knowing. Also, how would you change said credentials should they get leaked and need changing?

You could always build multiple copies of the binary (one for each environment); however, you're back to testing different versions of the software.

There are many industry-standard approaches to this problem, but the simple approach (which seems to work well for a vast amount of businesses) is to have this kind of data held in a startup script or system configuration file (which, of course, is under version-control) and have the software load it up at runtime. If you restrict access to these configs files/scripts, you have a good chance of keeping them *secret*. Whatever approach you choose, you should ensure that it allows you to use the same binary.

As previously mentioned, use of a binary repository will also allow you to store multiple versions of a given binary, which means a rollback to the previous version is pretty painless.

Now that we've looked at how to deliver the software to each environment, let's see how many environments you need.

How many environments is enough?

This question has been around since software development became a thing. Unfortunately, there is no simple answer, although there are some common-sense and tried-tested-and-trusted approaches that have worked over the years. When I talk about environments, I'm not just referring to servers here; I'm referring to the servers, infrastructure, network, firewalls, first- and third-party integration, and so on. In essence, everything you need to run one copy of your software platform.

Going back to the question at hand, the (rather underwhelming) answer is: the number of environments you **need** depends on your ways of working, your engineering setup, and, of course, the architecture of your platform. There's also another factor to consider: the overhead to manage and look after multiple environments along with the cost of keeping them running and healthy. Suffice it to say that you should not go overboard; try to work to a *less-is-more* approach where you can.

There may also be a temptation to have environments set up for different scenarios: development, functional testing, regression testing, user acceptance testing, performance testing, and load testing. If you are able to ensure all the environments can be kept up to date (including the all-important test data), can easily deploy to them, and, more importantly, **need** all of them, then this may be viable. The reality is that having too many environments can actually be counterproductive and can cause far too much noise and overhead.

The ideal number of environments is two:

- One for development
- One for production

This may sound like an accident waiting to happen, but if you think about it, many small businesses and start-ups manage fine with such a setup. What you'll find is that as a business grows, so does the need to be risk-averse, and hence the potential for multiple environments.

When ACME systems started out, two environments were sufficient. As they grew, so did the need for more environments, and they ended up with multiple development environments (one for each engineering team), an integration environment, a performance-testing environment, a load-testing environment, a pre-live deployment staging environment, and, of course, production environments. They also ended up with an entire team of people whose job was to keep these all running—actually, they ended up with two: one to look after the engineering and testing environments, and one to look after the production environments. Far from ideal or effective.

You may think that with virtualization technologies (including cloud-based) now in a highly-mature state and used by anyone and everyone, setting up and running hundreds of servers, is not as much as an overhead as it once was. There is truth in that thinking, but it's the challenge of keeping everything in line that is massive—versions of software, O/S patch levels, network configuration, firewall configurations, and so on. Therefore, virtualization can help in some ways, but the *how many environments* question still remains.

Whatever you decide, there may be a fly in the ointment: what if your production environments are locked away in a highly-secure datacenter to which you have little or no access, or, worse still, fully managed by a third party? This can have a massive impact on your *less-is-more* approach. If this is the case, then you really need to get those managing said environments closely looped into what you're trying to do—if you don't, it can derail your DevOps adoption.

Let's move on to a real-world example and see how ACME systems approached this. When they reviewed the environments **needed** for CD and DevOps, they settled on the following as being sufficient for their needs:

- **Development environments**: Cut-down versions of the platform with only a few other platform components that were needed for local testing
- **CI environment**: The place where the software is built and all automated tests are run on a regular basis
- **Pre-production environment**: Used for the occasional spot check/UAT (occasional being the operative word)
- **Production environment**: This is where all the action takes place

The following diagram depicts the environments used:

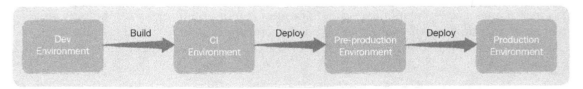

ACME systems 3.0 environment setup

ACME systems 3.0 environment setup

As you can see, this follows the less-is-more approach and allows for enough quality gates to ensure a given change was sufficient. When combined with all of the aforementioned engineering best practices (high levels of test coverage, build automation, CI tooling, and so on), the speed at which a given change could be delivered was minutes.

OK, so this is a bit of a utopia and you may be quite some distance from this now, but hopefully you can see how simple it can be, and hopefully you're slightly closer to answering the *how many environments* question.

Let's now have a look at another possible environment-related solution that can help speed up your delivery capabilities.

Developing against a like-live environment

There are many ways to ensure one version of a software binary works, or integrates, with other parts of your platform, but by far the easiest is to actually develop against an environment that contains live versions of your platform.

On paper, this may look like a strange statement, but if you think about it, you're making a change to one part of your overall platform and—as is the CD way—you want to validate and ship that change as soon as possible. What this also gives you is the ability to ensure that the dependencies you expect to be available within the production environment are actually there and function as you expect, along with the configuration and infrastructure.

This approach will give the most value when used in conjunction with component-based architecture, but some aspects will apply to legacy platforms as well.

The simplest approach would be to develop against the production environment, but this is very risky and the possibility that you could cause outage—albeit inadvertently—is quite high. There's also the security/access issues. The next best thing is, therefore, to have another like-live environment set up, which contains the versions of code that are running in the production environment.

You may be thinking that developing against a *like-live* environment is somewhat overkill, and you may be wondering why not simply develop against the versions of software that reside in the CI environment. There is a simple answer: you have no firm idea which of the changed binaries in the CI environment will be live before you. For example, if you are developing and testing against version 1.2.0.3 of the authentication component (to pick a name out of the air), and when your binary hits production and starts to talk to version 1.2.0.1, you may experience issues that you didn't see during the development/testing phase.

This is especially true if someone is testing out a breaking change where you need to ensure that you have covered all scenarios **before** you release it to production.

This like-live environment only needs to be *like-live* in terms of software (and infrastructure) versions. If you can populate it with live data, that would be good, but the reality is that you would need something as big as production in terms of storage and so on, which is costly. Saying nothing of the risk of exposing confidential data and breaching data protection rules and regulation, such as GDPR—unless you have a way to redact confidential data (which is a whole different challenge).

To give you a flavor of how this could work, the following diagram gives an overview of how ACME systems implemented such a setup:

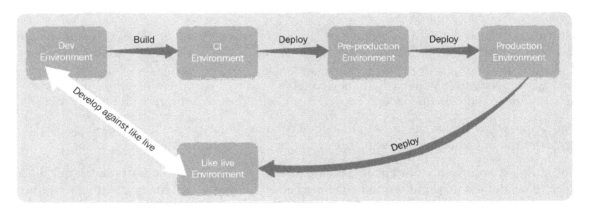

The like-live environment used by ACME systems 3.0

As you can see, the like-live environment is tagged onto the end of the deployment pipeline. It is on the end for a reason: you only want to deploy to this environment once the deployment to production is successful.

It should be noted that when we talk about a like-live environment, this need not be a physical set of servers. You could look at virtualization (cloud or desktop-based), whereby you can pretty much spin up a copy of your production environment on a developer's workstation (on the presumption that there's enough horse power and storage available).

Now that you are starting to get all of the building blocks in place to realize your goal of adopting CD and DevOps, we have a few additional blocks you'll need, those being how you actually take the fully-built and tested software component through the environments in a controlled, reliable, and repeatable way. This is where CD tooling comes into play.

CD and DevOps tooling

There is another collection of tools that may not be as readily available to you as the aforementioned tools (automated build and testing, CI, and so on). These are the tools that you will use to control and orchestrate the entire software-delivery life cycle from building the binaries (via CI), deploying said binaries to the various test environments, and if all goes well, pushing the same binary to production. At a very simple level, these tools act as workflow engines wherein each step is defined to do a specific action, and then the flow moves on to the next tasks. They also have basic logic built in to catch exceptions during the flow (for example, if tests fail, then don't go any further and send a notification). This workflow analogy is normally referred to as the CD pipeline, delivery pipeline, or just pipeline.

Over the past few years, the CD and DevOps tooling market has grown from almost nothing to a full-blown multi-million-dollar global business. There are now a plethora of tools and vendors wanting to sell tools to you, and it's become quite difficult to choose the one (or two) that will fit your needs. Just like any tool or technology you use within your software development life cycle, you need CD and DevOps tools that will be reliable, help more than hinder, and will grow with you as your adoption matures. I would also hazard a guess that you will already have some tooling that manages your software delivery/deployment, so you may need to look at something that will either integrate with the existing tooling or replace it completely.

The tooling you choose will be used day in and day out and will be heavily relied upon, so you had better make sure it fits your needs and will be there when it's needed. To assist in this, you could use something similar to the following, which could assist during your tool/vendor selection and due diligence.

The following are some example questions you should ask of your CD and DevOps tooling/vendor:

- Can it deploy the same binary to multiple environments?
- Can it access the binary and source repositories we're using?
  Can it remotely invoke and control the installation process on the server it's been deployed to?
- Is there functionality to allow it to orchestrate my current tooling?
- Is it capable of deploying database changes?
- Does it have functionality to allow for the queuing up of releases?
- Can it run parallel pipelines?
- Does it contain an audit of what has been deployed, when, and by whom?
- Is it secure?
- How is it hosted (SaaS, PaaS, on-premise, and so on)?
- Can it interact with the infrastructure to allow for no-downtime deployments?
- Can it/could it orchestrate automated infrastructure-provisioning?
- Can it interact with other systems and solutions, such as email, collaboration tools, change-management, issue-management, and project-management solutions?
- Does it have simple and easy-to-understand dashboards that can be displayed on big screens around the office?
- Can it interact with and/or orchestrate CI solutions (our current solution and other industry leaders)?
- Will it grow with our needs?
- What skills/experience do we need to run this?
- Is it simple enough for anyone and everyone to use?
- What support/SLA do we get?
- What set up/implementation support do we get included in the price?
- What about HA/failover?
- What is the process for upgrading the tooling itself?

At this point, it would be very helpful if I just listed most of the market-leading tools and gave you an idea of their pros and cons. However, depending on when you read this, that information could be very out of date. This is really something you need to be doing yourself anyway—you know your needs, problems to solve, and budget better than I. It should go without saying, but I'll mention it just in case: the tooling choice should be done in true DevOps style, with both Dev and Ops heavily and equally involved.

There are a few things you should take into account when selecting CD and DevOps tooling: don't skimp on budget as the tooling will become the backbone of your delivery pipeline; don't just stick with the big boys in the marketplace, as they may be too constraining in the long run; and if there are gaps you can fill with bespoke solutions, you should seriously consider that without creating another legacy to look after.

You may have noticed that one of the considerations noted here is automated provisioning. Let's now look into what this means.

Automated provisioning

The norm over the past few years has been to move from traditional tin-and-string physical servers and infrastructure to virtualized equivalents, be that on-premise, datacenter-hosted, or cloud-based. I won't dwell too much on the advantages of one over the other—again, there's plenty of rich information available should you wish to read up—but I will focus on one element that is not always front and center when planning to move to a virtualized environment solution: the ability to use automated provisioning as part of your CD and DevOps pipeline.

Provisioning is nothing new; as long as cloud providers have been a thing, they have been providing their customers with cloud-based virtualized servers that can be provisioned pretty much as and when needed. One also has the freedom in defining the configuration and setup of the servers in terms of horsepower, storage, networking, operating system, and location/region. In addition to this, when the servers are no longer needed, they can then be deleted (sometimes referred to as teared down).

Now consider how useful it would be to have automated provisioning as a step within your CD pipeline. You would then have the ability to not only control and orchestrate the software-delivery life cycle, but you can also create environments on the fly, install your software, run your tests, and then tear it all down. The massive advantages this gives you are predictability and repeatability. If you can guarantee that **every time** you initiate the CD pipeline you will have exactly the same vanilla environment created from scratch, then you can pretty much eliminate what some like to call environmental issues—something we'll be looking at later—which continually cause noise and false negatives (or positives) within the testing step.

As you would expect, there are many industry buzzwords floating around to complicate this sort of activity—the most common ones being **Infrastructure-as-a-Service (IaaS)** and PaaS—but what it boils down to is being able to programmatically interface with a provisioning system, tell it what you want in terms of spec, configuration, and so on, and get it to spit one out the other end. When you're done, you programmatically interface again and get the environment removed.

The list of requirements fed into a provisioning system that defines the server spec, CPUs, GPUs, RAM, storage, and so on is normally referred to as the recipe—there are some variations depending on the tools, but they are all pretty much the same thing.

Something to consider with automated provisioning is the time lag you may encounter within the CD pipeline. For example, if you were to take a binary and deploy it to a prebuilt server, then the time taken is simply the act of deploying. Add automated provisioning into the mix and the CD pipeline will have to wait for the new virtual server(s) to be provisioned before you can deploy your binaries. What you need to weigh up is the importance of quality, repeatability, and predictability over speed and convenience. Just because something is faster doesn't make it better. What you can do to overcome this is to pre-bake some vanilla virtual server images that can be added to the environment via the automated provisioning tooling as part of the CD pipeline. That way, you have a fresh virtual server in a fraction of the time. In fact, this is how many leading cloud providers operate. There is an overhead with this approach; someone needs to keep these vanilla virtual server images fresh and updated, with operating-system patch levels being the pain they are. Again, you need to weigh up the pros and cons.

One massive advantage of automated provisioning is blue/green deployments. Strictly speaking, this approach was around before automated provisioning became mainstream, but automated provisioning has made it far easier to realize. I won't go into too much detail—again that's homework for you. However, in simple terms, blue/green deployments allow you to provision a new server with the latest version of software or configuration changes or database updates offline within the environment, then switch old for new via a small network/routing change. Essentially, you do the hard work and prep upfront, and the release simply becomes the switchover. It's very effective and quick, and allows for near-instant rollback if problems are found (for example, switching back from new to old). I would highly recommend adding this to your reading list.

You may be thinking that the automated provisioning approach will only work for environments that are used for development and testing, but this self-same approach can (and should) be considered for your production environment. After all, if you have set up a CD pipeline, what's the point (or value) of stopping short of the goal. I wouldn't recommend doing this on day one; you need to build up your confidence in the tooling and iron out any kinks before taking the plunge. Based upon experience, I can guarantee that once you have automated provisioning in place, you will not look back.

Another massive but little-mentioned benefit of automated provisioning is the ability to overcome the bane of most IT departments and software houses around the globe: having to take your production system offline to upgrade it.

No-downtime deployments

One of the things that comes with large releases of software (legacy or otherwise) is the unforgivable need to take the production platform offline to upgrade it. Yes, I did say unforgivable, because that's exactly what it is. It is also wholly avoidable. It's the IT equivalent to having an out-of-order sign on the elevator:

There are two simple reasons for taking a production system offline to upgrade it: there are far too many unreleased changes that have been bundled up together, or you don't trust the quality of the software being delivered. Both of these can be overcome through CD and DevOps adoption.

Let's consider you are operating a real-time online service and you inform your customers that you have to take the system offline for an upgrade. You can bet a pretty penny that your customers will not take kindly to not being able to access your system (or more importantly, their data) for a few hours so that you can upgrade some parts of it. To minimize the impact, you will no doubt schedule the upgrade out-of-hours, which means you'll need to have people on-call to support the upgrade—but being out-of-hours, I doubt you'll have all of the engineers that made the changes available on the night, so you already have a risk.

One important thing in relation to out-of-hours is this: unless you are running a B2B solution and have customers in the same time zone, you may struggle to find a suitable out-of-hours time window. For example, if your solution and business is B2C, you're pretty much offering a 24/7 solution, so unless you know for sure when your consumers sleep, finding the time window is going to be tough. If your customers are global, you will find it even harder to find a suitable window. You will no doubt have included something in your terms of service and/or contracts to cater for taking the live platform offline, but this amounts to admitting to your customers that your business processes are inadequate.

If you also consider how many news stories are reported on a regular basis regarding major issues following a massive down-time IT upgrade, there is also a very strong possibility that your customers will look upon this big-bang approach with distrust as they'll be pretty sure something will go wrong once the service is up and running again. This distrust will be amplified if you go beyond the time window. From experience, I can say with confidence that something will go wrong, and depending on the severity, you will have to quickly move into damage-limitation mode to keep customers happy, T&Cs and contracts aside. It might even get to the stage where your customers may shop around to find a competitor who does not need planned downtime.

OK, so this is a bit doom and gloom, but that is the stark reality. Customers and consumers don't care about your process problems or complexities in your SDLC; they have become accustomed to having the IT services they use on a daily basis being available when they need them. Try to remember when one of the major search engines or social media platforms was offline. When release issues happen, it's now extremely difficult to contain the bad news, especially with the prevalence of social media, 24-hour news, and the like. You have to remember that bad news travels faster than anything else known to man, so the last thing you need is bad news generated because of a release.

The ultimate goal for CD and DevOps adoption is to repeatedly deliver value as quickly, consistently, and reliably as possible. Removing the need for down-time deployments completely is a massive bonus for you.

One thing to point out which may not be obvious is that it's not just the production environment that should have maximum uptime. Any environment that you are reliant on for your development, testing, and CD should be treated the same. If the like-live environment is down, how are you going to develop? If your CI environment is down, how are you going to integrate and test? The same rules should apply across the board—without exception.

Previously, we covered open and honest ways of working as part of engineering best practices. Openness and honesty are just as important when it comes to CD. A good way of providing this level of transparency is to monitor everything and have it available to all.

Monitor, monitor, monitor

One of the most important ways to ensure whether CD and DevOps is working is to monitor, monitor, and then monitor some more. If all of the environments used within the CD process are constantly being observed, then the impact of any change (big or small) is easy to see—in other words, there should be no hidden surprises. A simple rule of thumb here: if it moves, monitor it.

If you have good coverage in terms of monitoring, you have much more transparency across the board. There is no reason why monitoring should be restricted to the operations teams; everyone in the business should be able to see and understand how any environment—especially the production platform—is performing and what it is doing.

There are plenty of mature and industry-standard monitoring tools available, but it can be quite difficult to get a single view that is consistent and meaningful. For example, some tools are geared up for monitoring infrastructure and servers, whereas others are geared up for collecting application metrics, and still others for measuring application and/or database performance. Unless you can tie this data together into a coherent view, things will look disjointed. Ideally, you should try to aggregate the data from these tools—or at least try to integrate them—and present a unified view of how any given environment and the software/services running within are coping and functioning.

You will be surprised how much very valuable data you can get and how it can direct your engineering work, as the engineers can see exactly how their software or infrastructure is behaving in real time with real users.

If it moves, monitor it. If it doesn't, monitor it just in case

Monitoring is a must for CD and DevOps to work correctly, as things will be continually changing (software, services, infrastructure, and so on), and both halves of the Dev and Ops relationship will need to see what is going on and assist when/if problems occur.

Another, less obvious, positive that monitoring can bring you is proof that CD is not having an adverse impact on the production platform. If you're using some *graph-over-time* solution, you can get your CD tools to add a *spike* or a marker to the graph when a deployment takes place. You can then visually see the impact (or not) of the change.

So far, we have mainly focused on technical solutions and tools for the adoption of CD and DevOps. These solutions and tools may help to provide you with much of what you need in your toolbox. However, there is still room for simple manual processes.

When a simple manual process is also an effective tool

Even if you have enough tooling to shake a stick at, you will no doubt have some small and niggling challenges that cannot be overcome with tooling and automation alone. To be honest, tooling and automation can be overkill in some respects, and can actually create barriers between certain parts of the organization you are trying so hard to bring together—here, I am talking about the Dev and Ops partnership that forms DevOps.

If tooling and automation completely negate the need for human interaction and discussion, you may well end up back where you started. You may also find that it is almost impossible to automate your way out of a simple problem.

Let's take, for example, the thorny issue of dependency-management. As a software platform matures, many interdependencies will form. If you are deploying your code using a CD process, these many interdependencies become ever-moving targets wherein components are being developed and deployed at different rates. You can try to capture this within your CI process, but something somewhere might be missed and you could end up inadvertently bringing down the entire platform because component B was deployed before component A.

You can try to map this out and build into the tooling rules to restrict, or at least minimize, these moving targets, but the rules may end up being more complex than the original dependencies. Or you could simply agree on a process whereby only one change happens at any given point in time. To feed into this, you can implement a simple queuing mechanism written on a whiteboard and reviewed regularly by all of the engineering and Operations teams.

This approach worked extremely well for ACME systems. The following is what they did:

- They obtained a blanket agreement from everyone that only one change would go through to production at any given point in time. They called this a deployment transaction.
- To highlight the fact that someone was making a change to production (either a deployment or operational change), that person held the production environment token, which was in the form of a plush toy animal and was given the name the build badger. If you had the build badger, you were changing production.

- They implemented a simple prioritized queue system using a whiteboard and a pen. Each morning, whoever wanted to make a deployment would come along to the deployment stand-up and agree with everyone there the order in which deployments (or changes) would be made that day.
- Screens were installed throughout the office (not just the Dev and Ops areas), showing a real-time dashboard of what was going on.

All very simple, but what this gave ACME systems was a way to overcome dependency hell (for example, if they could only change one thing at a time, there was an implied logical order of which change went before another) and built a sense of collaboration throughout all of the teams involved.

The following diagram should give you some idea of what the deployment transaction covered, in terms of a deployment:

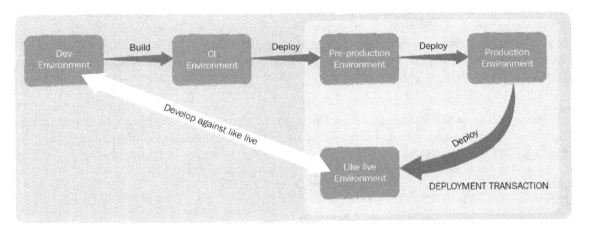

The deployment transaction

Eventually, ACME managed to engineer out the dependencies that plagued them in the early days so this manual process could be decommissioned, although it helped them keep moving with their CD and DevOps adoption.

Other very simple manual solutions you can use could include the following:

- Use collaborative tools for real-time communication between everyone and integrate this into your CD tooling so that deployments are announced and can be followed by all.
- If your management is uneasy about having developers deploy to production without involving the Operations team, make sure you have a DevOps team doing the release.
- If instant rollback is needed should a deployment fail, look into simple ways of rolling back, such as simply deploying the previous version of the component using the CD tooling.
- Consistently inspect and adapt through regular retrospectives to see what is working and what is not.

As you can tell, it's not all about technical solutions. If simple manual processes or tweaks to the ways of working are sufficient, then why bother trying to automate them?

And so ends the lesson—for now. Let's recap what we have covered.

Summary

As stated at the beginning of this chapter was a lot to cover and a lot to take in. Some of it is relevant to you now and some of it will be relevant for the future.

At this point you should have a greater understanding and appreciation for how agile engineering best practices (including use of source control, CI, incremental delivery, test automation, failing fast) along with modern architectural approaches, delivery methods and in-depth monitoring will ease your CD and DevOps adoption. Above all you should have learned that it's not all about technical tools and techniques, sometimes simple processes can solve problems.

We'll now move on from ways to advance your CD and DevOps adoption to the kinds of issues which will trip you up along the way, how to spot them and how to get passed them.

6
Avoiding Hurdles

Up until this point in the book, we have mainly been focusing on the core tools, techniques and approaches you'll need in your toolbox to ensure that your adoption of CD and DevOps starts well and continues smoothly. We've also covered a few of the potential hurdles you'll come across along the way which you'll have somehow to get over.

We'll now apply a little more focus to these hurdles and looks at ways that they can be overcome, or at least ways to minimize the impact they have on pushing forward towards your goal and vision. Throughout this chapter we will be looking into:

- The common hurdles you may (will) encounter along the way
- Where to apply your energies and who should get the most attention
- Change is scary and how people react and perceive it should not be taken lightly
- Geography is problematic
- Things will go wrong so you should prepare for that

Please take into account that what follows is by no means an exhaustive list, but there is a high probability that you'll encounter a good number of these hurdles along the way. As with any major change you will encounter the occasional storm throughout your journey, so you need to understand how you can steer your way around or through them and ensure that they don't run the adoption aground, scupper your progress or completely run the adoption into the rocks—to use a nautical analogy for some reason.

What are the potential issues you need to look out for?

What you need to look for really does depend on your culture, environment, ways of working, and business maturity. I know that's a bit of a cop-out, but it is, unfortunately, true. We've already covered some of this, but it does need pointing out that if you have an unhealthy culture, environment, or behaviors, there may be more potential hurdles than you can shake a stick at. Which is why it's pretty important that you address those areas.

Hopefully, this will not be the case and you will have a nice, smooth adoption, but just in case I'm being too optimistic, let's go through some of the more obvious potential hurdles. The sorts of things you will encounter will include the likes of the following:

- Individuals who just don't see why things have to change and/or simply don't want to change how things are
- Individuals who want things to go quicker and are impatient for change
- The way people react to change at an emotional level can help and/or hinder your progress
- A lack of understanding or visibility of what you are trying to achieve may throw a wrench in the works when business priorities change
- Red tape and heavyweight corporate processes grinding the process to a halt
- Geographically diverse teams and gaps/silos between then
- Unforeseen issues with the tooling (technical and non-technical)
- Skill gaps and resource constraints
- Political upheaval due to leadership changes

The list could be (and is) much longer, but there's only so much space in this book, so we'll focus on more obvious potential issues, which could, as previously mentioned, run the CD and DevOps adoption into shallow waters or, worse still, onto the rocks. We'll start by focusing on individuals and how they can have an impact, both negative and positive, on your vision and goal.

Dissenters in the ranks

Although the word dissenters may seem like a rather powerful one to use, it is quite representative of what can happen should individuals decide what you are proposing and/or doing doesn't fit with their view of the world.

As with any new concept, idea, or change, you will have some people who are uncomfortable. Most will hopefully be rational, and, will try to understand and accept that things change. However, you will have some individuals who decide, for no seemingly-rational reason, that they are against what you are doing. The whys and wherefores can be examined and analyzed to the nth degree, but what is important for you to realize is that this will happen. It's also important to understand that if a relatively small number of individuals are loud and disruptive enough, they can make a vast amount of unwanted noise and can distract your attention from your vision and goal. This is exactly what they want, so it's very important that you don't let them get their way.

As I say, you expend a vast amount of effort and time digging into the psychological reasons for this, but simply knowing and expecting this will happen is a good place to be. Forewarned is forearmed, and all that.

I should mention that this is nothing new, nor anything directly attributed to CD and/or DevOps adoption. If you look back at the early days of agile adoption, there are plenty of examples of this phenomenon. The individuals involved in the adoption of agile within an organization broadly fall into three types: a small number of innovators trailblazing the way, a larger number of followers who are either interested in this new way of doing things or can see the benefits and have decided to move in the direction that the innovators are going in, and the laggards who are undecided or not convinced it's the right direction to go in. The following diagram illustrates these three types:

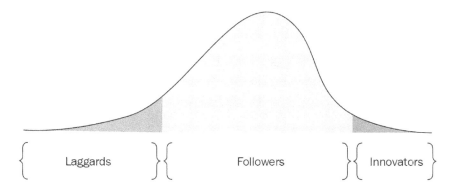

The three types of individuals identified during the early years of agile adoption

The general consensus is that effort and attention should be focused on the innovators and followers, as this makes up the majority of the individuals involved and are proactively moving adoption forward. The followers who are moving up the curve may need some help to get over the crest, so more attention should be given to them. To focus on the *laggards* may take too much attention away from the majority, so the painful truth is that they either shape up or ship out—even if they're senior managers or leaders. This may seem rather brutal, but this approach has worked for a good number of years so there must be something in it.

Let's consider our dissenters or laggards in terms of CD and DevOps adoption: what should you do? As previously pointed out, if they are loud and disruptive enough, they can make more than enough noise to derail things, but not for long. If the majority of the organization has bought into what you are doing—don't forget that you are executing a plan based upon their input and suggestions—they will not easily become distracted, and therefore you should not become distracted. If you have managed to build up a good network across the business, use this network to reduce the noise and if possible convert the *laggards* into *followers*.

If these *laggards* are in managerial or leadership positions, this may make things more difficult—especially if they are good at playing the political games that go on in any business. However, as stated previously, they will ultimately be fighting a losing battle as the majority will be behind the goal and vision. If you have an executive sponsor or someone influential within leadership who is in the innovators or followers camp, ask them to get involved. You just need to ignore the political games, be diligent, and stick to what you need to do.

One of the things on you need to do list is keep your eyes peeled and your ear to the ground so you will be able to tell when trouble is brewing. I would recommend that when this happens, you divert some effort to nip it in the bud and stop it becoming a major issue. The nip-it-in-the-bud part can be in the form of a simple, non-confrontational face-to-face discussion with the potential troublemaker over a coffee—that way, the *dissenter* feels that they are being listened to and you get an understanding of what the noise is all about. As a last resort, a face-to-face discussion with their boss might do the trick. Don't resort to email tennis, as this does not work!

All in all, you should try wherever possible to deal with dissenters as you would the naughty child in the classroom; don't let them spoil things for everyone, don't give them all of the attention, and use a calm, measured approach. After a while, people will stop listening to them or get bored with what they are saying anyway (especially if it's not very constructive).

No news is no news

Something that may increase the risk of *dissenters* spoiling the party is a lack of visible or demonstrable progress in terms of the CD and DevOps adoption, or, to be more concise, the perceived lack of visible or demonstrable progress. It may be that you're busy with some complex process change or implementing tooling or focusing on virtualizing the legacy solution, and, as such, there is a perceived lull in visible activity.

If you have individuals within your organization who are very driven and delivery-focused, they may take this lull as a sign of the adoption faltering or they may even think that you're finished. As we covered previously, being highly visible, even if there's not a vast amount going on, is very important. If people can see progress being made, they will continue to follow. If there is a period of perceived inaction, then the followers may not know what way you are heading and may start taking notice of the *dissenting* voices.

Any form of communication and/or progress update can help stop this from happening—even if there's not a vast amount to report, the act of communication indicates that you are still there and still progressing toward the goal. The no news is good news analogy is wrong; no news is no news.

Let's see what our personas can do to help:

Good approach	Not-so-good approach
Victoria (the Veep) should publicly be seen and heard as a innovator (or follower) and should openly encourage her department to decide where they stand without fear of retribution	Victoria (the Veep) opening accepts without question the voices of the laggards and / or announces she is one of them
Stan (the manager) should back up Victoria's message and ensure he understands who the laggards are within his peer group and team(s) and ensure their voices don't become too loud	Stan (the manager) ignores the noise generated by the laggards and the impact that has on the innovators and followers
Devina (the developer) and Oscar (the Ops guy) should also understand where they sit and be mindful of noise from laggards that could easily sway the innovators and followers in their peer group	Devina (the developer) and Oscar (the Ops guy) simply sit in their bubble of blissful ignorance and leave it to the leadership to sort out

We briefly covered the fact that some people will be uncomfortable with change and they may react in unexpected ways. We'll now look into how change can impact individuals in different ways and what you need to be aware of.

The change curve

Let's get one thing out in the open, and this is important: you need to recognize and accept that the identification of a problem and subsequent removal of it can be quite a big change. You have been working with the business to identify a problem and you are now working to remove it. This is change, pure and simple.

Earlier in the book, we stated that the brave men and women of ACME systems who helped the business adopt DevOps and CD ways of working were a catalyst for change. This wording was intentional, as change did come about for the ACME systems team—a very big change as it turned out. The adoption of CD and DevOps should not be taken lightly, and the impact on individuals should not be taken lightly; even if they originally thought it was the best thing since sliced bread.

Those of you who have been in, or are currently in, management or leadership roles may well understand that change can be seen as both a positive and negative thing, and sometimes it can be taken very personally, especially where a change directly impacts individuals and their current roles. How individuals perceive change is normally at an emotional level rather than a logical, rational level.

Let's look at some fundamentals in relation to how humans deal with change.

Any change, large or small, work-related or not, can impact individuals in many different ways and, as mentioned, at many different levels. Some people welcome and embrace change, some are not fazed by it and accept it as something that happens, some are concerned and worried by it but also open to see what happens, and some are downright hostile and see change as something personal. More importantly, some people are all of these—not necessarily all at the same time, of course. If one is mindful of these facts before one implements change, there's a good chance that one will have a clearer idea of what challenges to overcome during the implementation to ensure it is successful.

There has been much research into the subject of how people respond to change, and many papers have been published by learned men and women over the years. I don't suggest for one minute that I know all there is to know on this subject, but there is some degree of common sense required when it comes to change, or transition as it is sometimes called, and there are some very obvious and understandable traits to take into account.

One of my preferred ways to visualize and understand the impact of change is something called the change or transition curve. This depicts the stages an individual will go through as a change/transition is being implemented.

The following diagram is a very good example of a change/transition curve:

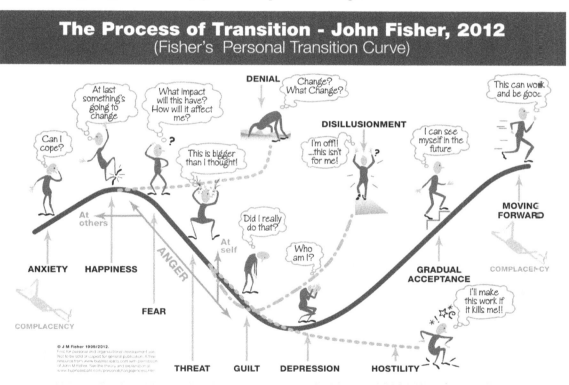

John Fisher's personal transition curve diagram courtesy of John Fisher

You can clearly see that as change is being planned, discussed, or implemented, people will go through several stages. We will not go through each stage in detail (you can read through this at your leisure at `https://www.c2d.co.uk/techniques/process-of-transition/`); however, there are a few nuggets of information that are very pertinent when looking at the adoption of CD and DevOps:

- An individual may go through this curve many times, even at the very early stages of change
- Everyone is different and the speed at which they go through the curve is unique
- You and those enlightened few around you will also go through this curve
- Those that do not/cannot come out of the dip may need more help, guidance, and leadership
- Even if someone is quiet and doesn't seem fazed, they will inevitably be at some stage in the curve, so they shouldn't be ignored—it's not just the vocal ones to look out for

The long and short of it is that individuals are just that, they will be laggards or followers or innovators, and they will also be somewhere along the change curve. The leaders and managers within your organization need to be very mindful of this and ensure that people are being looked after. You also need to be mindful of this, not least because this will also apply to you.

You should also consider that individuals who started the project as followers or even innovators may go through the change curve more than once as the initial euphoria gives way to the realization that things are actually changing. This will explain why some individuals act in one way at the beginning, yet they change their approach and outlook as you go through the execution of the plan and vision.

At a personal and emotional level, change is both good and bad, exciting and scary, challenging and daunting, welcomed and avoided. It all depends how an individual feels at any given point in time. CD and DevOps is potentially a very big change; therefore, emotions will play a large part. If you are aware of this and ensure you look for the signs and react accordingly, you will have a much better time of it. Ignore this and you will have one hell of a battle on your hands.

Let's see what our personas can do to help:

Good approach	Not-so-good approach
Victoria (the Veep) should be very aware of the impact of change upon her organization and ensure she publicly acknowledges this. She should also consider engaging with her HR team to assist where needed	Victoria (the Veep) simply sees CD and DevOps adoption as another project that doesn't warrant any special attention
Stan (the manager) should back up Victoria's message and ensure he carves out time to help, support and assist his team(s) throughout	Stan (the manager) mirrors Victoria's view and ignores the impact the adoption of CD and DevOps has on his team(s)
Devina (the developer) and Oscar (the Ops guy) should accept that things will be changing and that their peers may struggle with this and may well need support	Devina (the developer) and Oscar (the Ops guy) simply sit in their bubble of blissful ignorance and leave it to the leadership to sort out

On that light note, we'll move onto the subject of what to do about those people within your organization who are not involved in your journey or may not even be aware that it is ongoing. We'll call them the outsiders.

The outsiders

The percentage of those involved with the adoption of CD and DevOps will largely depend on the overall size of your organization. If you are a start-up, the chances are that pretty much everyone within the organization will be involved. If you are an SME (small-to-medium enterprise), there is a good chance that not everyone within your organization will be involved. If you are working within a corporate business, the percentage of those actively involved will be vastly smaller than those not.

The following diagram illustrates how distance from the core team working on the CD and DevOps adoption correlates directly to the knowledge of what's actually going on:

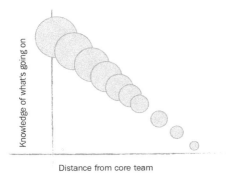

Individuals closer to the core team will have a greater knowledge of what is going on

Those whose involvement is further out from the day-to-day will have little or no idea of what is going on. This may (and will) lead to people on the outskirts, through this lack of knowledge, inadvertently putting hurdles in the way of progress. It should be pointed out that this is nothing new and does not specifically apply to the adoption of CD and DevOps; this is a reality for any far-reaching business change project. If individuals, especially those in decision-making roles, don't know what is going on, then CD and DevOps will not be one of the first things they consider.

To give you an example, let's take a look at ACME systems and see how this situation impacted their implementation.

During phase 2.0 of their evolution, ACME systems became part of a large corporate. They ended up as a satellite office, the corporate HQ being overseas and, on the whole, were left to their own devices. They beavered away for a while and started to examine and implement CD and DevOps. They were doing so, when viewed at a global corporate level, in isolation. Yes, they were making far-reaching and dramatic changes to the ACME systems organization, but they were a small cog in a very big wheel. No one outside of the ACME systems offices had much visibility or in-depth knowledge of what was going on. Consequently, when a new, far-reaching, corporate strategic plan related to the global downsizing of the operations organization was announced, little or no consideration was given to what ACME systems were up to, as, in all honesty, no one making the decisions really knew. As a result, the progress of the CD and DevOps implementation very quickly ground to a halt. As luck would have it, once the dust had settled, the need for DevOps became even greater than it was originally, which lead to a greater focus and acceleration in adoption.

In the case of ACME systems, the impact turned out to be positive with respect to the CD and DevOps adoption and actually provided an additional boost. If you experience wide-reaching changes during your journey, and people are ignorant of what you're doing, your story may not end so well. Bear that in mind.

The moral of the story is this: not only should you keep an eye on what is happening close to home, but you should also keep an eye on what is happening in the wider organization. We've already looked at how important it is to communicate what you are doing and to be highly visible. This communication and visibility should not be restricted to those immediately involved in the CD and DevOps adoption; you should try to make as many people aware as possible. If you are working within a corporate environment, you will no doubt have some sort of internal communications team who publish regular news articles to your corporate intranet or newsletter. Get in touch with these people and get them to run a story on what you are doing. A good bit of public relations will help your cause and widen the circle of knowledge.

This may seem like quite a lot of work for little gain, but you may be surprised how much benefit it can bring. Say, for example, you get the article written and published and it is read by the CEO or an SVP who then decides to visit and see what all the fuss is about. That is a major moral boost and good PR. Not only that, but it may help with your management dissenters—if they see the high-ups recognizing what you are doing as a positive thing, they may reconsider their position.

We're primarily considering outsiders as individuals outside of your immediate sphere of influence who are ignorant of what you are doing and where you're heading. You may have others who are well aware, but are either restricted by or hiding behind corporate red tape and/or bureaucracy. Let's spend some time looking into this potential hurdle and what can be done to overcome it.

Corporate guidelines, red tape, and standards

The size and scale of this potential hurdle is dependent on the size and scale of your organization and the market in which you operate. If you work within the service sector and have commercial obligations to meet certain SLAs, or you work within a financial institution and have regulatory guidelines to adhere to, you will be in some ways hampered in how you implement and adopt CD and DevOps. This, as they say, comes with the territory.

What you need to do is work with those setting and/or policing the rules to see what wiggle room you have. You may find that some of the rules and guidelines set in place for the business are actually overkill and have only been implemented because it was easier to stick to what it said in the book than it was to refine it to fit the business needs.

The need for such rules, guidelines, and policies mainly revolves around change-management and auditability. In simple terms, they offer a safety gate and a way to ascertain what has recently changed should problems occur. You may find that those managing or policing these rules, guidelines, and policies will consider CD and DevOps to be incompatible with their ways of working. This may be true, but that doesn't mean it's correct.

During the investigation stage, their organization/department may have been highlighted as an area of waste within the product-delivery process (I would put money on it), so they may be defensive about change. It may even be the case that they simply don't know what they can change without breaking a rule or corporate policy. Work with these people and help them understand what CD and DevOps is about, and help them research what parts of their process they can change to accommodate it. Do not simply ignore them and break the rules, as this will catch up with you down the road and could completely derail the process. Open, honest, and courageous dialogue is the key.

That said, open and honest dialogue may be hindered by geography, so let's look at how we can address that.

Geographically diverse teams

We previously touched on the subject of setting up an open and honest physical environment to help reinforce open, honest, and collaborative ways of work. This is all well and good if the teams are collocated, however trying to recreate this with geographically diverse teams can be a tricky problem to solve. It all depends on the time zone differences and, to some extent, the differences in culture.

I use the word culture again here on purpose. As previously stated, culture is very important to the success of CD an DevOps adoption, and we focused on corporate and organizational culture. When it comes to things that can and will trip you up, geographical, geo-political, or social-group culture differences can be high on the list. When you have teams or team members involved that don't necessarily share the same outlook or values as you (or the majority of the organization) do, there is a risk that they could easily become dissenters, or at the very least innovators or followers who truly believe they are contributing but may have interpreted your intentions in their own way and may actually end up hindering. You therefore need to pay attention and ensure they feel as if they are treated the same as physically-present team members.

That segues quite nicely to physical presence. Not having a physical presence is always a barrier. There have been many studies, and no doubt will be more, on the subject of remote versus collocated teams, and none seem to point to which method produces the best results. What these studies do sometimes omit is how some external factors also help (or hinder) remote versus collated teams: organizational maturity, cultural synergies, shared experience and knowledge, and common language. If some of these factors have a negative impact on how collocated teams work together, there's a strong chance that these negatives will be magnified when you add remote teams into the mix.

It should be noted that most research has focused on the Dev side of the DevOps partnership. There is sometimes an acceptance that having Dev and Ops teams separated is the norm, however if you consider that DevOps is most effective when both are working closely together, then you should be applying the whole geographically-diverse teams thing to both.

From experience, the most effective and efficient teams are collocated simply due to the fact that humans are social creatures and therefore tend to prefer having other humans nearby to work with, talk to, argue with, or simply share a joke with. Unless you have a budget that allows for everyone to work in the same physical location, you need to look at ways to replicate this for teams and team members who are not physically in the same location. Here are a few things that you should consider to help remove the barrier:

- Try to think of all team members as simply that—members of the same team who should be treated equally.
- Ensure both local and remote teams have regular (ideally daily) teleconference (ideally video-conference) calls.
- If you're using scrum (or a similar methodology) and decide to have a daily scrum of scrums, get the remote teams(s) to join as well—even if you call them on your cellphone and have them on speakerphone.

- Set up a Skype (or equivalent software) PC within both office spaces and use them as a virtual wall/window between the offices. These should be left on during norm office hours so team members on each side of the virtual wall/window can simply walk up and have a face-to-face conversation as if they were in the same room.
- If budget allows, try to get people swapped across the offices via secondments, placements, and so on for short periods of time.
- Do not rely on email as a form of collaboration/communication, instead invest in collaboration tools (we covered that previously).

Another potential barrier to be mindful of is time zones. This can (will) wreak havoc on things such as team meetings and daily stand-ups (from experience, these normally happen first thing in the morning, which may be problematic if the teams are on different sides of the globe). With some creative thinking, you can overcome these small issues, for example pick "first thing in the morning" based upon a time zone midway between the teams.

Coming back to culture again, there is another thing to take into account. In some parts of the world, the culture may not be the fast and loose western culture where everyone has a voice and isn't afraid to use it. Instilling openness, honesty, and transparency may be more difficult for some and you should be mindful of this. I would suggest you work with the local HR or management team, explain what you're trying to do, and see how they can with this.

We'll now look at what you should do if you encounter failure during the execution of your goal and vision.

Failure during the evolution

As you go along your journey, things will occasionally go wrong, this is inevitable and is nothing to be afraid or ashamed of. There may be situations that you didn't foresee, or steps in the existing process that were not picked up during the elephant exposure. It might be as simple as a problem within the chosen toolset, which isn't doing what you had hoped it would or is simply buggy.

Your natural reaction may be to hide such failures or at least not broadcast the fact that a failure has occurred. This is not a wise thing to do. You and your team are working hard to instill a sense of openness and honesty, so the worst thing you can do is the exact opposite. Think back to what we covered previously in relation to failing fast in terms of finding defects; the same approach works here as well.

Admitting defeat, curling up in a fetal position, and lying in the corner whimpering is also not an option. As with any change, things go wrong, so review the situation, review your options, and move forward. Once you have a way to move around or through the problem, communicate this. Ensure you're candid about what the problem is and what is being done to overcome it. This will show others how to react and deal with change—a sort of lead-by-example.

You might be concerned that admitting failures might give the laggards more ammunition to derail the adoption; however, their win will be short-lived once the innovators and followers have found a solution. Hold fast, stand your ground, and have faith.

If you're using agile techniques such as scrum or Kanban to drive the CD and DevOps adoption, you should be able to change direction relatively quickly without impeding progress.

Okay so this is all a very **positive mental attitude** (PMA) and may be seen by some of you who are more cynical than the rest as management hot air and platitudes, so let's look at another example.

ACME systems implemented a deployment transaction model (covered in a previous chapter) to manage dependencies and ensure only one change went through to the production system at any one point in time. This worked well for a while, but things started to slow down. Automated integration tests that were previously working started to fail intermittently, defects were being raised in areas of functionality that were previously seen as bulletproof. This slowdown started to impact the wider R&D team's ability to deliver and the noise level started to rise, especially from the vocal laggards. Open and honest discussions between all concerned ensued and, after much debate, it transpired that the main source of the problem was a very simple dependency, and change management was not keeping up with the speed of delivery. In essence, there was no sure way of determining which software asset change would be completed before another software asset change and there was no simple way to try out different scenarios in terms of integration. What it boiled down to was this: if changes within asset A had a dependency on changes within asset B, then asset B needed to go live first to allow for full integration testing. However, if asset A was ready first, it would have to sit and wait—sometimes for days or weeks. The deployment transaction was starting to hinder CD.

Here's a reminder of the simple process that ACME systems called the deployment transaction:

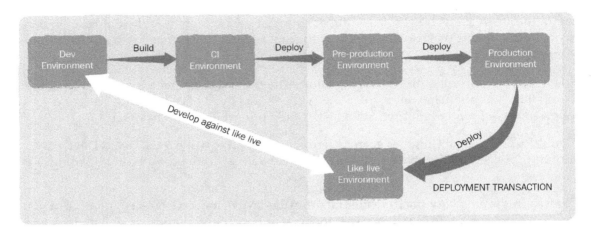

You'll recall that everyone had agreed that the deployment transaction worked well and provided a working alternative to dependency hell. When used in anger, however, it exposed a flaw that started to cause real and painful problems. Even if features could be switched off through feature flags, there was no way to fully test integration without having everything deployed to production and the like live environment. This had not been a problem previously, as the speed of releases had been very slow and assets had been clumped together. ACME systems now had the ability to deploy to production very quickly and now had a new problem: which order to deploy? Many discussions took place and complicated options were looked at, but in the end the solution was quite simple: move the boundary of the deployment transaction and allow for full integration testing before assets went to production. It was then down to the various R&D teams to manually work out in which order things should be deployed.

The following diagram depicts the revised deployment transaction boundary:

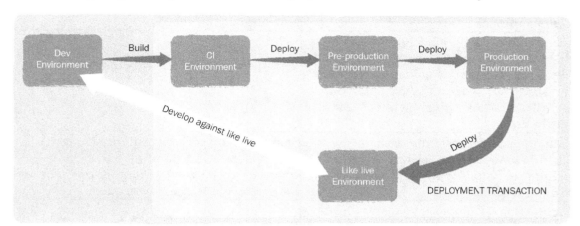

So ACME had a potential showstopper, which could have completely derailed their CD and DevOps adoption. The problem became very visible and many questions were asked. The followers started to doubt the innovators, and the laggards became vocal. With some good, old-fashioned collaboration, and open and honest discussions, the issue was quickly and relatively easily overcome.

Again, open and honest communication and courageous dialogue is key. If you keep reviewing and listening to what people are saying, you have a much better opportunity to see potential hurdles before they completely block your progress.

Let's see what our personas can do to help:

Good approach	Not-so-good approach
Victoria (the Veep) publicly acknowledges that things can and will go wrong at points in the adoption and should encourage her department to work together to iron out any issues collaboratively without fear of retribution	Victoria (the Veep) does not tolerate any form of failure and is openly critical of problems that occur
Stan (the manager) should back up Victoria's message and ensure he carves out time to help, support and assist his team(s) when needs be	Stan (the manager) sees failure as a sign of incompetence and stamps it out at every opportunity. Anyone who raises problems or issues are told to keep them quiet
Devina (the developer) and Oscar (the Ops guy) should not be afraid of failure when trying something new or risky. When problems surface they should work together to solve them and ensure their leadership are fully aware	Devina (the developer) and Oscar (the Ops guy) simply sit in their bubble of blissful ignorance and leave it to the leadership to sort out

Another thing that may scupper your implementation and erode trust is inconsistent results.

Processes that are not repeatable

There is a tendency for those of a technical nature to automate everything they touch, such as the automated building of an engineer's workstation, automated building of software, and automated switching on of the coffee machine when the office lights come on. This is nothing new and there is nothing wrong with this approach as long as the process is repeatable and provides consistent results. If the results are not consistent, others will be reluctant to use the automation you spent many hours, days, or weeks pulling together.

When it comes to CD and DevOps, the same approach should apply, especially when you're looking at tooling. You need to trust the results that you are getting time and time again.

Some believe that internal tooling and labor-saving solutions or processes that aren't out in the hostile customer world don't have to be of production quality as they're only going to be used by people within the business mostly by techies. This is 100 percent wrong.

Let's look at a very simple example: if you're a software engineer, you will use an IDE to write code and you will use a compiler to generate the binary to deploy, and if you're a **database administrator** (**DBA**), you'll use a SQL admin program to manage your databases and write SQL. You will expect these tools to work 100 percent of the time and produce consistent and repeatable results; you open a source file and the IDE opens it for editing, and you execute some SQL and the SQL admin tool runs it on the server. If your tools keep crashing or produce unexpected results, you will be a bit upset (putting it politely) and will no doubt refrain from using said tools again. It may drive you insane.

Insanity: doing the same thing over and over again and expecting different results.

Albert Einstein

The same goes for the tools (technical and non-technical) you build and/or implement for your CD and DevOps adoption. These tools have to be as good as (if not better) the software your teams are creating. The users of the tool/processes implemented need to be confident that when they do the same actions over and over again, they get the same results. As that confidence grows, so does the trust in the tool/process. Ultimately, the tool/process will start to be taken for granted and people will use it without a second thought.

Consequently, people will also trust the fact that if the results differ from the last run, something bad has been introduced (for example, a software bug has been created) that needs immediate attention.

Consider how much confidence and trust will be eroded if the tool/process continually fails or provides different and/or unexpected results. You therefore need to be very confident that the tooling/processes are fit for purpose.

We have already covered the potential hurdles you'll encounter in terms of corporate guidelines, red tape, and standards. Just think what fun you will have convincing the gatekeepers that CD and DevOps is not risky when you can't provide consistent results for repeatable tasks. Okay, maybe fun is not the correct word; maybe pain is a better one.

Another advantage of consistent, repeatable results comes into play when looking at metrics. If you can trust the fact that to deploy the same asset to the same server takes the same amount of time each time you deploy it, you can start to spot problems (for example, if it starts taking longer to deploy, there may be an infrastructure issue or something fundamental has changed in the configuration).

All in all, it may sound boring and not very innovative, but with consistent and repeatable results, you can stop worrying about the mundane and move your attention to the problems that need solving, such as the very real requirement to recruit new people into a transforming or transformed business.

Bridging the skills gap

This might not seem like a big problem, but as the organization's output increases, the efficiency grows, and the organization starts to be recognized as one that can deliver quality products quickly (and it will), then growth and expansion may well become a high priority—this, I think you'll agree, is a good problem to have. You now need to find individuals who will work in the new way and exhibit the behaviors that everyone has worked so hard to instill and embed throughout the organization. This is not as easy as you might think and it will take some time to find the people that not only have the skills, experience, and potential but also the mindset you're looking for. Simply adding *experience in CD and DevOps* to a job spec will not produce the results you want; even though CD and DevOps have been a thing for some time, there aren't that many people out there with the sort of experience you'll be looking for.

The other big problem you'll have is the level of knowledge throughout the recruitment and talent-acquisition world in terms what CD and DevOps actually is. They may have a rough idea based upon tech press and some conferences, but they won't know exactly what you are looking for. It's therefore very important to embark on more knowledge-sharing with those involved in your recruitment process to ensure that they understand what you're looking for (or at least have a grasp of what you're not looking for). You may need to do this number of times until it sinks in.

In terms of candidate-vetting, there are few things you can do to filter out those who get CD and DevOps and those who don't. For example, if you have a candidate whose main experience is in the Ops field, throw in some traditional development-focused questions, or for a developer ask them some questions traditionally targeted at Ops candidates. Mixing things up will give you a more rounded view of their grasp. One of my favorite interview questions is very simple:

As a software engineer, how would you feel if your code were running in the production environment being used by millions of customers 10 minutes after you commit it to source control?

The question is worded specifically to get an honest emotional response; the key word here being feel. You will be surprised by the responses to this; for some, it simply stops them in their tracks, some will be shocked at such a thing and think you're crazy to suggest it, and some will think it through and realize that although they have never considered it, they quite like the idea. If, however, the response is 10 minutes? That's far too slow, you may be onto a winner.

 Take your time and ensure you pick the right people. You need innovators and followers more than you need laggards.

We'll end this section with something that most wouldn't see as a problem, but can stop CD and DevOps adoption in its tracks, which is changes in leadership.

Changes in leadership

Each of us has, at some point in time, worked somewhere that has gone through a change of leadership. Normally, the higher up the food chain the change is, the more potentially disruptive that change will be. For example, a new CEO will, over a period of a few months, change the leadership reporting to them via hiring and firing or via organizational realignment (firing by moving chairs around). They will also have some new vision and business drivers to increase some business metric, which is why they got the job.

Most of the time, those lower down the food chain don't see an impact, at least not for a while, however, impact will come. You can guarantee it.

When you're looking at something that can be quite radical, such as the adoption of CD and DevOps, there is a massive risk that a decision in a board room could completely ruin things, especially in the early stages of adoption. As stated previously, CD and DevOps are more about ways of working, behaviors, and culture than box-ticking and business metrics. That said, there is a reason for the decision to adopt CD and DevOps—to improve the ability to deliver quality software solution quickly and repeatedly. This will not go away simply because an org chart has been updated.

Your best approach is to keep doing what you're doing and keep being open, honest, and transparent. If you have an executive sponsor who is still in situ, encourage them to go back on the charm offensive. Don't be afraid to cover old ground and reiterate the reasoning and history behind the decision. In addition, make sure you share good news stories and ensure that the new leaders are included in your regular communications. In essence, do whatever is needed to keep things rolling and ensure progress continues.

Summary

What new things have we learned throughout this chapter? The main message is that change is not something to be afraid of, is something that does and will happen and that there will be hurdles that you will experience along the way. As long as you plan for and are aware of this fact and you're able help and guide those involved and impacted by change get through it you should be in a relatively good place. When hidden boulders become apparent, be that in terms of communications, red tape, bureaucracy, hiring or geography, you will have some ideas how to overcome them. Another thing you have learned is that people, be they within the inner circle or far removed, are key to your success.

There will no doubt be other hurdles, hazards, and potential blockers along the way that have not been included within these pages but as long as you're prepared you will be successful. Talking of success, we'll now move onto the measurement of success and why it is so important—something we'll cover within the next chapter.

Vital Measurements

7

Over the previous chapters, we have looked at what tools and techniques you should be considering, the need to acknowledge how change will impact people in different ways, why culture, behaviors, and environment are important, what potential hurdles you'll need to overcome, and how all of this is needed to successfully adopt CD and DevOps. If you are taking this into account, creating plans to cater for and/or address this, you should be in a good shape to make wide strides forward.

We will now look at the important but sometimes overlooked—or simply dismissed—area of monitoring and measuring progress. We did touch on this subject previously, but what we considered was a small slice of the pie, figuratively speaking. What we're looking at now is the capturing, compiling, and sharing of metrics related to the impact that CD and DevOps has on the day-to-day ways of working and the business as a whole.

This, on the face of it, might be seen as something that is only useful to the management types and won't add value to those who will be dealing with the CD and DevOps adoption on a day-to-day basis. In some regards, that is true, but being able to analyze, understand, and share demonstrable progress will definitely add value to you and everyone else who is on the CD and DevOps journey. We're not just talking about simple project management charts, graphs, and PowerPoint fodder here; what we are looking at is measuring as many aspects of the overall process as possible. That way, anyone and everyone can plainly see and understand how far you have collectively come and how far from the ultimate goal you are.

To do this effectively, you'll need to ensure that you start this data capture very early into the CD and DevOps adoption, as it will be very difficult to see a comparison between then and now if you don't have data representing *then*. You will need to be vigilant and consistent in ensuring that you are continuously capturing these measurements so that you can compare the state of progress at different points in time. Some would consider this anal, but this whole CD and DevOps journey started because the data captured in the elephant exposure pointed to areas of waste—or, at the very least, ineffective processes.

In this chapter, you will learn the following topics:

- How to measure the effectiveness of your engineering process(es)
- How to measure the stability of the various environments you use and rely on
- How to measure the impact your adoption of CD and DevOps is having

We'll start, as they say, at the beginning and focus initially on engineering metrics.

Measuring effective engineering best practices

This is quite a weird concept to get your head around: How can you measure effective engineering, and more than that, how can you measure best practices? There's another often-asked question: what has this got to do with DevOps or CD? We'll look at the former in a moment, but now let's focus on the latter.

Let's take two scenarios:

- Your current software-engineering process is very waterfall and you have a vast amount of manual testing to validate your code just before it gets shipped—which happens every 3-6 months—and build in a buffer for bug fixing
- Your current software-engineering process is pretty agile and follows (mostly) industry best practices, however as there is plenty of time between releases you can sometimes let technical debt slip (including test automation) as there will be time to go back and mop up just before the next release—which happens every 3-6 months

OK, so this is pretty simplistic, but bear with me. As the CD and DevOps adoption starts to gather momentum, the time between releases will decrease. Therefore, the we can do that later window gets smaller and smaller. This can lead to engineers having to start cutting corners simply because they have run out of time to mop up the pre-release tech-debt tasks. The adoption of CD and DevOps ultimately allows you to deliver solutions quickly—there's nothing that categorically states that engineers will be given more time to write and test said solutions.

Let's consider what a large quarterly release looks like in terms of timeline and effort, as shown:

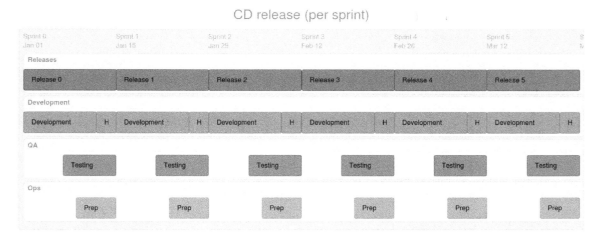

Now let's compare that to a CD-type release, as follows:

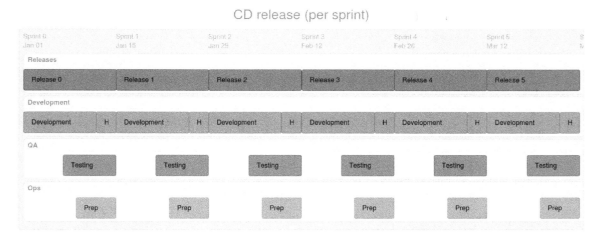

These are both very simplistic examples, but they highlight the impact that reducing the time between releases will have on the key players. The we can do that later window goes from days/weeks to hours.

In Chapter 5, *Approaches, Tools, and Techniques*, we looked at how the wider business perceives the relationship between features and releases. As your CD and DevOps adoption matures, the time between releases will decrease, which means that engineers will have less time to complete features. If the wider business has become accustomed to having features delivered within a given release, they will continue to expect this until things bed in.

Let's go back to the corners. These will normally be related to the non-cutting code, yet still time-consuming activities—skipping the odd unit test here, leaving the odd gap in integration tests there, forgoing documentation, reducing the tendency to refactor old code, and so on. In simple terms, the engineers will be under pressure to deliver and they will no longer have the time to address everything they did previously. This therefore becomes technical debt—which is something every software-engineering team tries to avoid at all costs, as it will come back to bite them later.

Going back to the main subject of measuring effective engineering best practices, it's not as strange or uncommon as you might think. There are a great number of software-based businesses around the globe regularly using tools to capture data and measurements for things such as:

- Overall code quality
- Adherence to coding rules and standards
- Code documentation
- Code complexity
- Code duplication
- Redundant code
- Unit-test coverage
- Technical debt
- Mean time between failures
- Mean time to resolution
- Bug-escape distance
- Fix-bounce rate

Measuring each of these in isolation might not bring a vast amount of value; however, when pooled together, you can get a very detailed picture of how things stand. In addition, if you can continuously capture this level of detail over a period of time, you can then start to measure and report on progress. Why this is important to the adoption of CD and DevOps is quite simple: if the quality of your software decreases due to the fact that things are being shipped faster, the laggards will have a field day. If those laggards are in influential and/or decision-making positions, the whole adoption could be derailed.

As stated previously, if you can spot this as it starts to happen, you have a fighting chance of stopping it. There is also another side to this; if your quality currently sucks and you can prove that CD and DevOps adoption helps to increase quality, then that's a massive good news story—we can ship quicker and the quality is vastly better. Take that, laggards!

It all sounds very simple, and to be honest, it can be, but you need to be mindful of the fact that you will need to apply some time, effort, and rigor to ensure that you gain the most value. There will also be a degree of trial and error and tweaking as you go, to ensure you can capture the data in a reliable and repeatable way—more inspecting and adapting—so you need to ensure that you factor this in. Not only will these sorts of measurements help your engineering team(s), they will also help with building trust across the wider business. For example, you'll be able to provide open, honest, and truthful metrics in relation to the quality of your software, which, in turn, will reinforce the trust they have in the team(s) building and looking after the platform.

One thing to seriously consider before you look at measuring things such as software code metrics is how the engineers themselves will feel about this. What Devina is thinking might be a typical reaction:

A typical reaction to this approach

Some engineers will become guarded or defensive, and may see it as questioning their skills and craftsmanship in relation to creating quality code. You need to be careful that you don't get barriers put up between you and the engineering teams or let them slip back into the *laggards* camp. You should *sell* these tools as a positive benefit for the engineers. For example, they have a way to definitively prove how good their code actually is; they can use the tools to inspect areas of over-complexity or areas of code that are more at risk of containing bugs; they can highlight redundant code and remove it from the codebase; and they can visually see hard dependencies, which can help when looking at componentization.

If you have vocal laggards, get them actively involved in the setup and configuration of the tools (for example, they could take ownership of defining the threshold of acceptable code coverage or choose the tools to be implemented)

If nothing else, you need to ensure that you have the innovators and followers from the engineering community brought in. To add some clarity, let's look at a few items from the preceding list—which, by the way, is not exhaustive—in a little more detail, and examine why they are potentially important to your CD and DevOps adoption. Let's start with code complexity.

Code complexity

Having complex code is sometimes necessary, especially when you're looking at extremely optimized code where in resources are limited and/or there is a real-time UI—basically, where every millisecond counts. When you have something such as an online store, login page, or a finance module, having overly complex code can do more harm than good. Some engineers believe they are special because they can write complex code; however, complexity for complexity's sake is really just showing off.

Overly complex code can cause lots of general problems—especially when trying to debug or when you're trying to extend it to cater for additional use cases—which can directly impact the speed at which you can implement even the smallest change. The premise of CD is to deliver small, incremental, quality changes. If your code is too complex to allow for this, you are going to have issues down the line—normally referred to the maintainability, testability, and readability of the code base.

I would recommend that you put some time aside to look into this complex (pun intended) subject in more detail before you dive into implementing any process or tooling. You really need to understand what the underlying principles are and the science behind them; otherwise, this will become messy and confused. Some of the science is explained in the `Appendix A`, *Some Useful Information*.

One suggestion would be to take one of the various code-analysis tools available and run a trial to profile your code base, which will help highlight some existing pain points. From this, you can start to formulate a plan.

The next thing you could consider is code coverage.

Unit-test coverage

Incorporating unit tests within the software-development process is uniformly recognized as best practice—Chapter 6, *Avoiding Hurdles*. There is a vast amount of information available on this subject, so I won't spend too much time focusing on this here, but I would recommend that you apply some time and effort into investigating this subject and how you can adopt this approach within your SDLC.

So as not to short-change you, I will provide some insight and background into this subject in relation to CD and DevOps.

At a simplistic level, unit tests allow software-engineering teams to exercise and validate code paths and logic at a granular level during the development process; this, in turn, can help spot and eradicate software defects very early on. Incorporating these tests within CI (see the Chapter 6, *Avoiding Hurdles*, for information on CI) and having them stop the build can help stop defects escaping into downstream phases of the CD pipeline. This can also be used as an early warning for regression; for example, if the unit test that was previously working starts to fail, there is a high probability that regression has been introduced.

The premise of CD is to be able to ship changes frequently. If you have good unit test coverage across the codebase, you will have a greater level of confidence that you can ship that code frequently with reduced risk.

Analyzing the coverage is a good indication as to how much you can rely upon unit tests to spot problems. You can also use this data to map out the areas of risk when it comes to shipping code quickly (for example, if your login page is frequently changed and has a high level of coverage, the risk of shipping this frequently becomes lower).

There is one thing you do need to take into account regarding coverage measurements—that being the mix of legacy versus new code. What you'll usually find is that legacy code—especially that based on older technologies—may have little-to-no unit-test coverage. If this type of code makes up the majority of your code base, the coverage measure will be pretty low. If the wider business gets too hung up on this measure, they may perceive a low score as a major risk. Although this is technically true, you can't really expect to have older code fully covered from day one. You therefore need to ensure you set the context of the data and have a plan for increasing the coverage over time. One approach would be to set a rule that all new code or refactored code should have a high degree of coverage (ideally 100% as long as this is attainable without slipping into the realm of. diminishing returns), and that the overall coverage figure must grow as refactoring of legacy code increases.

Let's now look at the effectiveness of measuring the frequency of commits.

Commit and merge rates

Regular commits to source control is something that should be widely encouraged and deeply embedded within your ways of working. Having source code sitting on people's workstations or laptops for prolonged periods of time is very risky and can sometimes lead to duplication of effort or, worse still, might block the progress of other engineers.

There might be a fear that if engineers commit too frequently, the chance of defects being created increases, especially when you think there's an outside risk that unfinished code could be incorporated into the main code branch. This fear is a fallacy. No engineer worth their salt would seriously consider doing such a thing—why would they? If you have checks and balances in place, such as regular code reviews or a pull-request approval process, the risk of buggy code being merged will be vastly reduced. Add in unit tests and code analysis and you're looking at next-to-no risk.

Opposite to this is the very real risk of delays between commits and code merges. The more code there is to be merged, the greater the risk and the higher the potential for code conflicts, defects, and incomplete functionality to be introduced. The CD approach is based on delivering working software often. This should not be restricted to software binaries; delivering small incremental chunks of source code little and often is also a good practice.

Most source control systems will have tools and or logs that can be analyzed by third-party tools. The sort of data you should be analyzing will include such things as number of commits and merges per engineer per day, time between merges, and which areas of the code base are changed most frequently.

From this data, you can start to see patterns, such as seeing who is playing ball and who isn't, and what areas of the code base carry the most risk. A word of warning: don't use this data to reward or punish engineers, as this can promote the wrong kinds of behaviors and can be as damaging as ignoring engineering best practices.

Next, we'll look at the thorny issue of code violations and adherence to rules.

Adherence to coding rules and standards

You may already have coding standards within your software-development teams and/or try to adhere to an externally-documented and recognized best practice. Being able to analyze your code base to see which parts do and don't adhere to the standards is extremely useful as it helps highlight areas of potential risk. If you continue to capture this data over time, you can start to spot trends—especially when these figures start to fall.

There are a number of tools available to help you do this, some of which are listed in `Appendix A`, Some *Useful Information*.

 This type of analysis will take some setting up, as it is normally based on a set of predefined rules and thresholds (for example, info, minor, major, critical, and blocker), and you'll need to work with the engineering teams to agree on and set these up within your tooling.

Measuring adherence to coding rules and standards goes some way to stopping defects in your code leaking, but software is software and defects will sneak through. What you therefore need to do is analyze what happens when they do.

Quality metrics

Quality is something that everyone involved in writing and delivering software should want to uphold and build into their solutions. The preceding sections included some elements of quality metrics, but you should also consider some specific measurements targeted on time.

The ones that are pertinent to CD and DevOps are **Mean time between failures (MTBF)**, **Mean time to resolution (MTTR)**, and defect-escape distance, which are explained as follows:

- **MTBF**: This will help you measure how often problems (or failures) are found by end users—the longer the time between failures, the greater the stability and quality of the overall platform
- **MTTR**: This will help you measure the time taken between an issue being found and being fixed
- **Defect escape distance**: This will help you measure when an issue is found and by whom—for example, defects found by the engineering team are close to the source of the defect (for example, one of the team), whereas UAT spotting a defect is farther out from the source

The first two give some good indication as to how CD and DevOps adoption is going as they relate to the speed of delivery. For example, one would expect MTBF to go up and MTTR to go down over time if CD and DevOps adoption is working well. If they don't, there's something wrong that needs looking into.

The third of the trio—defect-escape distance—is a good indication of engineering best practices and how well the CD pipeline is picking up issues early. If the engineering team is spotting defects early on in the process—for example, a CI step fails due to a failing unit test—then the distance and impact is small. If a defect escapes to a downstream process—for example, the UAT team—then the distance and impact is larger. If a defect gets all the way to the production environment then ... well, I think you get the gist.

One way to represent this is to add a $ value to a defect based upon the environment it is found in and the time it took to find it. For example, let's assume we have four environments used as part of the CD pipeline: Dev, QA, UAT, and Prod. We then apply a sliding scale of cost for each environment based upon the distance from the source:

Env	Cost
Dev	1
QA	2
UAT	8
Prod	16

Let's now consider the cost of each defect using a multiplier based upon the lead time between the defect being created and it being spotted. You'll end up with something such as this:

Defect#	Env	Env cost	Lead time (days)	Defect cost
DE1	Dev	1	2	2
DE2	Dev	1	5	5
DE3	QA	2	10	20
DE4	Dev	1	0.5	0.5
DE5	Prod	16	20	320
DE6	Prod	16	50	800
DE7	UAT	8	5	40
DE8	QA	2	7	14
DE9	Dev	1	15	15
DE10	UAT	8	12	96

This is a snapshot in time that gives you an indication of the cost of defects. This doesn't mean you should totally eradicate defects—the only way to do that is to stop writing software—but you should focus on eradicating the high-cost defects. After all, the cost of defects found by customers in real life is far greater than a defect found during the SDLC.

We'll now take a look at the meaning of lead (and cycle) times.

Cycle and lead times

These are more time-based metrics that are very useful to measure the progress and effectiveness of the changes you make during CD and DevOps adoption. These two metrics are pretty simple to understand:

- **Lead time**: The measurement of time between a requirement being identified and it being delivered to a customer
- **Cycle time**: The time between someone starting work on a given work item/story/defect and it being delivered to a customer

The following diagram should give you a better idea of what this means:

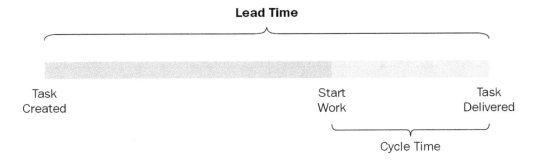

The observant among you may notice that for defects, the lead time is pretty much the same as for MTTR, which means that one simple data point can be used for two measurements. Two for the price of one is good value.

Regularly taking snapshots of lead and cycle time gives a very good indication of whether things are working well (or not, as the case may be). It should be noted that lead time can be dependent on changes in business priorities and time-based commitments—for example, a feature may be deprioritized when something more urgent comes into the backlog—so there may be some fluctuation in the value over time. What you should be striving toward is an overall reduction in lead time. Cycle time, on the other hand, is more within the control of the engineering team, and therefore reducing that is within their hands. As CD and DevOps adoption takes hold, the act of delivery should be much simpler, so the average cycle time should decrease. If it doesn't, you should be looking at what is causing the pain points. Some of that may be related to quality issues.

Quality gates

Not only does capturing data help build up a picture over time and spot trends, but you can also use the data to stop quality issues from leaking. What I mean by this is that once you have some data captured and analyzed regarding such things as code coverage, adherence to coding standards, code complexity, or code documentation levels, you could set some thresholds within the CD pipeline, which, if exceeded, will stop the pipeline in its tracks. You can also implement quality gates based upon the results of automated tests—again, if the tests fail, the CD pipeline stops.

For example, let's assume that you have decided that any new piece of software must have 100 percent unit-test code coverage and must not contain any documented security vulnerabilities; then you can implement a code analysis/linting tool within the CD pipeline to check each commit or merge. If the tools report that the code in question doesn't pass the checks, the CD pipeline will stop and let the team know.

 When referring to the CD pipeline, I would include the CI solution being part of the whole pipeline—just in case you were thinking they are separate things.

Implementation of such tools will not only ensure your code is up to scratch, it can also help reduce things such as escaping defects and ensuring code that flows through the CD pipeline with minimal interruption. Capturing this data will also give you some historical insight in relation to when quality gates pass/fail, which may correlate with another event—for example, failures may grow during the frantic period before a major release.

Some of you may be thinking that this all sounds like hard work—on top of all the other hard work—so is it actually worth it? Yes, it is!

Where to start and why bother?

As stated earlier, there are many things that you can and should be measuring, analyzing, and producing metrics for, and there are many tools that can help you do this. You just need to work out what is most important and start from there. The work and effort needed to set up the tools required should be seen as a great opportunity to bring into play some of the good behaviors you want to embed: collaboration, open and honest dialogue, and trust.

I would advise implementing these types of tools early in your CD and DevOps adoption so that you can start to track progress from the get-go. Needless to say, it is not going to be a pretty sight to begin with, and there will no doubt be questions around the validity of doing this when it doesn't directly drive the adoption forward—in fact, things might look pretty awful, especially early on.

It might not directly affect the adoption, but it offers some worthwhile additions, which are explained here:

- Having additional data to prove the quality of the software will, in turn, build trust that the code can be shipped quickly and safely
- There is a good chance that having a very concise view of the overall code base will help with the re-engineering to componentize the platform
- If the engineers have more confidence in the code base, they can focus on new feature development without concerns about opening a can of worms every time they make a change

We'll now move our focus from measuring the act of creating software and look at the importance of measuring what happens when it's built.

Measuring the real world

Analyzing and measuring your code and engineering expertise is one thing; however, for CD and DevOps to really work, you also need to keep a close eye on the overall environment, platform, the running software, and the progress of CD and DevOps effectiveness. Let's start with environments.

Measuring the stability of the environments

You may have a number of different environments that are used for different purposes throughout the product-delivery process: development, CI, QA, UAT, performance/load testing, and so on. As your release cycle speeds up, your reliance on these various environments will grow—if you're working in a 2-to-3-month release cycle, having an issue within one of the environments for half a day or so will not have, in the grand scheme of things, a vast impact on your release, whereas if you're releasing 10 times per day, a half-a-day downtime is a major impact.

There seems to be a universal vocabulary throughout the IT industry related to this, and the term environmental issue crops up time and time again, as we can see here:

The universal environmental issue discussion

We've all heard this, and some of us are just as guilty of saying these things ourselves. All in all, it's far from helpful and can be counterproductive in the long run, especially where building good working relationships across the Dev and Ops divide is concerned, as the implication is that the infrastructure (which is looked after by the operations side) is at fault even though there's no concrete proof.

To overcome this attitude and instill some good behaviors, we need to do one of two things:

- Prove beyond a shadow of a doubt that the software platform is working as expected, and, therefore, any issues encountered must be based on problems within the infrastructure
- Prove beyond a shadow of a doubt that the infrastructure is working as expected, and, therefore, any issues encountered must be based on problems within the software

When I said quite simple, I actually meant not very simple. Let's look at the options we have.

Incorporating automated tests

We've looked at the merits of using automated tests to help prove the quality of each software component as it is being released, but what if you were to group these tests together and run them continuously against a given environment? This way, you would end up with a vast majority of the platform being tested over and over again—continuously, in fact.

If you were to capture the results of these tests, you can quickly and easily see how healthy the environment is, or, more precisely, you could see whether the software is behaving as expected. If tests start failing, we can look at what has changed since that last successful run and try to pinpoint the root cause.

There are, of course, many caveats to this:

- You'll need a good coverage of tests to build a high level of confidence
- You might have different tests written in different ways using different technologies, which do not play well together
- Some tests could conflict with each other, especially if they rely on certain predetermined sets of test data being available
- The tests themselves might not be bulletproof and might not show issues, especially when they have mocking or stubbing included
- Some of your tests might flap, which is to say they are inconsistent and for one reason or another fail every now and again
- It could take many hours to run all of the tests end-to-end (on the assumption that you are running these sequentially)

Assuming that you are happy to live with the caveats or you have resources available to bolster up the tests so that they can be run as a group continuously and consistently, you will end up with a solution that will give you a higher level of confidence in the software platform.

 I would suggest you apply some focus to flapping and/or tests that do not provide the same results after execution, as these will impact confidence. The rule of thumb is that if you can't trust the test, either refactor it or remove it from the suite.

If you extend this thinking, you could also use the same approach to build confidence in your environment(s). For example, if you run the same test suite a number of times against the same environment without changing anything in terms of software, configuration, or environment, you should get the same results each time. Therefore, you should be able to spot instability issues within a given environment with relative ease—sort of.

Combining automated tests and system monitoring

Realistically, just running tests will only give you half the story. To get a truer picture, you could combine your automated test results with the output of your monitoring solution (as covered in Chapter 5, *Approaches, Tools, and Techniques*). Combining the two will give you a more holistic view of the stability—or not, as the case may be—of the environment as a whole. More importantly, should problems occur, you will have a better chance of pinpointing the root cause(s).

OK, so I've made this sound quite simple, and to be honest, the overall objective is simple; the implementation might be somewhat more difficult. As ever, there are many tools available that will allow you do to this, but again, time and effort is required to get them implemented and set up correctly. You should see this as yet another DevOps collaboration opportunity.

There is, however, another caveat that we should add to the previously mentioned list: you might have major issues trying to run some of your automated tests in the production environment

Unless your operations team is happy with test data being generated and torn down within the production database many times per hour/day and they are happy with the extra load that will generate and the possible security implications, this approach might be restricted to non-production environments.

This might be enough to begin with, but if you want a well-rounded picture, you need to look at another complementary approach to gain some more in-depth real-time metrics.

Real-time monitoring of the software itself

Combining automated tests and system monitoring will give you useful data, but will realistically only prove two things: the platform is up, and the tests pass. It does not give you an in-depth understanding of how your software platform is behaving or, more importantly, how it is behaving in the production environment being used by many millions of real-world users. To achieve this, you need to go to the next level.

Consider how a Formula One car is developed. We have a test driver sitting in the cockpit who is generating input to make the car do something; their foot is on the accelerator, making the car move forward, and they are steering the car to make it go around corners. You have a fleet of technicians and engineers observing how fast the car goes, and they can observe how the car functions (that is, the car goes faster when the accelerator is pressed and goes around a corner when the steering wheel is turned). This is all well and good, but what is more valuable to the technicians and the engineers is the in-depth metrics and data generated by the myriad of sensors and electronic gubbins deep within the car itself.

This approach can be applied to a software platform as well. You need data and metrics from deep within the bowels of the platform to fully understand what is going on; no amount of testing and observation of the results will give you this. This is not a new concept; it has been around for many years. Just look at any operating system; there are many ways to delve into the depths and pull out useful and meaningful metrics and data. Why not simply apply this concept to software components? In some respects, this is already built in; look at the various log files that your software platform generates (for example, HTTP logs and error logs), so you have a head start; if only you could harvest this data and make use of it.

There are a number of tools available that allow you to trawl through such output and compile them into useful and meaningful reports and graphs. There is a but here: it's very difficult to generate this in real-time, especially when there's a vast amount of data being produced, which will take time to fetch and process.

A cleaner approach would be to build something into the software itself that can produce this kind of low-level data for you in a small, concise, and consistent format that is useful to you—if truth be told, your average HTTP log contains a vast amount of data that is of no value to you at all. I'll cover some examples in Appendix A, *Some Useful Information*, but simply put, this approach falls into two categories:

- Incorporate a health-check function within your software APIs; this will provide low-level metrics data when called periodically by a central data-collection solution
- Extend your software platform to push low-level metrics data to a central data-collection solution periodically

You will, of course, need something to act as the central data-collection solution, but there are tools available if you shop around and work in a DevOps manner to choose and implement what works best for you.

Monitoring utopia

Whatever approach (or combination of approaches) you adopt, you should end up with some very rich and in-depth information. In essence, you'll much have as much data as your average Formula One technician (that being lots and lots of data). You just need to pull it all together into a coherent and easy-to-understand form. This challenge is another one to encourage DevOps behaviors, as the sort of data you want to capture/present is best fleshed out and agreed on between the engineers on both sides.

If you're unsure whether you should measure a specific part of the platform or the infrastructure, but feel it might be useful, measure it anyway. You never know whether this data will come in handy later. The rule of thumb is: if it moves, monitor it; if it doesn't move, monitor it just in case.

Ultimately, what you want to be able to do is ensure that the entire environment (infrastructure, configuration, and software platform) is healthy. This way, if someone says it must be an environmental issue, they might actually be correct.

If we pull all of this together, we can now expand up on the preceding list:

- Prove beyond a shadow of a doubt that the software platform is working as expected, and, therefore, any issues encountered must be based on problems within the infrastructure
- Prove beyond a shadow of a doubt that the infrastructure is working as expected, and, therefore, any issues encountered must be based on problems within the software
- Agree that problems can occur for whatever reason and that the root cause(s) should be identified and addressed in a collaborative DevOps way

We'll now move on from the technical side of measuring and look at the business-focused view.

Effectiveness of CD and DevOps

Implementing CD and DevOps is not cheap. There's quite a lot of effort required, which directly translates into cost. Every business likes to see a return on investment, so there is no reason why you should not provide this sort of information and data. For the majority of this chapter, we've been focusing on the more in-depth, technical side of measuring progress and success. This is very valuable to technical-minded individuals, but your average middle manager might not get the subtleties of what it means, and to be honest, you can't really blame them. Seeing a huge amount of data and charts that contain information, such as **Transactions per second** (TPS) counts, response times for a given software component, or how many commits were made, is not awe-inspiring for your average suit. What they like is top-level summary information and data, which represents progress and success.

As far as CD and DevOps is concerned, the main factors that are important are improvements in efficiency and throughput, as these translate directly into how quickly products can be delivered to the market and how quickly the business can start realizing the value. This is what it's all about. CD and DevOps is the catalyst to allow for this to be realized, so why not show this?

With any luck, you will have (or plan to have) some tooling to facilitate and orchestrate the CD process. What you should also have built into this tooling is metrics; the sort of metrics that you should be capturing are:

- A count of the number of deployments completed
- The time taken to take a release candidate to production
- The time taken from commit to the working software being in production
- A count of the release candidates that have been built
- A league table of software components that are released
- A list of the unique software components going through the CD pipeline

You can then take this data and summarize it for all to see—it must be simple, and it must be easy to understand. An example of the sort of information you could display on screens around the office could be something such as the one shown in the following screenshot

	This wk	This month	YTD
Number of releases candidates:	10	32	102
Number of releases:	8	30	99
Average time from release candidate build to live:	20 min	32 min	30 min
Most released service:	CUSTORDERS	PAYMENTS	CUSTORDERS
Quickest time for release Candidate to live:	10 min	14 min	10 min
Quickest time for commit to live:	120 min	160 min	120 min

An example page summarizing the effectiveness of the CD process

This kind of information is extremely effective, and if it's visible and easily accessible, it also opens up discussions around how well things are progressing and what areas still need some work and optimization.

What would also be valuable, especially to management types, is financial data and information, such as the cost of each release in terms of resources. If you have this data available to you, including it will not only be useful for the management, but it could also help provide focus for the engineering teams, as they will start to understand how much these things cost.

Access to this data and information should not be restricted and should be highly visible so that everyone can see the progress being made and, more importantly, see how far they are from the original goal.

We've looked at the effectiveness; let's now look at the real-world impact.

Impact of CD and DevOps

Implementing CD and DevOps will have an impact on your ways of working and business as a whole. This is a fact. What would be good is to understand what this impact actually is. You might already be capturing and reporting against things such as business **key performance indicators** (**KPI**) (number of active users, revenue, page visits, and so on), so why not add these into the overarching metrics and measurements? If CD and DevOps is having a positive impact on customer retention, wouldn't it be nice for everyone to see this?

At a basic level, you want to ensure that you are going in the right direction.

Before we move away from measuring and monitoring, let's look at something that, on the face of it, does seem strange: measuring your DevOps culture.

Measuring your culture

I know what you're thinking: measuring software, environments, and processes is hard enough, but how can you measure something as intangible as culture? To be honest, there are no easy answers, and it really depends on what you feel is most valuable. For example, you might feel having developers working with system operators 20 percent of their time is a good indication that DevOps is working and is healthy, or the fact that live issues are resolved by developers and the operations team is a good sign.

Capturing this information can also be tricky, but it doesn't need to be overly complex. What you really need to know is how people feel things are progressing and whether they think things are progressing in the correct way.

The simplest way to capture this is to ask as many people as you can. Of course, you'll want to capture some meaningful data points—simply having a graph with the words it's going OK doesn't really give you much. You could look at using periodical interviews or questionnaires that capture data such as:

- Do you feel there is an effective level of collaboration between engineers (Dev and Ops)?
- How willing are engineers (Dev and Ops) to collaborate to solve production issues?
- Do you feel blame is still predominant when issues occur?
- Do you feel operations engineers are involved early enough in feature development?
- Are there enough opportunities for engineers (Dev and Ops) to improve their ways of working?
- Do you feel you have the tools, skills, and environment to effectively do your job?
- Do you feel that CD and DevOps is having a positive impact on our business?

There might be other example questions that you can think up; however, don't overdo it and bombard people—KISS (see the `Chapter 3`, *Culture and Behaviors are the Cornerstones to Success*). If you can use questions that allow for answers in a scale form (for example, 1 being strongly agree, 2 being agree, 3 being disagree, and 4 being strongly disagree), you'll be able to get a clearer picture, which you can then compare over time.

Again, if you pool this data with your technical data, this might provide some insights you were not expecting. For example, maybe you implemented a new process that has reduced the escaped defects by 10 percent, but releases per day have dropped by 5 percent and the majority of the engineering team is unhappy. In such a case, you might have a problem with the process itself or the acceptance of it at a grass-roots level.

Summary

Throughout this chapter, you learned that capturing data and measurements is important, as this gives you a clear indication of whether things are working and progressing in the way you planned and hoped for. Whether you're interested in the gains in software quality over time, reduction in bugs, performance of your software platform, or number of environmental issues in the past quarter, you need data. Lots of data. Complementing this with business-focused and real-world data will only add value and provide you with more insight into how things are going.

You are striving to encourage openness and honesty throughout the organization (see the Chapter 4, *Culture and Behaviors*); therefore, sharing all of the metrics and data you collect during your CD and DevOps implementation will provide a high degree of transparency. At the end of the day, every part of any business turns into data, metrics, and graphs (financial figures, head count, public opinion of your product, and so on), so why should the product-delivery process be any different?

The sooner you start to capture this data, the sooner you can inspect and adapt. You need to extend your mantra from monitor, monitor, and then monitor some more, to monitor and measure continuously and consistently.

Let's now move from measuring everything that can and should be measured to see how things look once your CD and DevOps adoption has matured. In Chapter 8, *You Are Not Finished Just Yet*, we'll be covering some of the things you should be considering when CD and DevOps become the norm.

You Are Not Finished Just Yet 8

Up until this point we have been on a journey, from surfacing the issues that caused the business pains through defining the goal and vision to remove them, addressing cultural, environmental, and technical impediments, adopting much-needed tools and techniques, overcoming hurdles, to measuring success.

Let's wind the clock forward and presume at this point that all of the advice in the preceding chapters and pages has helped—along with some more specialist advice, complimentary publications, and maybe some assistance—and that you have implemented the necessary tools and process changes. Let's also presume that the adoption of CD and DevOps is in full swing throughout your organization.

If you're reading this at the start of your journey, then I would ask you to continue reading and use your imagination to visualize how things could be with CD and DevOps adoption under your belt.

If all has gone to plan, the business has started to see the benefits and reap the rewards in terms of the ability to deliver quality features to the market far sooner that they could previously. On the face of it, you're almost done achieving your goal and realizing your vision, but—and it's a very important but—this is not the end.

The journey you have all been on has been a long one, and just like the five-year-old who has been sitting in the back of the car on the long road trip to grandma's house, you will now have people within your organization repeatedly asking things such as are we there yet? How much longer? When do we stop spending money on this DevOps thing? And I need to pee! Okay, maybe not so much the last one, but I think you get the point. This is as good a time as any to pause for a moment and take stock of where you are.

Reflecting on where you are now

Yes, you have come a long way; yes, things are going much more smoothly; yes, the organization is working more closely together; yes, the Dev and Ops divide is less of a chasm and more of a small crack in the ground; and yes you have almost completed what you set out to do. What you have done is reduce the process of delivering software from something complex, painful and cumbersome to something as simple as the following:

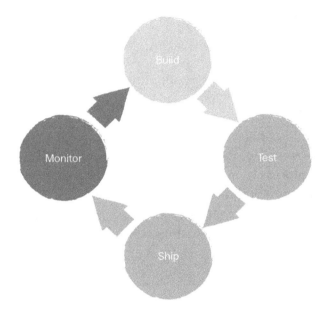

The problems you originally set out to address revolved around the waste within the process of delivering software, the long-winded and pointless processes, the political posturing, and more specifically, the waste that comes from large, infrequent releases. Adopting CD and DevOps has helped you overcome (most of) these problems.

As a result, you will now start to hear comments such as we can deploy quickly, so we must have implemented CD, or our developers and operations people are working closely together, so we must have implemented DevOps.

Some would suggest that once you start to hear this, it must mean that you have indeed completed what you set out to do. In some respects, this is true; however, in reality, this is far from the truth.

What these comments do illustrate is the fact that the major issues highlighted at the beginning of the journey have now started to become dim and distant memories. The business has grown to accept CD and DevOps as the way we do things around here, and has at last started to grasp their meaning, which is good. However, there's still work to be done and problems to solve; albeit different work and different problems. As you did at the beginning of the journey, it is again time to inspect and ascertain what problems are important now and adapt to solve them. To explain this, we have to go off on a bit of a tangent.

Streaming

Let's compare your software-release process to a flowing river (I did say it was a bit of a tangent):

- At the very beginning, many small streams flowed downhill and converged into a river. This river flowed along, but the progress was impeded by a series of locks and a massive manmade dam:

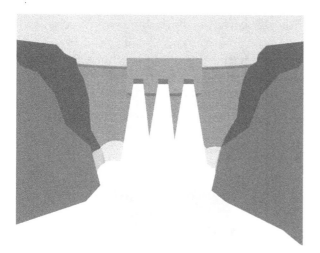

- The river then backed up and started to form a reservoir.
- Every few months, the sluice gates were opened and the water flowed freely, but this was normally a short-lived and frantic rush.

- As you identified and started to remove the manmade obstacles, the flow started to become more even, but it was still hindered by some very large boulders further downstream:

- You then set about systematically removing these boulders one by one, which again increased the flow; this, in turn, started to become consistent, predictable, and manageable.
- As a consequence of removing the obstacles to increase the flow, the water level starts to drop and small pebbles start to appear and create eddies, which restrict the flow to a small degree, but not enough to halt it:

- The flow goes on increasing, the water level goes on decreasing, and it soon becomes obvious that the pebbles were actually the tips of yet more boulders hidden in the depths of the river.

So, what's this got to do with your adoption of CD and DevOps? Quite a lot if you stop to think about it:

- Before you started, you had many streams of work, all converging into one big and complicated release—these were the streams into the river that backed up into the reservoir.
- At the beginning of your journey, you had a pretty good idea of what the major issues and problems were. These were pretty obvious to all and were causing the most pain—these were the locks and dams.
- You removed these obstacles and the flow started to be more consistent, but it was being hindered by the boulders—these are the lack of engineering best practices, bad culture and behaviors, the lack of an open and honest environment, and so on.
- You systematically addressed and removed each of the boulders and started to get a good, consistent flow, but new unforeseen issues start to pop up and impede your progress—these are the pebbles that turn out to be more boulders under the waterline.

If you cast your mind back, your original goal and vision was focused on the major issues highlighted during the elephant exposure inspect stage (the manmade locks and dams)—the things you *knew* were problems when you started out. As you systematically worked to address these, your delivering-software river started to flow more freely and you and the wider business started to see some positive and interesting results. Over time, hurdles (the boulders) that were not as obvious or important became more visible and a cause for concern. You then changed focus to remove these, which, in turn, improved the overall flow once again.

 Due to the nature of improvement, the more efficient and effective you make a process, the more the small niggling issues (pebbles) become hurdles (boulders). This is nothing specific to CD, DevOps, or IT; this is just something that happens.

This is by no means all doom and gloom, nor something to be concerned about. You and the business have faced bigger challenges, and you now have a level of organizational maturity that means you can deal with these new boulders with ease. That's a sign of being successful.

A victim of your own success

Humans are very fickle beings. As businesses are mostly staffed by humans, they are also fickle. A moment of success soon passes and fades into the collective memory, and problems that were not problems a few weeks/months ago start to become the talk of the town, boardroom, water cooler, or washroom. Another problem with success is that this becomes the baseline, which means that even the smallest of problems can start to become a major issue relatively quickly. These problems can be relatively simple things, such as:

As adoption matures, relatively small issues can become the new problems

In the space of a few months, the vast majority of the team members originally working within the constraints of big release cycles—which took many weeks or months to pull together, test, and push into the production environment—have all but forgotten, dark old days and are now finding new things to worry and grumble about. This is nothing unusual; it happens within every project, be it a major business change project or a relatively simple software-delivery project. It's nothing unusual, but if you think about it, it is a positive problem to have.

Up until recently, the engineering teams were severely restricted and unable to truly innovate, experiment, or flex their engineering muscles due to the bureaucracy, complexity, and constraints of the big release process. They no longer have to worry about the process of releasing software, as this has become an everyday background noise that just happens over and over again without the need for much effort—mainly due to the excellent work you have all done.

The seemingly small problems that are now being raised would have been, in the dark days, simple annoyances that would have been dismissed or ignored as low priority. They were pebbles deep under the waterline. Now, they are something real and boulder-shaped, and they need to be addressed; otherwise, there is a risk that things will slow down and the days will again become darker.

You and the wider business may at this point start asking the following types of question (I have included my responses as well, if that helps):

Question	Answer
Does the fact that new problems have surfaced mean that your original goal has not been met and you have failed?	No, it doesn't! It just means that the landscape has changed.
Was it all a waste of time, as we seem to have as many problems as we had to begin with?	No. The problems you encountered previously—and were exposed to, such as the elephant way back when—were much larger, far-reaching, and for all intents and purposes ignored, or at least accepted. These new problems are insignificant in direct comparison—especially in terms of cost to the business—and are out in the open for all to see.

How much more money do we need to spend?	That depends on the size and relative priority of the new problems. However, as CD and DevOps are now simply part of the standard SDLC, you should be investing as you would in any other part of your business processes and tools.
Did we miss something?	No, most of the *new* problems were unforeseen and/or simple niggles at the beginning of the journey.
Does this mean you need to change the goal, create a new plan, and start all over again?	Not necessarily. What you now need is some PDCA.

So, what exactly is PDCA? Let's find out.

[P]lan, [D]o, [C]heck, [A]djust

There are a number of variations of this acronym; however, the most widely used one is **Plan**, **Do**, **Check**, and **Adjust**. You might also find PDCA being referred to as the Deming circle or the Shewhart cycle. Whatever definition you prefer, the idea behind the PDCA approach is quite simple; it is a framework and approach that you can use for continuous and iterative improvement. The following simple diagram should help explain this:

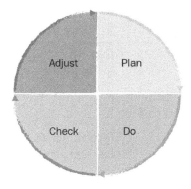

The iterative PDCA process

Simply put, this approach is an expansion of the inspect-and-adapt approaches that have been mentioned many times previously—although, if truth be told, it's been around for much longer. The concept is pretty easy to grasp and follow, and it can be applied to almost every aspect of your CD and DevOps adoption. Let's look at an example:

- **Plan**: You realize that your current process to deliver software is broken and decide that you need to find out why by running workshops to map out the entire process
- **Do**: You run the workshops and capture input and data from across the business
- **Check**: You analyze the output to ascertain whether the data provided gives you an insight into where the pain points are within your process
- **Adjust**: You highlight some areas of waste and agree on corrective actions
- **Plan**: You set a goal and pull together a plan of attack to address the major pain points
- **Do**: You execute against this plan
- **Check**: You review the progress against the goal
- **Adjust**: You make tweaks to the approach as more information and unforeseen hurdles are unearthed
- **Plan**: You realign the plan to ensure that the goal is still achievable, given the new information you have gathered
- **Do**: I think you can fill the rest in yourself

As with most of the tools and techniques covered in this book, using the PDCA approach over any other is your call; however, it is a well-proven and well-recognized framework to use—especially when you're looking at implementing something that is as wide-reaching and business-changing as CD and DevOps—so I would suggest you don't simply dismiss it.

If you took heed of the importance of collecting data and metrics, as covered in Chapter 7, *Vital Measurements*, you should now have a good collection of data to call upon for the Check stage of PDCA, which will make the Adjust stage easier to define. You may even spot issues that were not as obvious. For example, if you see cycle times spiking on regular occasions (Check) that also correspond with unplanned downtime of the QA environment, which in turn is caused by the storage filling up, then someone should look into why this is from happening and stop it happening (adjust)—which might be as simple as (plan)ning to add more storage (Do).

One major advantage of PDCA is that it has the luxury of being simple to understand at all levels of the business, and it is also highly adaptable—for example, this book has been developed using the self-same approach:

- I planned out the overall structure and content of the book as whole
- I then documented this as a proposal
- I passed this to the publisher to check and provide feedback
- I assessed the feedback and made adjustments to the overall plan
- I started to plan out chapter one
- I wrote chapter one
- My editor reviewed it and provided feedback
- I adjusted chapter one
- I planned out chapter two—I think you get the rather labored point

If PDCA isn't your preferred framework or approach, I encourage you to do some research before any action is taken. I specifically said any action is taken rather than you act, as you should now take a step back and take stock of where *you* are and what *you* need to do next.

Exit, stage left

After many long hours, days, and months, the business has become used to the changes you and those working alongside you have all spent many long hours, days, and months implementing. The fickle business is now experiencing and reporting new issues that they feel are important. The question is, who should address these newfound challenges? The answer is quite simple—not *you* or those who have been working alongside *you* spearheading the adoption of CD and DevOps.

You have helped embed the new collaborative ways of working, helped bridge the gap between Dev and Ops, helped implement new tools and optimized processes, drank lots of coffee, and had little sleep. You have done your bit, and it's now time for those you have been helping to take off the training wheels, step up, and take the reins (to mix quite a few metaphors):

The training wheels are no longer needed

Way back in Chapter 2, *Understanding Your Current Pain Points*, we looked at how to identify the problems and issues the business faced. We called this the elephant in the room. You helped the wider business understand and learn how to use retrospection and other tools to look back and plan forward, and taught them how open, honest, and courageous dialogue would help to find the correct path. As stated a few times, the *new* issues and problems are just that: *new*.

These new issues and problems do need to be addressed, but if you compare where the business was at the start of the journey to where it is now in terms of organization maturity, there is one major and very important difference: the business now has the tools and capabilities to identify the new elephant-shaped boulders very quickly, and now has the tools, knowledge, confidence, experience, and expertise to remove them quickly and painlessly on their own. If you don't believe me, re-run the CD and DevOps evolutionary scale quiz from Chapter 1, *The Evolution of Software Delivery*, and see how the business scores now compared to many months ago.

As discussed previously, you have pretty much reached the original goal (or as near as, damn it), so your swan song is to help others help themselves. It was fun while it lasted, but all good things must come to an end, so now is a good time to consider your exit strategy. This isn't to say that you should run away, hide, and not be involved at all; it just means that to fully encourage the fledgling ways of working, you need to be the responsible parent and let the kids grow up and learn by themselves.

Your focus should now change from driving the adoption (doing) to coaching and guiding the continuation (leading). Those who were the innovators of the adoption of CD and DevOps—yourself included—should now start encouraging the innovators and followers who benefited from the adoption to step into the light and take responsibility for their own boulders. This will not happen overnight, but you need to be pretty clear on your intentions so that people understand that you are handing over the baton. Simple things such as handing over the organization of regular CD and DevOps meetings to someone else or booking some time off when the next big tooling upgrade is scheduled to take place would suffice. The old "out of sight, out of mind" adage can be a useful thing when you need it.

Just like a good parent, you have set up a safe environment for growth and self-discovery, and therefore, you should only need a light touch, a bit of guiding here, some advice there, and the odd prod in the right direction.

One major part of this newfound parental leadership role is to look again at the wider and less tangible areas of CD and DevOps to ensure complacency doesn't set in.

Resting on your laurels (not)

So, you've done a lot and progressed further, and the business and those working within it are all the better for it. This is a good thing—you and all those involved should be very proud of what has been achieved. However, this is no reason for the business to rest on its laurels; it might be tempting, but there are still things that need to be kept in check.

Previously, I highlighted that there would be new problems and issues that will surface from below the waterline that will keep the new generation of innovators and followers busy. With you and the previous generation coaching and guiding them, they'll be fine and will solve these new challenges. Alongside this will come complacency as the new becomes the normal. You have helped the business evolve, but you have to be very mindful of the fact that the business can start to devolve just as easily and quickly if there seems to be a vacuum and complacency seeps in to fill it.

Horror vacui (more commonly known as 'Nature abhors a vacuum') - Aristotle

As with any far-reaching project or business change, if the frantic rate of change starts to peter off or be seen to stop, things will start to stagnate and old ingrained habits will start to resurface. In this environment, the *laggards* might start to become vocal again, and the followers might start to listen to them. You will have actively and notably shifted your position from doer to facilitator and influencer; as such, your role will be to make sure things are running smoothly and to keep your eyes and ears open for new threats. You have built up a good network, so start using this to get some early warning.

When compared to what you have achieved, this might seem simple, but it can be much harder at times; you're used to being actively involved in driving others and doing stuff yourself, and now have to keep your distance and watch others doing stuff that you are still passionate about. It's sometimes harder, but just as rewarding. Think of it as taking the next step in your personal evolution. As such, you are in a good position to look beyond the initial goal to see whether there are opportunities to assist in a wider capacity.

Summary

Adopting CD and DevOps is a long and hard journey. If you think it's not, you are deluded. You'll circumvent elephant-filled rivers and other unforeseen challenges as you near the journey's end. Parental guidance is needed to steer the business in the right direction while you plan how to step out of the limelight and make room for those who have benefited from the achievements you have collectively made. New problems will emerge and threaten the adoption progress; however, the business is wiser and should now have the tools, maturity, and experience to cope. Keeping an eye on things is worthwhile and admirable however there's much bigger and better things to focus your attention on. In Chapter 9, *Expanding Your Opportunity Horizon*, we'll be looking at some examples of these bigger and better opportunities that come from a mature CD and DevOps culture.

Expanding Your Opportunity Horizon

9

As you may have guessed by this point, we have largely been focused on traditional software delivery within a traditional, established business that delivers traditional web/server software-based solutions and products rather than the young, trendy, and innovative start-up software businesses out there, the reason being that they normally have the agility and opportunity to be creative in the way they deliver software built into their DNA. Most tech startups—especially those formed in the last few years—normally build CD and DevOps into their normal day-to-day ways of working.

It may be that you currently work within such a hipster business, but CD and DevOps wasn't built into the ways of working from the start. That shouldn't be a problem, as this book should have given you some good ideas and guidance with regards to addressing this gap.

The vast majority of businesses that deliver software on a day-to-day basis are not so lucky—the intention might be there, but the will to act might be lacking. Hence, the focus is on the traditional. There's a strong possibility that you yourself work within one of these traditional businesses.

Having followed the advice provided in this book and successfully adopted CD and DevOps, there's a very good chance that you would have caught up with the whippersnappers and your business is able to be just as agile and creative in how it delivers software, and maybe even more so.

At the tail end of `Chapter 8`, *You Are Not Finished Just Yet*, we turned our focus onto *you* and how *you* could take your newfound knowledge, skills, and experience forward, beyond the initial goal of embedding the CD and DevOps ways of working within your organization. Let's look at what this could actually mean.

What about me?

Let's presume at this point in the narrative that you have been instrumental in the successful adoption of CD and DevOps and have delivered what you set out to do. Things are working well, even better than you envisaged. The business is all grown up, can tie its own shoe laces, and doesn't need you to hold its hand anymore—well, not quite.

As mentioned in Chapter 8, *You Are Not Finished Just Yet*, you should take a moment or two to consider where most of the individuals within the business were at the beginning of the journey and where they are now. Consider the changes in ways of working, communication, collaboration, and behaviors. Think of the proportion of innovators, followers, and laggards in the early stages of the evolution and what the proportion is now. Taking all of this into account, you will most probably find that in reality, the majority are now at the same point that you were when you started out—they are just starting to fully realize that there is another way to do things and that it is a better way. Sure, there's still work to be done to make things as effective and efficient as possible, and there are still a few kinks to iron out, but things are, on the whole, good.

Now, look at how far *you* have personally come in comparison; as far as most of the people you have been working with and coaching and teaching in the ways of the CD and DevOps think, you are akin to a figure way off in the distance:

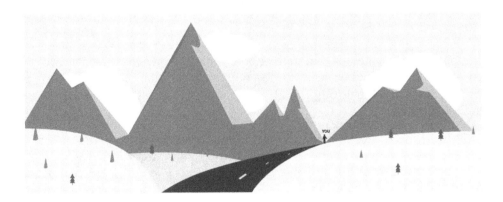

Others' perception of you

Regardless of your role at the beginning of the journey, be that a developer, a system admin, a manager, or something else, your role has now changed. Like it or not, you have become the holder of knowledge, expertise and experience. You are the CD and DevOps subject-matter expert. You know your stuff.

You may feel that your fellow early-adopting innovators are also standing shoulder to shoulder with you, but for the sake of simplicity, you are the one reading this, and therefore you are the one standing in the distance.

You have traveled far, the landscape has changed quite dramatically from where you started, and you have new hills to climb—these are the new opportunities that the business is now ready to look at. Maybe these were challenges that the business could not overcome earlier; maybe they simply didn't know these opportunities existed, but with newfound knowledge, they are keen to try new things. Maybe your **Chief Technology Officer (CTO)** has been chatting with his young and trendy counterparts at the golf club. Whatever the reason, now is the time to apply *your stuff* to these new challenges and opportunities. What follows are some examples of how you can bring to bear your skills, expertise, and experience beyond traditional software delivery.

What follows are some examples of doors that can open following that successful adoption of CD and DevOps. Some of these may be achievable without CD and/or DevOps, but from experience, the results will not be as good without as they would with them. These are the sorts of new challenges and opportunities that you—should you accept them—could apply some focus, attention, and time to.

Performance and load-testing

The more observant among you might have noticed that there is little mention of performance or load-testing throughout this book. This is intentional as, in my mind, attempting this activity without the close collaboration, tooling, and techniques that come from adopting CD and DevOps is a fool's errand. Yes, there are many established and traditional approaches, but these normally amount to shoehorning something into the process just before you want to ship your code—which might well result in the code not shipping due to the fact that performance issues were found at the last minute. You may have overcome this problem by implementing a process that periodically takes a build of the software and runs some intensive automated tests against it within a controlled and highly-monitored environment. This can help, but unless you have set up the automated tests to **exactly** mirror real-world usage, you're basically giving everyone false hope that no performance issues will be found once the code is live.

I would also hazard a guess and say performance/load-testing was seen as a burden, or even an area of waste, during the elephant-exposing inspection stage. It needn't be, and shouldn't be the case.

Once you have adopted CD and DevOps, the act of performance/load-testing can become relatively simple and straightforward. You just need to change the way you think about and approach it.

There's a very simple and understandable way to consider load- and performance-testing; by far the best place to ascertain how your software is performing under real-world load and usage is within your production environment. You may be reading this and thinking, has the author lost his mind? This may be true, but I would ask you to bear with me and decide for yourself.

Let's presume that you have implemented extensive monitoring of your overall production environment and the software running within (as mentioned in Chapter 7, *Vital Measurements*), from which you can observe in great detail what is going on under the covers in terms of hardware, infrastructure, and software. From this, you can form a very clear idea of how things should look during normal day-to-day operations.

With this data, you should then be able to safely run controlled experiments and observe the results in terms of overall platform performance. For example, you could run an experiment to incrementally apply additional load to the platform while it's being used, either by routing more user activity to a specific node or server or by running some non-intrusive automated test that will generate load in a controlled manner. As you turn up the dials and the load increases, you will start to see where the pain points are—a heat map of sorts—in near real-time. As both Dev and Ops are working closely together, observing the platform as a whole, they should be able to work out where the problems are by comparing normal day-to-day stats with those generated under load.

If and when issues are pinpointed, they could easily be overcome by applying patches in real time using the CD tooling used on a daily basis while the load is still in place—giving instant feedback. Alternatively, they might witness an overall slowdown of the platform, but the monitoring solution doesn't highlight anything specific. This could mean that there is a gap in the overall monitoring coverage, which again can be pinpointed and addressed in a collaborative way. Either way, simply turning the dials back down will put things back to the normal day-to-day load.

Some of you may be reading this and thinking that the production environment is sacrosanct and should not be used for such activities as this could impact customers using the platform at the same time. My view is that unless you are purposefully restricting the number of people who can access the production environment, then this increase in load will happen without your knowledge in an uncontrolled manner—especially if your CD and DevOps adoption directly attributes to an increase in customer satisfaction and growth. Why not make sure your production environment is ready for this growth before it happens?

All in all, trying to run performance- or load-testing without extensive monitoring in place and/or a high degree of collaboration between the Dev and Ops teams will not provide the results you expect or need. Doing so anywhere other than the production environment will give mixed results. This is not an obvious benefit of adopting CD and DevOps, but it is a very powerful and compelling benefit, as is reducing complexity.

Reducing feature-flag complexity

There are many established approaches to allow for different use cases or user flows to be switched on and off in real time, but most revolve around some sort of feature flag or configuration setting within the platform. Although this is a viable approach, it does add something to the code base, which can, over time, become a massive headache. That something is complexity.

Not only does this add complexity to the code base, it also adds complexity to related activities such as testing and the setup/support of the overall platform, especially if you start to chain the feature flags together. For example, let's assume you have a new reporting feature (let's call it feature C) that is automatically enabled if the reporting menu feature (let's call it feature B) is manually enabled **and** the legacy-reporting feature (let's call that feature A) is manually disabled. If feature A **and** B are manually enabled, then feature C is automatically disabled. However, if feature A and B are manually disabled, then the third-party reporting feature (feature D) becomes automatically enabled.

The following may make the example easier to understand:

Reporting-menu (B) flag	Legacy-reporting (A) flag	Result
ON	OFF	New reporting (C) automatically enabled
ON	ON	New reporting (C) automatically disabled
OFF	OFF	Third-party reporting (D) automatically enabled

It all seems simple enough and based upon simple logic gates, but consider what will happen when you have a platform that has feature flags controlling dozens or hundreds of features—some independent of each other, and some forming a weird, convoluted daisy-chain feature tree. Testing of all of these combinations and trying to support a production system that can be set up in hundreds (and sometimes thousands) of different states will be a nightmare, saying nothing of the pretty pointless task of trying to debug a given problem when it arises.

 I worked on one product that had in excess of 50,000 feature flags—the origins of and features being controlled by the majority had been lost in the mists of time, and therefore new flags were continually being added to control newly-added features. Complexity gone mad!

Having successfully adopted CD and DevOps, you will be regularly and consonantly shipping code with ease, and you'll have the Dev and Ops team working as one. Therefore, it would be far simpler to consider using the CD approach to enable and disable features or functionality. In other words, to enable a given feature, you just ship the code with it in—no messing around with flags, settings, or daisy-chaining. You'll of course test this first to ensure there's no unforeseen negative impacts, but there is a very simple way back: ship the previous version that didn't have the new feature/functionality (if you follow the "never break your consumer" advice from `Chapter 5`, *Approaches, Tools, and Techniques*, rolling back should not cause any issues). Nice and simple to comprehend, develop, and support, I think you'll agree.

OK, so this is may actually be an overly simplistic view, but with CD and DevOps, you can start looking at these sorts of problems in new and innovative ways. The advantages might not be immediately obvious, but reducing complexity, if nothing else, will save you time, money and effort, as well as reducing waste in the process.

One of reasons for using feature flagging within software is to enable A/B testing. Let's now look at what A/B testing actually is and how CD and DevOps can help improve this approach.

A/B testing

A/B testing has been around for a while and is an extremely effective way of trying out changes to user journeys and/or logic flows within a software solution. The simple premise being that you can—through configuration, feature-flagging, or clever traffic-routing—send a predetermined number of users (or the transactions generated by use of the software itself) down different paths. This can help try out new features and/or functionality under controlled conditions normally within a production environment to prove or disprove certain hypotheses.

I won't go into too much depth regarding this subject—there are plenty of books and online resources focused on this subject that I encourage you to read.

Let's, for example, say that your business wants to see what the impact would be if they introduced a new design or subtle web page layout change. If you can, in some way, redirect specific users or groups of users down path A and the rest down path B, you can then monitor and compare the user behavior via analytics and metrics to see which worked best.

The following diagram provides a simplistic overview of this approach:

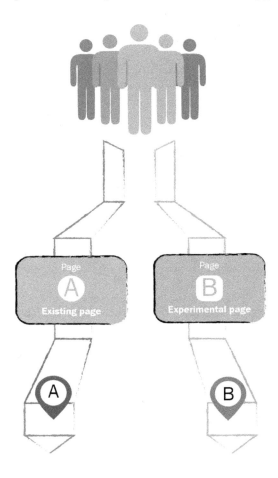

A simplistic example of A/B testing

Another useful approach would be to run A/B experiments covertly. For example, if you have a new recommendation service that you want to trial, you could force some user traffic and transactions to this new service and see how it works compared to the incumbent service. You could even use the same mechanism to route data to a specific service as part of load-testing. The possibilities are endless.

You don't necessarily need CD or DevOps to implement A/B testing; however, both do give you some major benefits:

- The ability to ship code extremely quickly—for example, you want to implement the code to split traffic to A or B across all servers in minutes so that all users start using the same code at the same time.
- You have Dev and Ops closely working together, monitoring everything that is going on. If gaps are found in the data used to analyze the results, you have the ability to address this with relative ease.
- You have the option to roll everything back relatively quickly with little/no impact if things take an unexpected turn or you have completed your experiment.

Without CD and DevOps, you would need to plan this kind of activity very closely in advance and hope nothing is missing or amiss when you implement it. Unless you have the ability to make small patch releases, you will no doubt need to include any changes—however small—within a full release cycle so the normal risk-averse process will kick in. The same will apply for rolling the changes back when you're done.

Another variation (or at least a close relation) of A/B testing is alpha and beta testing (sometimes referred to as closed or pre-release testing). This gives us the ability to try out wide-reaching UI, UX, and functional changes alongside the existing solution. Normally, this is narrowed down to specific users and/or via invitation only. Where A/B testing is traditionally targeted as small and specific changes, this type of testing is normally more far-reaching in nature. The basic premise still applies: the ability to try out new features and functionality in a controlled manner. Again, this can be achieved without CD and DevOps, but it will be far more complex, risky, and prone to failure as old-school processes will get in the way, slow things down and—based on experience—ultimately be blamed for the failure of the test. Consider what it would take to maintain two versions of the entire UI and run them in parallel without a mechanism to react to issues in a timely manner.

As stated, A/B testing pretty much boils down to proving or disproving certain hypotheses, whether due to changes in market conditions or as part of a strategic direction change. Whatever the reason behind it, running an A/B test is normally time-critical. Without CD and DevOps to help you deliver quality software frequently, the ability to successfully run A/B tests will be hampered as the world may have moved on while you struggle to get releases planned and executed, and the use case you originally wanted to test may no longer be relevant. As they say, time waits for no man, women, or A/B tests.

We'll now move from testing to colors—blue and green, in fact.

Blue-green deployments

Some of you *au fait* with CD will no doubt have heard of blue-green deployments, which are one of the cornerstones of the original CD approach. For those of you not in the know, blue-green deployments allow you to deploy (as the name suggests) a new version of software (or a new server with updated O/S, or new configuration or DB engine, and so on) while the incumbent version/server is up and running, and then seamlessly switch new for old. This is a very simplistic overview of the approach, but suffice it to say it's quite an easy concept to get your head around.

This approach vastly improves your ability to not only reduce/remove the need for downtime (see `Chapter 5`, *Approaches, Tools, and Techniques*), but also to try side-by-side versioning (for example, running two different versions of the same thing within the same environment)—which is something that can also help A/B testing:

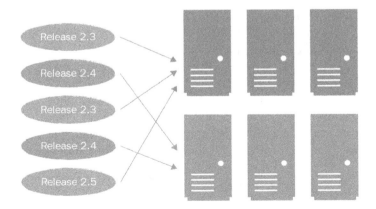

Although this approach is very much tied to CD, the adoption of DevOps as well will make this so much easier to manage, plan, and coordinate. Without close collaboration and trust between the Dev and Ops team, there is potential for things to go badly wrong—especially when dealing with the production environment. For example, what if a developer inadvertently deploys a breaking change within an API alongside the existing API but the consuming service (see `Chapter 5`, *Approaches, Tools, and Techniques*) starts to talk to both? This will lead to very inconsistent results and some head-scratching. With DevOps, finding the root cause will be relatively easy and fixing the potential data issues can be sorted collaboratively.

Rather than going into too much detail, I highly recommend you do some research and reading into CD—there's a list of reference materials in the `Appendix A`, *Some Useful Information*—but, suffice it to say that blue-green deployments is a very powerful tool.

Something else that I would highly recommend is leveraging CD and DevOps to ease the burden of security-patching.

Security-patching and bacon-saving

It seems that every day the news is full of reports about the latest business that has been hacked in some way, or has suffered a **distributed denial-of-service** (**DDOS**) attack. These, of course, are only the ones we know about—research suggests that there are a good number of business that don't publicly admit to large-scale IT security issues (and why would they?). In recent years, this has made businesses—especially at the executive level—extremely wary of change and very focused on ensuring their IT systems are fully (mostly) up to date in terms of security patches. Most times, this is at the expense of software delivery.

When a business has adopted CD and DevOps, the implementation and validation of security patches simply becomes another change to deliver. If the patch is at the operating-system (O/S) level, then the configuration-as-code approach covered in `Chapter 5`, *Approaches, Tools, and Techniques*, will cater for this. The same would apply for networking, infrastructure, and runtime frameworks (for example JAVA, .NET, and so on). If the patch is at the software level (for example, found within some open source software used), then there is a tried and tested method of shipping software changes via a CD pipeline.

To keep the narrative simple, let's assume that a business has been hacked and customer data has been stolen within the attach due to a security flaw within their network and unpatched OS.

Let's now apply this scenario to a traditional listed business that has **not** adopted CD or DevOps. Consider the following questions and think of the answers that would apply:

1. How quickly do you think they would apply a patch to overcome the problem?
2. How calm do you think their operations team feels with their CEO, VP of PR, and SVP of operations all breathing down their necks wanting to know when the IT system will be patched?
3. How confident are the Ops team that hastily applying an OS and network patch that should have been applied months ago will **not** impact the software platform?
4. How happy do you think the development team will be when the SVP of engineering tells them that they can't go home until they have sorted out a fix to overcome the issues introduced by hurriedly applying an OS patch?
5. How much market value do you think is wiped off a listed company when news gets out that they have been hacked and customer data has been stolen?
6. How many heads will roll?

It doesn't take a PhD to guess the answers to these questions. Situations such as this are not as isolated or uncommon as they used to be, and the fallout in recent years has been very widespread, expensive, and career-limiting for those caught up in it all.

Now imagine the same situation for a business that has adopted CD and DevOps. The answers to the preceding questions would be something like this:

1. As quickly as they can normally release—minutes or hours, at the most.
2. Perfectly calm, and, to be honest, the senior management wouldn't know anything about it until they've been informed that an issue had been found during routine monitoring and is in the process of being addressed.
3. Very confident, as they can collaborate with the development team to ensure that there are no impacts and/or work on a plan to address the impacts in parallel.
4. They won't have to.
5. If the message delivered is, "We found an issue and have already applied a fix. The impact was minimal and we can assure our customers that their data is perfectly safe," the news isn't very newsworthy and the markets might not even care. In fact, they might even see it as good news and want to invest more in the business. (OK, I can't quantify this, but it is plausible.)
6. None.

If your CD and DevOps adoption has matured, the probability of a hack due to outdated security-patching would be quite small as the monitoring for and implementation of regular security patches will be incorporated into the day-to-day ways of working, either via configuration-as-code or as part of the software delivery pipeline. However, there will always be unforeseen security holes, so it's good to know that there's a rapid way to address these situations as and when they arise.

As you can see, adopting CD and DevOps can provide some major bacon-saving benefits. That isn't to say that you couldn't achieve the same results without CD and DevOps, but having the ability to deliver quickly and having a very close working relationship across the Dev and Ops teams will make it much easier to spot and fix live issues before anything breaks—or your business becomes the top story on the evening news.

As previously stated, there will always be unforeseen events that can impact the running production system, and keeping ahead of this can be difficult. However, there is an approach that can help to surface these problems before they manifest themselves. This involves actively trying to break the live platform. On purpose.

Order-out-of-chaos monkey

It doesn't matter how much care and attention you apply to your platform; something can and will inevitably go wrong when you least expect it. For example, a server will fail, a process might start looping, a network switch will decide it doesn't want to be a network switch anymore, the SAN will decide it likes to function in single-user mode, the latest security patch will cause issues in the software platform, or someone will decide to hack you because you're a nice big target. As the saying goes, you should always expect the unexpected.

Most businesses will have some sort of business contingency plan in place to cater for the unexpected, but there's a strong possibility that they don't try to purposely force the issue, at least not to the extent that something bad actually happens—they just hope nothing bad will ever happen, and if it does, they hope and pray that they'll be ready and the plan works.

What if you had a set of tools that could safely initiate a failure at will in a controlled manner with the goal of observing what happens and, more importantly, where the weak spots in your platform are? This is exactly what some bright spark did a few years ago, and this has been widely adopted as the **chaos monkey approach**. There are a few variations, but what it boils down to is this: a set of tools that you can run within your closely-monitored environment whose *raison d'être* is to try and break it.

If you do some research into this subject, you'll find that the majority of the tools currently available are very much focused on cloud-based installations. That isn't to say that such tools cannot be used within an on-premise environment, but the effectiveness may be lower and the risk higher, so you should bear that in mind.

If you attempted this approach without a strongly-embedded CD and DevOps culture, you would end up in a complete mess—to be honest, I doubt if you would be even be allowed to try it in the first place without getting someone very high up in the organization to understand why this should be done, and be willing to take the risk. With close collaboration, in-depth monitoring, and the trust-based relationships that come from CD and DevOps, attempting to break the platform to observe what happens is relatively (but not totally) risk-free.

 There is one caveat to this approach: you need to be confident that your platform has been designed and built to gracefully allow for failure. You should avoid committing platformicide in public with core dumps and HTTP 500 messages available for all to see. Again, this can be addressed in a DevOps way by ensuring the environment and software that runs within it fail gracefully.

One other advantage to the chaos monkey approach is that it's also a great way to share knowledge of how the overall platform works across both the Dev and Ops teams. As any creative and technically-minded person will tell you, the best way to understand how something works is to push it to its breaking point to see what makes it tick. Going back to our F1 racing car analogy in `Chapter 7`, *Vital Measurements*, the engineers and drivers regularly push the cars and components to the limit during testing and practice laps to ensure the car will work as designed when it needs to. The information gleaned from this activity can mean the difference between a podium finish and being lapped.

We'll now move away from the potentially destructive power of CD and DevOps, and consider how CD and DevOps can make the lives of your customers and other teams within your organization so much better.

End user self-service

Over the course of this book, we have been focused on a unidirectional process of pushing software out to given environments (including production). This in essence revolves around a software-engineering team having confidence in their changes, and therefore triggering the process to ship it or an Ops team who are confident to ship a config as code change.

What if you were to turn this around and allow the users of your software platform to initiate the *pulling* of your software at will? It might sound strange, but there are a few legitimate scenarios in which this could be required.

Let's look at a few scenarios:

- You have an implementation team that supports the on-boarding of new customers, and they would like to test out different scenarios and use cases so that they can ensure their manual test scripts, FAQs, and training documentation are up to date.
- The SecOps team needs to run a set of deep security scans and some DDOS scenarios against a copy of the platform within their locked-down test lab.
- The PR and marketing team needs to take screen grabs of the current beta platform for a press release.
- The sales team is about to demo to an important new client and wants a local copy of the software platform running in a VM on their Mac as there is no reliable Wi-Fi available in the conference center.
- An internal auditor is investigating a data breach from six months ago and wants an exact copy of the platform as it was then.

Using traditional techniques and approaches, each of the previous scenarios would involve quite a large amount of mundane work (and that's putting it very mildly) to set up a dedicated environment and get all of the software needed installed and working as it should—saying nothing of the infrastructure setup. This mundane work would have to be prioritized according to the workload the various teams already have, and therefore it may take a very long time—most probably far beyond the date when the environments are **needed**. I'm pretty sure that you will have experienced this frustration yourself—I know I have many times.

Now consider how much mundane extra work it would entail if these teams/users could press a button and have an entire environment automatically set up for them? What if they could also specify the exact version they wanted (for example, production, beta, current work in progress, a snapshot in time, and so on) via a self-service portal?

With CD and DevOps embedded into your ways of working, there's no obvious reason you shouldn't be able to do this. It will take some work to set up, but you have the tooling that can reliably provision environments, deploy software assets, and provide in-depth monitoring. If the automation goes a little astray or doesn't cater for one of the scenarios, you have a DevOps team who are used to collaborating and are, therefore, happy to help solve the problems.

Extending the user self-service beyond your organizational boundary is also something CD and DevOps can help you realize.

Thing as a service

As software solutions mature, the businesses that invested in them continually look for new and interesting ways of leveraging said investment. In plain terms, they want to make more money from the software they have already paid for.

There are a number of well-established ways of doing this, but **PaaS (Platform as a Service)** or **SaaS (Software as a Service)** are the most popular and are very much in vogue in terms of new and interesting ways of making more money out of an existing software platform. You may recall that we briefly touched upon these in Chapter 3, *Culture and Behaviors—The Cornerstones to Success*, in relation to third-party tools. The premise is pretty simple; you expose via **Application Programming Interfaces (APIs)** certain parts of functionality to a first or third party who that uses APIs to extend their software platform to include the functionality you provide. For example, if your software platform specialized in car rental bookings, you could expose APIs to a price comparison web site to allow their users to seamlessly book a car via your software platform.

This type of approach has been around for many years, and sometimes referred to as B2B or similar), but has always been seen as something that is painful to implement, maintain, secure, monetize, and support—especially by businesses that deliver software in the traditional way. There's also complexity in terms of making any changes that could impact the APIs, which can lead to technical debt mounting up and/or upset customers/clients who use said APIs (see "never break your consumer" in Chapter 5, *Approaches, Tools, and Techniques*). Counter to this is the problem that any API changes required are slow to deliver—more of a problem when the first/third party has adopted CD and DevOps and can move far quicker than you. This can sometimes lead to them looking at the completion for their next partner.

I wouldn't say that CD and DevOps adoption will enable this approach without some effort and investment, but it will drastically simplify the ability to get it up and running and then keep it running. This in turn should remove the perception that SaaS/PaaS is too painful to implement and should be seen as something that legitimately is a new and interesting way of leveraging your software platform. In addition, you'll tend to find that organizations that have already adopted CD and DevOps are more likely to work with suppliers who work in a similar way, as they know that new requirements can be implemented quickly and reliably and that collaboration is something that just happens.

Summary

Throughout this chapter, we've focused on your evolution beyond leading the adoption of CD and DevOps and how you can help the business evolve beyond simply delivering quality software frequently. We've looked at some examples of how CD and DevOps can further improve the ways of working for everyone involved in product delivery and how either/both can help open up new opportunities for the business.

You can probably think of scenarios and interesting problems more pertinent to your situation, organization, or business, but the point is that with CD and DevOps embedded within your ways of working, you are able to take the load off the Ops and Dev team, help them solve new problems, and improve the satisfaction of your customers both internally and externally.

Thus far, we have been sticking to the kinds of web/server-based software delivery that the founders of the CD and DevOps movements sought to optimize, streamline, and make far less painful. In our closing chapter, we'll look at how CD and DevOps can be used outside of their comfort zone, and how you could add yet more value to your organization and business.

10
CD and DevOps Beyond Traditional Software Delivery

CD and DevOps are normally associated with delivering web server-based solutions—that's not to say it is exclusively the case, however; this is the norm. As you have learned, CD and DevOps are not specifically associated with tools or techniques. A true adoption of CD and DevOps is based on enhancing culture, behaviors, and ways of working to smoothen the flow of changes so that value can be delivered continuously. This means that they don't need to be constrained to the usual flavor of software delivery. Once your business has adopted CD and DevOps as the way we do things around here, you could, should, and can apply the same approaches to solve other business problems.

The most obvious would be to apply the CD and DevOps approach to something that is normally painful for most businesses that delivery software solutions: mobile apps.

CD, DevOps, and the mobile world

CD and DevOps are based on culture, behaviors, and ways of working, and therefore applying these approaches to delivering mobile applications—which is a large and ever-growing industry—can work. That isn't to say that it's a cookie-cutter adoption; there are a few caveats in terms of how delivering mobile-application software differs from web-based/server-based software delivery, the main ones at the time of writing being as follows:

1. Delivering software to a web platform 10 times per day seamlessly without impacting the end user is achievable—you are in full control of the infrastructure and the mechanism for releasing it. Doing the same with a mobile application will have a major impact on the end user—can you imagine what would happen if you sent a mobile app to end users' smartphones 10 times per day?

2. There is no Ops team living within the end user's smartphone/tablet, speakers, fridge, lights, door locks, dog cams, and so on; therefore, the Ops side of the DevOps partnership doesn't strictly exist.

3. You cannot guarantee the spec, size, network capabilities, and so on, of the device you'll be deploying to.

4. You are not, strictly speaking, in control of the final distribution of your software.

So, how do you square this circle? Let's go through each in turn.

In relation to the first point, you wouldn't realistically want to ship more frequently than every few weeks—even if you do have the capability—as this would simply spam the end user. You should therefore apply the release train approach. In essence, this amounts to incrementally building up the changes (which are all independently built, tested, and published via your CD pipeline) until such a point that you feel enough time has passed to ship. There is one exception to this: you can (and should) be shipping very frequently to internal beta test/dogfooding users so that they can try out the latest version whenever they want.

In relation to the second point, unless you can miniaturize the Ops team and clone them millions of times, there's not a vast amount you can do. However, if you have followed the advice in `Chapter 5`, *Approaches, Tools, and Techniques*, and `Chapter 7`, *Vital Measurements*, you will have embedded analytics and metrics within your software and have in-depth monitoring in place, so you'll be able to spot issues out in the wild in exactly the same way as you would with the software running on your servers. If something is spotted, the Dev and Ops team can collaborate, work out what's wrong, and rectify it.

In relation to the third point, you could try to cater for this in your testing, but in all honesty that's a thankless task. I would recommend focusing on the bestsellers, and based upon analytics and metrics captured, ascertain which sizes, specs, and types of devices your users prefer—if you see usage of a specific device type trending up, then you should consider adding this to your list of supported devices and include it in your test-automation suite. Either that or look at using external solutions/providers that specialize in mobile-device testing—many can be driven via APIs, which means your testing solution can orchestrate and control the test's execution.

As regards the last point, there's not much you can do about it. The leading app stores are now very established and reliable, and have good global coverage. The advantage CD gives you is that the app store is in reality a binary repository, which is something your CD pipeline is already used to publishing to, so the mechanism of publishing your shippable app is very similar to that of your server-based software. In addition, most app stores will allow for automated updates, which means when you publish a new version of your app, the end users should get it soon after. There are, however, no guarantees, so you need to take into account that you'll have a few versions still out in the wild that need supporting.

 This is realistically skimming the surface, but it goes some way to highlight how similar traditional server-based apps and mobile apps are in terms of the SDLC process.

Now, you may be reading this and thinking that there are a vast number of tech companies that are building and shipping mobile apps without formally following the CD and DevOps approach we've been going through within this book, so why should you bother? Because you can, and it will add value. The work undertaken to embed collaboration, trust, and honesty within your organization can easily be applied to your mobile apps. You have implemented tools and techniques to automate the process of building, testing, shipping, and monitoring your server platform, so extending these for your mobile apps should be (relatively) straightforward.

Added to this is the fact that mobile apps can now be written in the same technologies as you would use on a server-based website and built into native mobile apps. This, in turn, means that the same code base could potentially be shipped to both server and mobile; therefore, using the same techniques, tools, and approaches will make the process seamless and save a hell of a lot of time, effort, and money.

Another non-traditional area to which you can apply CD and DevOps ways of working is completely outside the world of software delivery.

Expanding beyond software delivery

So far, this book has been espousing the advantages of the adoption CD and DevOps to vastly improve the capability to deliver software seamlessly, quickly, and continuously. CD and DevOps need not be restricted to software/product delivery.

The tools, processes, and best practices that come with this way of working can be extended to include other areas of the business. There will, of course, have to be some tweaks and changes to some of the tools and techniques, but on the whole it's the behavioral, cultural, and environmental elements that are important.

Let's look at some areas outside of software delivery that can benefit from the CD and DevOps ways of working approach, starting with UX and design.

UX and design

Most business that deliver software—especially software that includes user interfaces (web sites, desktop apps, and so on)—will have some form of UX and/or design team involved in working on the UI and user experience assets (wireframes, and so on). Even the most agile of organizations will—on the whole—work in a waterfall way when it comes to UX and design. For example, most UX and design teams normally sit outside of software engineering. The usual approach is to have the assets created up front—before development starts—which are fed into the product backlog. Agile software-development approaches go some way to overcoming this, but the thing that most don't focus on is the need for close collaboration and the importance of culture, behaviors, ways of working, and delivering continuously.

You can (and should) take your newfound experience and skills and apply them to improving the way in which design and UX assets are built and delivered. If you collaborate with the UX/design team and get them to consider how these assets can be broken down into smaller logical chunks—as you did with your software platform—and have them delivered incrementally, you may find that things become smoother, more streamlined, and less wasteful. In terms of tools, there are plenty of well-established and mature design/UX software solutions that incorporate collaboration features and agile delivery.

Business process improvements

Let's presume that you have followed the advice within this book and have identified and removed the waste from your product delivery process, which is now optimal and efficient due to the adoption of CD and DevOps, but there are business functions and processes that sit before and/or after the actual product delivery process that are starting to slow things down.

For example, you may have a team managing the sales leads and business portfolio/requirements-gathering, which feeds into product delivery or post-delivery implementation/support teams, both/either of which are struggling to keep up with the rapid volume of changes.

There is no reason why using the same techniques covered earlier in this book cannot be used to address wider-reaching business problems. As an organization, you now have the experience, confidence, and respect to take something that is unwieldy and cumbersome and streamline it to work more effectively, so why not apply this further afield?

TYPICAL BUSINESS PROCESS FLOW

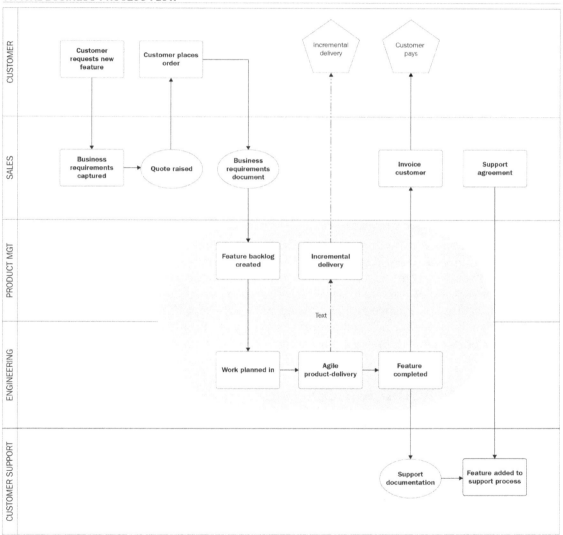

Going back to the previous example, you should be able to isolate business processes that precede and follow your product delivery process and go through a similar process of inspection (finding the elephant), address behavioral, cultural, and environmental issues, and define and implement tools, techniques, and approaches to streamline and measure outcomes.

Doing this could provide even greater business value and allow more parts of the business to realize the huge benefits of the CD and DevOps ways of working. The more seamless your overall business process is, the greater the overall impact. If you can capture customer requirements in an effective and efficient way, you can deliver what they want and provide the level of service they expect.

Business growth

Previously, we covered PaaS and Saas as models of delivering software solutions to your customers, but what about looking at new business opportunities? If you have successfully implemented automated provisioning, you may want to look into extending your business to provide IaaS to your customers—after all, you have the expertise to do this for yourselves, so why not your customers?

Other areas of business growth could come from leveraging the skills and experience now embedded within your organization. Think back to when you needed the help of experts in the field of CD and DevOps. On the presumption that you acquired some assistance, I would wager that it was not cheap. What if your customers themselves delivered their own software but needed assistance getting started with adopting CD and DevOps? You may be able to offer such assistance as a value-add—maybe you should suggest they buy a few copies of this book? Don't blame me for trying.

Optimized feedback loops

This phrase has been knocking around for a while in relation to agile software delivery approaches. For those not in the know, this relates to reducing the time taken to get feedback from users in terms of how the software you have supplied functions, works, and operates. This can come in many forms—NPS (net promoter score) functionality, feedback forms, rating score— but the main thing is to get this feedback as soon as possible. If you have adopted CD and DevOps and have the ability to deliver changes rapidly, then you really need feedback in a timely manner to ensure what has been delivered matches expectations (and quality standards). There's pretty much no point in getting feedback two or three months after the feature has been built as the world may have moved on and the feedback is therefore worthless.

The simplest form of optimized feedback loops is to leverage the enhancing culture, behaviors, and collaboration now embedded within the organization to get open and honest views from internal team members (or anyone else within the organization) as the features and functionality are incrementally being delivered through the CD pipeline. You can utilize the self-service functionality mentioned in Chapter 9, *Expanding Your Opportunity Horizon*. However, the greater value will come from getting feedback from the target end users in a timely manner.

With CD and DevOps adoption giving you the ability to ship software quickly, repeatably, and reliably, you should be able to incorporate tooling to capture feedback (such as those mentioned previously) from end users, which, if combined with the metrics and analytics you have embedded (see Chapter 7, *Vital Measurements*), will give you some very rich feedback and associated data. Traditionally, this feedback would be collected and/or collated by a team outside of software engineering, whereas with the CD and DevOps ways of working, the software engineering team will be used to working with such data so they can react relatively quickly.

As I say, CD and DevOps is not just about delivering software; the way things get done, the collaboration, the open and honest environment, the trust-based relationships, and even the language used, can and will help revitalize and enhance any business process.

What about me?

The preceding are simply examples, but none will have the chance of becoming a reality without someone helping the business and steering it in the right direction. Like it or not, you will have the experience, skills, and reputation as the go-to person for things related to CD and DevOps.

You now have the opportunity to start a new journey and help the business help itself by driving forward the sort of changes that can only be realized with a mature and strong CD and DevOps culture.

If this doesn't float your boat, then maybe keeping up with the ever-changing and ever-growing CD and DevOps landscape is your thing. Just trying to keep up with the new ways to do things, new tools, new ideas, and new insights could take most of your time and attention. More and more businesses are realizing the huge value of having evangelists in their ranks— especially when it comes to software and product delivery.

You might have hooked yourself into the global CD and DevOps communities, which will give you an opportunity to share or present your experiences with others and, more importantly, bring others' experiences and knowledge back into your business. Maybe you could even capture this and publish it on public blogs and forums, or even get it printed in book form. Stranger things have happened.

Whatever you choose to do, you will not be bored, and nor will you be able to go back to how things were. You have learned a very valuable lesson: there is a better way, and CD and DevOps is it.

What have you learned?

I keep making references to your experience, knowledge, and expertise, but until you have actually gone through the motions of adopting and implementing CD and DevOps, this will amount to what you have read. Let's take a final chance to recap what we have covered:

- CD and DevOps are not just about technical choices and tools; a vast amount of the success is built on the behaviors, culture, and environment.
- Implementing and adopting CD and DevOps is a journey that might seem long and daunting at first, but once you've taken the first step and then put one foot in front of the other, you'll hardly notice the miles passing.
- Teams who have successfully adopted CD and DevOps seldom regret it or are tempted to go back to the bad old days when releases were synonymous with working weekends and late nights—working late nights and weekends should be synonymous with innovation and wanting to create some killer app or the next world-changing technological breakthrough.
- You don't have to adopt both CD and DevOps at the same time, but one complements the other. You don't have to, but you should seriously consider it.
- Where you do need to make technical choices, ensure that you implement something that enhances and complements your ways of working—never change your ways of working to fit the tooling.

- It can be big and scary, but if you start with your eyes wide open, you should be able to get through. CD and DevOps are now very well-established and there is a global community available that can help and give advice, so don't be afraid to reach out.

- Don't start implementing CD or DevOps just because it's the next big thing that everyone else is doing. You need to have a good reason to adopt both/either, or you will not reap the benefits, and nor you will truly believe in what you are doing.
- Although we have covered a vast amount, you don't have to implement everything you have read about; take the best parts that work for you and your situation and go from there—just as you would with any good agile methodology.
- Just because you can ship software doesn't mean you are done. CD and DevOps are ways of working, and the approaches within can be applied to other business areas and problems.
- Share failures and successes so that you learn and others have the opportunity to learn from you.

Summary

This book, like all good things, has come to an end. As pointed out numerous times, we've covered quite a lot in these pages. This book is by no means the definitive opus for adopting CD and DevOps; it is a collection of suggestions laid out in a logical order based on real-world experience and war stories. I recommend you put some effort into fleshing out your knowledge with other reading materials and books, or even attending a conference or two.

Even if you are simply window-shopping and looking at what is needed to implement and adopt CD and DevOps ways of working, you should now have a clearer idea of what you are getting yourself and your organization into. Forewarned is forearmed, as they say. It's not an easy journey, but it is worth it.

So, go grab yourself a hot beverage, a notepad, and a pen; skip back to `Chapter 2`, *Understanding Your Current Pain Points*, and start mapping out why you need to adopt CD and DevOps and how you are going to do it.

Go on then. Stop reading and go!

Good luck!

Some Useful Information

Although this book provides some (hopefully) useful information, there's only so much space available. Therefore, I've compiled a list of additional sources of information that will complement this book. I've also included a list of the many subject-matter experts out there who might be able to provide further assistance and guidance as you progress along your journey. Additional resources can be found on my website at `http://www.swartout.cc.uk`.

What follows is by no means an exhaustive list, but it is a good start.

Tools

Some of the following tools are mentioned within this book, and some are considered the best of breed for CD and DevOps:

Tool	Description	Where to find more information
Jenkins		`https://jenkins.io/`
GIT	A free and open source distributed version-control system	`https://git-scm.com/`
GitHub	An online-hosted community solution based on GIT	`https://github.com/`
Graphite	A highly scalable real-time graphing system that allows you to publish metric data from within your application	`http://graphiteapp.org/`
Tasseo	A simple-to-use Graphite dashboard	`https://github.com/ obfuscurity/tasseo`
SonarQube	An open platform to manage code quality	`https://www.sonarqube.org/`
Ganglia	A scalable distributed monitoring system for high-performance computing systems	`http://ganglia.sourceforge. net/`

Tool	Description	Where to find more information
Nagios	A powerful monitoring system that enables organizations to identify and resolve IT-infrastructure problems before they affect critical business processes	`https://www.nagios.org/`
Puppet Labs	A tool to automate the creation and maintenance of IT infrastructure	`https://puppet.com/`
Chef	Another tool to automate the creation and maintenance of IT infrastructure	`https://www.chef.io/chef/`
Vagrant	A tool to build complete development environments using automation	`https://www.vagrantup.com/`
Docker	An open platform for distributed applications	`https://www.docker.com/`
Kubernetes (`https://kubernetes.io/docs/concepts/overview/what-is-kubernetes/`)	An open source system for automating deployment, scaling, and management of containerized applications	`https://kubernetes.io/`
Octopus deploy	A rather good tool that can be used as a CD pipeline	`https://octopus.com/`
Yammer	An Enterprise private social network (think of it as a corporate Facebook)	`https://www.yammer.com`
Slack	A mature and widely used collaboration tool and platform	`https://slack.com/`
IRC	The granddaddy of collaboration and chat tools	`http://www.irc.org/`
Hubot	An automated bot that can be set up within most chatroom systems	`https://hubot.github.com/`
Trello	An online scrum/Kanban board solution	`https://trello.com/`

People

What follows is a list of people who are actively involved in the agile and continuous delivery and DevOps communities:

- Patrick Debois is seen by many in the DevOps community as the daddy of DevOps and the founder of the DevOpsDays movement (`http://devopsdays.org/`). This relatively small get-together of like-minded individuals in 2009 has grown into a global gathering.
- John Botchagalupe Willis is a regular and renowned contributor to the DevOps community and has inspired many with his honest way of sharing his wisdom.
- Jez Humble is the co-author of the Continuous Delivery book that is used by many as the definitive reference material when investigating or implementing continuous delivery. He also actively contributes to the continuous-delivery blog at `http://continuousdelivery.com/`.
- John Allspaw is the SVP of Operations at `https://www.etsy.com/` and seems to understand the value of DevOps-even though he's one of the senior management types.
- Gareth Rushgrove is a self-confessed web geek, who seems to somehow find time to produce the DevOps weekly email newsletter (`http://devopsweekly.com/`), which is full of useful and insightful information.
- Gene Kim, co-author of *The Phoenix Project*, is the founder and former CTO of Tripwire. He is passionate about IT operations, security, and compliance, and how IT organizations successfully transform from good to great.
- Mitchell Hashimoto is a self-confessed DevOps tools mad scientist and the creator of Vagrant, Packer, Serf, Consul, and Terraform.
- Rachel Davies is an internationally recognized expert in coaching teams on the effective use of agile approaches and has a wealth of knowledge when it comes to retrospective techniques and games.
- Ken Schwaber and Mike Cohn are the godfathers of scrum and agile.
- John Clapham is an all-round nice guy and agile/DevOps evangelist.
- Karl Scotland is a renowned agile coach who specializes in lean and agile techniques.
- Keith Watson is well known throughout the UK DevOps community and I have the privilege of working closely with him.

Recommended reading

The following books are well worth a read, even if you don't decide for some strange reason to adopt CD and/or DevOps:

Resource	Description	Link
Agile Coaching	A nice introduction on how to become a good agile coach	`https://pragprog.com/book/sdcoach/agile-coaching`
Agile Retrospectives: Making Good Teams Great	An excellent book that covers most of what you need to know to run effective retrospectives	`https://pragprog.com/book/dlret/agile-retrospectives`
Continuous Delivery: Reliable Software Releases Through Build, Test, and Deployment Automation	The CD bible	`http://www.amazon.com/dp/0321601912?tag=contindelive-20`
The Phoenix Project	A unique take on DevOps adoption in fiction form, well worth a read	`http://itrevolution.com/books/phoenix-project-devops-book/`
Agile Product Management with Scrum	View scrum and agile from the product managers' point of view	`http://www.amazon.com/exec/obidos/ASIN/0321605780/mountaingoats-20`
The Enterprise and Scrum	This book provides some addition insight into the challenges of adopting an agile approach and ways of working	`http://www.amazon.com/exec/obidos/ASIN/0735623376/mountaingoats-20`
The Lean Startup	Real-life experiences and insights into how to transform your business, culture, and ways of working	`http://amzn.com/0307887898`

Getting Value out of Agile Retrospectives	Gives a good introduction on retrospectives and provides a good, long list of games/exercises	`https://leanpub.com/ gettingvalueoutofagileretrospectives`

Retrospective games

Retrospectives are normally the inspect part of the agile inspect and adapt. If you are aware of or are using scrum or some other agile methodology, then running retrospectives should be nothing new. If you have never run a retrospective before, then you would have some fun things to learn.

The remit of a retrospective is to look back over a specific period of time, project, release, or simply a business change and highlight what worked well, what didn't work well, and what improvements are needed. This process can traditionally be a bit dry, so retrospectives tend to be based on games (some people refer to these as exercises, but I prefer the word "games"), which encourages collaboration, engagement, and injects a bit of fun.

As with any game, there are always rules to follow. Here are some example rules:

- Each session should be strictly time-boxed
- Everyone should be given a voice and a chance to actively contribute
- Everyone should be able to voice their opinion but not at the expense of others
- Whoever is facilitating the session is in charge and should control the session as such
- The session should result in tangible and realistic actions that can be taken forward as improvements

As with the value-stream mapping technique mentioned in Chapter 2, *Understanding Your Current Pain Points*, the only tools you really need are pens, paper, a whiteboard (or simply a wall), some space, and some sticky notes.

I've already introduced you to timeline and value-stream mapping. Let me now introduce you to one of my favorite games, StoStaKee.

StoStaKee

This stands for stop, start, and keep. Again, this is an interactive time-boxed exercise focused on past events. This time, you ask everyone to fill in sticky notes related to things they would like to stop doing, start doing, or keep doing, and add them to one of three columns (stop, start, and keep). You then get everyone to vote—again, with sticky dots on the ones they feel most strongly about. Again, you should encourage lots of open and constructive discussions to ensure that everyone understands what each note means. The end goal is a set of actions to take forward. The following diagram depicts a typical StoStaKee board:

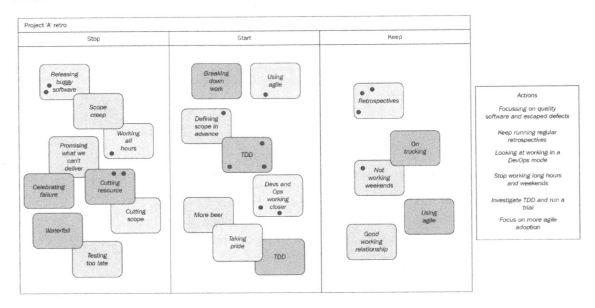

A typical StoStaKee board

The preceding examples are a mere subset of what is available, but both have proven time and time again to be the most effective in investigating and, more importantly, understanding the issues within a broken process.

Vital measurements expanded

Chapter 7, *Vital Measurements*, introduced you to a number of different ways of measuring certain aspects of your processes. We will now expand on some of these and look in more detail at what you could/should be measuring. We'll start by revisiting code complexity and the science behind it.

Code complexity – some science

As mentioned in Chapter 7, *Vital Measurements*, having complex code in some circumstances is fine and sometimes necessary; however, overly complex code can cause you lots of problems, especially when trying to debug or when you're trying to extend it to cater to additional use cases. Therefore, being able to analyze how complex a piece of code is should help.

There are a few documented and recognized ways of measuring the complexity of source code, but the one most referred to is the cyclomatic complexity metric (sometimes referred to as MCC or McCabe Cyclomatic Complexity) introduced by Thomas McCabe in the 1970s. This metric has some real-world science behind it, which can, with the correct tools, provide quantifiable measurements based on your source code. The MCC formula is calculated as follows:

$$M = E - N + X$$

In the preceding formula, M is the MCC metric, E is the number of edges (the code executed as a result of a decision), N is the number of nodes or decision points (conditional statements), and X is the number of exits (return statements) in the graph of the method.

Code versus comments

Including comments within your source will make it much more readable, especially in the future when someone other than the original author has to refactor or bug fix the code. Some tools will allow you to measure and analyze the ratio of code versus comments.

That said, some software engineers don't believe that comments are worthwhile and believe that if another engineer cannot read the code, then they're not worth their salt. This is one view; however, including comments within one's source should be encouraged as a good engineering practice and good manners.

One thing to look out for should you implement a code-versus-comments analysis is those individuals who get around the rules by simply including things such as the following code snippet:

```
/**
 * This is a comment because I've been told to include comments in my
 * code
 * Some sort of code analysis has been implemented and I need to
 * include comments to ensure that my code is not highlighted as poor
 * quality.
 *
 * I'm not too sure what the percentage of comments vs code is
 * required but if I include lots of this kind of thing the tool will
 * ignore my code and I can get on with my day job
 *
 * In fact this is pretty much a waste of time as whoever is reading
 * this should be looking at the code rather than reading comments.
 * If you don't understand the code then maybe you shouldn't be trying
 * to change it?!?
 */
```

This might be a bit extreme, but I'm sure if you look close enough at your code base, you might well find similar sorts of things hidden away.

One other good reason for comments—in my experience—is for those situations when you have to take the lid off some very old code (by today's standards, very old could be a couple of years) to investigate a possible bug or simply find out what it does. If the code is based on outdated design patterns or even based on an old language standard (for example, an older version of Java or C#), it might be quite time-consuming trying to understand what the code is doing without, at least, some level of commenting.

Embedding monitoring into your software

As mentioned in `Chapter 7`, *Vital Measurements*, there are a few ways you can include and embed the generation of metrics within the software itself.

Let's assume that your software components contain APIs that are used for component-to-component communication. If you were able to extend these APIs to include some sort of a health-check functionality, you could construct a tool that simply calls each component and asks the component how it is. The component can then return various bits of data, which indicates its health. This might seem a bit convoluted, but it's not that difficult.

The following diagram gives an overview of how this might look:

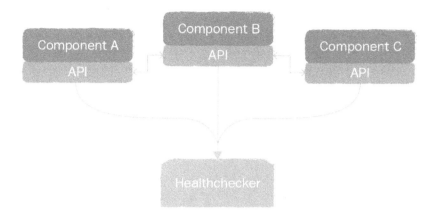

A health-checker solution harvesting health-status data form software components

In this example, we have a health-checker tool that calls each component via the APIs and gets back data that can then be stored, reported, or displayed on a dashboard. The returned data can be as simple or complex as you like. What you're after is to ascertain whether each component is healthy. Let's say, for example, one element of the data returned indicated whether or not the software component could connect to the database. If this comes back as false and you notice that the system monitor looking at the free disk space on the database server is showing next to zero, you can very quickly ascertain what the problem is and rectify it.

This method of monitoring is good but relies on you having some tooling in place to call each component in turn, harvest the data, and present it to you in some readable/usable form. It's also restricted to what the APIs can return or rather how they are designed and implemented. If, for example, you wanted to extend the data collection to include something such as the number of open database connections, you will need to change the APIs, redeploy all of the components, and then update the tooling to accept this new data element. This is not a huge problem, but a problem all the same. What could be a huge problem, though, is the single point of failure, which is the tooling itself. If this stops working for whatever reason, you're again blind, as you don't have any data to look at, and, more importantly, you're not harvesting it.

There is an alternative approach that can overcome these problems. In this approach, the component itself generates the metrics you need and pushes the data to your tooling. Something like Graphite does this very well. Instead of extending the APIs, you simply implement a small amount of code; this allows you to fill up buckets of metrics data from within the software component itself and push these buckets out to the Graphite platform. Once in Graphite, you can interrogate the data and produce some very interesting real-time graphs. Another advantage of Graphite is the plethora of tools now available to generate and create very effective graphs, charts, and dashboards based on the Graphite data.

Other Books You May Enjoy

If you enjoyed this book, you may be interested in these other books by Packt:

Hands-On Security in DevOps

Tony Hsu

ISBN: 978-1-78899-5-504

- Understand DevSecOps culture and organization
- Learn security requirements, management, and metrics
- Secure your architecture design by looking at threat modeling, coding tools and practices
- Handle most common security issues and explore black and white-box testing tools and practices
- Work with security monitoring toolkits and online fraud detection rules
- Explore GDPR and PII handling case studies to understand the DevSecOps lifecycle

Effective DevOps with AWS - Second Edition

Yogesh Raheja, Giuseppe Borgese, Nathaniel Felsen

ISBN: 978-1-78953-9-974

- Implement automatic AWS instance provisioning using CloudFormation
- Deploy your application on a provisioned infrastructure with Ansible
- Manage infrastructure using Terraform
- Build and deploy a CI/CD pipeline with Automated Testing on AWS
- Understand the container journey for a CI/CD pipeline using AWS ECS
- Monitor and secure your AWS environment

Leave a review - let other readers know what you think

Please share your thoughts on this book with others by leaving a review on the site that you bought it from. If you purchased the book from Amazon, please leave us an honest review on this book's Amazon page. This is vital so that other potential readers can see and use your unbiased opinion to make purchasing decisions, we can understand what our customers think about our products, and our authors can see your feedback on the title that they have worked with Packt to create. It will only take a few minutes of your time, but is valuable to other potential customers, our authors, and Packt. Thank you!

Index

www.ingramcontent.com/pod-product-compliance
Lightning Source LLC
LaVergne TN
LVHW081520050326
832903LV00025B/1557